MISTRESS OF TWO FORTUNES AND A DUKE

A STEAMY REGENCY ROMANCE (PARVENUES & PARAMOURS BOOK 2)

TESSA CANDLE

Mistress of Two Fortunes and a Duke

Book 2 in the *Parvenues & Paramours* series

Print Edition

Published by

Copyright © 2017 by Tessa Candle. All rights reserved.

No part of this book may be reproduced in any form or by any electronic or mechanical means, now known or hereafter invented, including information storage and retrieval systems, without written permission from the author, except for the use of brief quotations in a critical article or book review.

Mistress of Two Fortunes and a Duke is a work of fiction. Names, characters, places, and incidents are either the product of the author's imagination or are used fictitiously. With the exception of well-known historical figures and places, any resemblance to actual persons, living or dead, business establishments, events or locales is entirely coincidental.

ISBN: 978-1-77265-014-3

Mistress of Two Fortunes and a Duke

or The Objection of His Affection

is dedicated to you, my true reader. You enjoy a good steamy romp with some naughty nobles and a witty heroine. You don't mind an occasional an occasional bit of off-coloured language, and you don't mind waiting for the characters to earn their sex scenes, so long as they are sexy. Perhaps most importantly, you are an early supporter of the Parvenues & Paramours series. Thank you.

I thought you might be interested in reading one of the novels that Lydia reads in Three Abductions and an Earl, and Tilly reads in this book. So as a little fun spinoff just for you, I have written Accursed Abbey. It is a steamy Regency Gothic romance, coming soon. You can read a little sample at the end of this book

Thank you for being my true reader. You are the person I write for.

ALSO BY TESSA CANDLE

Three Abductions and an Earl, Book 1 in the *Parvenues & Paramours* series. Get links to buy my books on all your favourite retailers on my website: www.tessacandle.com.

Accursed Abbey, a Regency Gothic Romance—coming soon! Sign up for updates on my website.

Three Abductions and an Earl, audio book, as read by the author—coming soon! Sign up for updates on my website.

CHAPTER 1

Tilly Ravelsham smiled at the rays of morning light peeking from the corner of the window, passing through the crystal jars on her table and casting little rainbows about the room. One of them played mischievously across the nose of Mr. Rutherford, her paramour, who was dozing beside her. She grinned and fought the urge to wake him by kissing it.

It was the first time in a month she had slept in her own bed. She loved Amsterdam, but this last trip had been exhausting, in part because it was dominated by tedious visits with her fiancé's puritanical grandfather. And then they had carted him back to London.

Grandfather Fowler was sickly, but wished to attend the upcoming nuptials of his heir—or his would be heir. There was first the little matter of matrimony and conceiving a child. Controlling old tyrant. She yawned and returned to watching the rainbows.

The constant travelling about was growing extremely tiresome. It was good to be home, and it had been an especially nice surprise when Rutherford, whom she missed more than she liked to admit, sneaked in through her bedroom window.

She finally gave in to temptation and kissed Rutherford on the cheek to wake him, then rolled over and popped a confection into her mouth from the tray by the bedside. He stirred beside her.

She beamed when his beautiful hazel eyes opened. "Mmm. Last night was just what I needed, darling. I see your technique has not suffered while I was away. And it is lovely to wake up to such a luscious specimen of manhood."

Rutherford smiled sleepily, then, as an afterthought, his entire face pursed into a scowl. "But it seems to me that you could have given a fellow a little more notice of your departure than merely sending a letter posted from the port before you made the crossing. *Dear Stallion, off to the continent. Back in a trice. Ta-ta!*"

"What, and have to look at a face like *that* for a fortnight before I left? I think not." She traced a finger affectionately over the scar on his bare shoulder.

He had been wounded last season while rescuing their mutual friend, Lady Aldley, from an abduction. The site was completely healed now, but the silver scar tissue formed a lopsided heart. It lent such an air of intrigue to his already intriguing, smooth, muscular and irresistible torso.

Tilly had hungered for him the whole time she had been away. But he had seemed a little blue-deviled when she returned. There had always been a slightly dark, sardonic twist to Rutherford's humour, but now it seemed short on the humour and long on the dark twist.

Rutherford was still pouting. "You know you do not love DeGroen. Why should you cart off and visit his relations at their whim?"

"Well, there is the trifling matter of our being engaged, I suppose."

"Do not remind me. I beg you." He rubbed the scar on his shoulder unconsciously, as if to soothe the little, lopsided heart.

"You do realize my parents were in Amsterdam, as well? And you know how important cultivating the relationship with Mr. DeGroen's grandfather is for our future prospects."

"You mean for your and *Mr. DeGroen's* future prospects. Quite. Inheriting all that extra money is not to be resisted. But how much ruddy money do you need, Tilly? You are already as rich as Lucifer. Why can you not just marry for love?" His eyes were wide, and his long lashes had tangled themselves together in the night. He looked, for a moment, like a little boy lost.

Tilly sighed. He looked so worn down that her heart twinged, but it was hard having this discussion with Rutherford over and over again. She wondered if she should just give him up, let him move on and be happy with someone else, someone with a less complex and secretive life.

He had seemed like a Corinthian rake in Lord Byron's clothes when she first met him. Invincible, completely indifferent to her engagement, roguish and ready for some fun. But he had since shown himself to be quite conservative in his views and idealistic in his hopes about marriage.

It was very sweet, but with a life like hers, Tilly could not afford anything as messy as true love. "You know very well that I am disinclined to marry for… affection. Marriage is about status, property and money. I am not a fanciful young girl, and I have never concealed this from you."

"No." His face was glum as he stood and began to dress. "You have been perfectly clear. I have just been foolishly kindling a little flame of hope that you would get tired of committing adultery and would commit to me instead."

"I am not committing adultery."

Rutherford laughed, then winced at how bitter it sounded. "What do you call this then?"

"If you must give it a label, it is *fornication*." She ate another sweet and contemplated whether she should tell him that she was not deceiving Mr. DeGroen. She dismissed the idea, as it would require explanations that she could not give. "And although the Church of England inexplicably seems to think the topic worthy of mention in wedding vows, the ten commandments could not be bothered to forbid it."

"You have a convenient interpretation of holy scripture."

She tossed her head and snorted. "Does not every one?" She was distracted for a few moments, watching him dress. It was almost as alluring as watching him undress, even if his choice of colours was shockingly loud. "And having attended church every Sunday whilst in Amsterdam, as well as having my fill of all the pious conversation Grandfather Fowler's failing health would permit, I find myself feeling quite devout." She assumed her blandest, butter-wouldn't-melt-in-her-mouth smile.

He rewarded her with a real laugh. "One of these days you will be struck by lightning, you saucy little libertine fraud."

She wiggled her brows and pertly replied, "That is the risk one runs in consorting with the god of thunder."

He fastened his trousers, then gave her a cheeky smile.

Could she give up this beautiful stallion of a man? It was surely in his best interest for her to do so. But as much as Tilly needed to have her intrusive little fingers in the lives of others for their own good, she was growing weary of always putting everyone else's happiness before her own.

As he finished putting on his clothing, he turned to look at her. His eyes were full of love and sadness. A beam of sunlight penetrated the partly open curtain and lit up his chestnut brown hair where it curled adorably around his ears. Rutherford sighed. "I wish I could stay, darling, but I must go see Aldley."

"It is just as well. I am to go pay call on Grandfather Fowler and see that he is settled in." She winced at Rutherford's expression as he rubbed his shoulder. Thoughtless. Why did she mention it? Her upcoming marriage was a dagger in his heart, and she knew it. He had to get used to it, but there was no need to keep throwing matters in his face. "Tell Lady Aldley that I miss her, and will come to call soon." She paused. "And I missed you, too, Rutherford."

Rutherford's smile fell flat. "Welcome home, my dearest one." He left.

She covered her face with her hands. This was supposed to be diverting, not painful. Why did watching him leave pull at her heart, so? Tilly shook her head and began to straighten herself. She could not be all maudlin. There was a lot to do today.

She sighed. There was a lot to do *every* day. She rang for her lady's maid.

CHAPTER 2

Rutherford went home and had his valet, Smythe, freshen him up before stepping out in his smart barouche and four. He brought along his two favourite dogs, Dolly, his best pointer, and Mack, the bloodhound who had helped locate him when he was injured the previous year while rescuing Lady Aldley.

Mack had saved his life and obtained a special place in his heart. Dolly was in a delicate condition, and Rutherford found in her a glimmer of happiness and hope for the future. He did not wish to be away from her for the long hours he would be at Aldley House. Aldley would surely understand.

He thus arrived at the Aldley home in style, with dogs, and only a little fuzzy from the previous late night and the dose of laudanum he had taken for the pain in his shoulder. Funny how it always seemed to flare up when he thought of Tilly's upcoming wedding.

He knew it was dangerous to keep using the medicine, for he had seen the effects of opium on Lord Aldley's brother-in-law, Lord Essington. But it was the only thing that helped his blasted shoulder when Tilly had left suddenly for Amsterdam.

"Rutherford! Good to see you!" The Earl of Aldley came to the door to greet his guest personally, then stood back and examined Rutherford's clothing. "And hard to miss you in that colourful ensemble. I see you have brought your dogs. Did we have some hunting appointment that has simply slipped my mind?"

"Of course not. But I could not leave them behind, for I have the most wonderful news." Rutherford smiled stupidly. "My bitch is pregnant!"

Aldley squinted in momentary confusion at his friend, then cast his eye to Dolly's belly which Rutherford was rubbing. "Ah, yes. Oh, I see. Well, that is excellent news, Rutherford. Wonderful. When is she due?"

"I should guess about a month from now. I had her bred just before Tilly left town." Rutherford frowned at the memory. He had wanted to share the experience with her, but discovered she had abandoned him. It was stupid, really. It wasn't a decent topic for a young lady. But then Tilly was no prude. He was certain that she would have seen the fun in it. Except that she was gone, left town without a word, and only sending a quick note from Dover.

He had taken a few stabs in his time, but that one had really hurt. He rubbed his shoulder, then stopped himself and petted Dolly and Mack instead. At least they were loyal. They would never abandon him.

He recovered and stood, slapping on a smile for Aldley. "The sire is a champion pointer. *Samson* they call him. Cost me a pretty penny for the appointment, but her babes are going to be champions, too." He scratched Dolly's ears and cooed to her. "Isn't that right, little princess? The best little pointer babies in all of England."

"Em. Not babies, old boy, pups." Aldley laughed, and gave Rutherford a quizzical look of superiority. "Get a hold of yourself, man."

Rutherford waved the comment aside and continued to beam at the future mother of his grand-puppies. "Not planning to offer me a drink, then?" he drawled lazily.

"Yes, of course." Aldley ordered champagne, and led Rutherford through to his den.

"Champagne, hmm?"

"Yes. I did not interrupt your announcement, for I did not wish to steal your thunder. And, frankly, the juxtaposition did not quite seem flattering to my wife. But I believe champagne is in order, for the countess and I are also expecting a new addition." Aldley could no longer contain his joy, and grinned openly at Rutherford.

"Ah. Congratulations, Aldley. That is wonderful news." Rutherford had been suspicious before, but as nothing had been announced, he had let himself believe that Aldley was just as devoid of paternal prospects as Rutherford was. But now—well, he would not permit himself to be jealous. He would not. Such thoughts were unmanly.

"Yes, only you must not say anything about it, for no one knows yet. And I cannot get Lydia to enter her confinement, so we have to be discreet. I love her to distraction, but she has a will of iron."

"A proper countess, then." Rutherford smirked. "I am not sure what you expected. She is an original, Aldley. She climbed trees for sport when you met her. Of course she would object to sitting about at home."

Aldley scowled. "You would take her side. You sport loving people all flock together. At least I have persuaded her to stop riding."

"Well, that is good." Rutherford looked glum, but the champagne had arrived, so he raised an ironic toast. "To the women. May God preserve us from madness."

"To the women." Aldley nearly agreed.

Rutherford savoured the drink and let the bubbles tease his nose, then finished it without realizing what he had done. Aldley refreshed his glass, and Rutherford continued, "Forgive me if I am not wholly sympathetic, Aldley. But the woman I love refuses to marry me, so I cannot think that you have it so terribly hard."

"Do not take this the wrong way, Rutherford, but I think you complicate things unnecessarily. I like Miss Ravelsham, truly I do, but I hate to see you so miserable. You are hardly yourself half the time. Why do you not just give her up and find someone respectable to marry?"

"I do not wish to marry someone respectable. Respectable maidens are total bores."

Aldley scoffed and refilled both glasses. "You sound like that rakehell that got blackballed from White's last month. And good riddance."

"Lord Screwe? I should imagine some hell fire club would suit him better. I am not so corrupt as all that, but surely you of all people understand how much more fun interesting women are."

Aldley wore his best sternly superior earl expression when he replied, "I will try to ignore the implication that my wife is *interesting.*"

The earl gave Rutherford a quizzical look over the rim of his glass as he sipped his champagne. "But if you are indeed so devil-may-care as that, then why should you marry at all? A man of your energies will surely tire quickly of the marriage state. It sounds like a recipe for more of your listless ennui, and *I* shall have the brunt of your doldrums. You are barely tolerable as it is."

"You are quite droll, but this is nothing to the point. It is not that I wish to be married. It is that I wish to marry *Miss Ravelsham.*"

"Well then, not to be blunt, but you had best get on with it, for she is scheduled to marry another rather soon."

"I know it." Rutherford's practised air of cool patrician boredom slipped away entirely, and he raked his hands though his hair. Dolly and Mack nuzzled his legs and stared up at him with adoring brown eyes. He patted their heads. "I have tried and tried to convince her. She is immovable."

Aldley opened the door and ordered another bottle. "I feel for you, my old friend." Then he smiled cheekily. "Have you considered getting yourself abducted? I understand Miss Ravelsham is compelled to help others when they find themselves in such straits. If someone absconded with you, she would no doubt marry you just to save your reputation."

Rutherford lowered his lids into a lazy glance. "Your wit is truly diverting, Aldley." Still, Rutherford thought his friend might have a point. After all, he was wounded and convalescing in bed when Tilly first started flirting with him. Was it possible that she had been attracted to him because he was helpless?

It seemed far-fetched. Still, being direct with her had got him nowhere. Other than compromising her virtue, he had never tried stratagems to trick her into accepting him. He scratched his chin thoughtfully.

"I can see the clockwork turning. I meant it in jest." Aldley shook his head. "I hope you are not seriously plotting a feigned abduction."

"No. I believe after last year, we have all had quite enough of abductions for a lifetime." Rutherford rubbed his shoulder. "You never thanked me for rescuing your wife, you know."

"Well, let me do so formally now. Thank you, Rutherford, for saving Lydia from that filthy swine Delacroix. But I had thought for a Corinthian buck like you, heroics were their own reward." Aldley chuckled. "Besides, she was not yet my wife. And at the time I was persuaded that you were trying to steal her away, while I was trotting about the continent, trying to recover my ramshackle brother-in-law. That must be some excuse for my forgetting to thank you."

"Ah, Lord Essington. Have you heard much of him, lately?"

Aldley's brows furrowed. "No, and I am becoming a little concerned. I thought for certain the loose screw would have crawled his way back to London by now."

"I should think that his absence would be glad tidings." Rutherford helped himself to more champagne.

"It is. But with some people, when they are too quiet one begins to wonder what they are up to."

"Hmm. Quite. Shall you drive out to Essington Hall and check in on your sister?"

Aldley rubbed his chin. "I am afraid I cannot bring myself to leave Lydia alone for so long as that. Not while she is in the family way. It would be hard enough if she were confined. But as long as she is out in the world, I cannot stop worrying. She actually chastised me this morning for smothering her."

Rutherford's lips pursed as he drawled, "I really cannot imagine."

"You are rather smug for a man who will not stop petting his dog's belly for more than five minutes at a time. I wonder how Smythe manages to dress you." Aldley paused to lift a brow at Rutherford's attire. "On the other hand, that might explain your hideous green waistcoat. What vile, daltonic genius has possessed Smythe to pair that with a beet red shirt and gold neckcloth?"

"I instructed him on the colour choice. It is *a la* Lord Byron."

"Oh, indeed?" Aldley's nose twitched. "I believe you may have exceeded your goal."

"True, you know nothing of the art of fine dress, and go about wasting perfect tailoring on depressingly bland colours. You and that Beau Brummel dandiprat. I cannot abide him. Puts a person to sleep with his attire and then rouses him into wakeful irritation with his rude comments and his damned quizzing glass."

"I am no follower of Mr. Brummel. But I believe there must be some alternative between dangling after dandies with upstart pretensions and," Aldley waved a hand at Rutherford's clothing, "whatever this is."

Rutherford flicked an imaginary crumb from his sleeve and replied with an air of boredom, "I am sure there is, for people who like half measures. But you know me well enough to know that I am not such as these."

"True. You tend to pursue things at full force." Aldley smiled. "I shall just hold out hope that you are some day seized by a profound love for dove grey, or perhaps an everyday sort of blue." He shook his head. "But where was I? Ah yes, I was about to share my wonderful idea with you."

"Indeed?"

"I thought you might need a little distraction. Get out of London, stop dangling after Miss Ravelsham, that sort of thing."

"My friend you are always thinking of my wellbeing. You are truly too good. Might I venture a guess that the destination you have chosen for my restorative journey is Essington Hall?"

"Rutherford!" Aldley grinned in mock surprise. "What a marvellous idea! I had not thought of it, but it would be an excellent opportunity both to relax your nerves and to see how my sister is faring with her dirty-dish of a husband."

"Quite." Rutherford held up his empty glass to Aldley. "How fortuitous that I thought of it."

CHAPTER 3

Tilly squeezed Mr. Degroen's hand as they stood by the great black oak door of the DeGroen house. She leaned into his ear and whispered, "He only lectured me on the supreme importance of chastity twice. I do believe Grandfather Fowler likes me."

Mr. DeGroen whispered back, "What a frightening thought. How *is* Mr. Rutherford?"

Tilly sighed and shook her head in reply. "I will see you at my brother's on Sunday, my dear. Be good." She kissed his cheek. "Do not take the old puritan out to any gaming hells, now."

"As much as I should like to see that," he smiled with a thoughtful squint, "I should be petrified of killing the old boy."

"True. That could complicate the *good character* clause attached to your inheritance." She winked.

He gasped. "Good Lord you are a bad one, Tiddly-wink. I knew there was something I liked about you."

"I had assumed it was my willingness to go along with this ridiculously long engagement."

"You do not have much to complain about. An engaged woman has a great deal of freedom. In fact," he shook his head in dismay, "that is the one among my grandfather's strange testamentary demands that I find least irksome."

Tilly huffed. "*Long engagements are a family tradition* my left buttock! I think he just likes controlling people and is compensating himself for the fact that he will not be around much longer to do it in person."

"You are awfully sweet to him, for someone who thinks him a bitter old tyrant." He grinned.

"Well, he is not so *very* awful. He is the only one of your relatives that does not treat you deplorably badly. And I cannot help being diverted by difficult characters. Beside all that, I was taught to defer to the elderly. Especially the rich elderly." Tilly gave him a significant look.

He put an arm around her shoulder and squeezed affectionately. "You are a gem among women, Tiddly." Then he smiled mockingly. "Both of your men are so lucky to have you."

Tilly left her fiancé and settled into her coach with her deaf companion, Mrs. Carlton. She permitted herself a moment to enjoy the scent of lavender from one of her many carriage-freshening sachets, before descending into a moment of sadness.

She wondered how Rutherford was supporting himself under the burden of her engagement. If only she could explain to him the real reason that she could not marry him. If only she could make him understand that her life was complicated and he was better off without her.

Or did she really want him to understand that? Did she really want him to be happy with another? Perhaps she was not quite as altruistic as she liked to suppose, for the thought immediately sent her overactive mind into machinations of how she might prevent such a match. She was roused from her thoughts by their rapid arrival at the London home of her brother, Frederick.

The entryway was lit by myriad candles, and the brass fittings seemed to gleam with a sort of well-polished self-satisfaction. Mrs. Carlton, her companion, smiled and nodded at Tilly before the servant showed the patient woman into the large parlour where she would wait by the great stone fireplace—so large it almost made one fearful—until Tilly returned from her meeting.

Tilly made her way unassisted to the main wine cellar. At the back of the extensive rows of dusty bottles stood a stack of crates that almost touched the low ceiling. She reached behind one corner and depressed a latch, which permitted a door concealed in the centre of the crates to spring open.

She went through, and was greeted on the other side by her brother and the two assistants she had recently hired. Both had got themselves into a spot of trouble last season, while aiding members of the Delacroix family in their plots against the Aldleys, and Tilly had helped them out and given them employment.

There was no point, after all, in imprisoning people who had shown themselves willing to go a long way for a small amount of money. That would be a wasted resource. Better to give them work, for their gratitude made them very loyal, and their history made them discreet. And loyalty and discretion were crucial.

Tilly only hoped her good friend Lydia, the Countess of Aldley, never discovered that she had hired them—particularly Crump, who had been involved in trying to abduct Lydia. She was uncertain she could make her friend see things clearly.

Tilly received a kiss on the cheek from her brother, before seating herself at the head of the oak table that took up most of the small room.

She nodded to Crump and Miss Wheeler. "Thank you all for waiting."

"It hain't been long, Miss." Crump checked the door to be sure it was latched, and then seated himself next to Miss Wheeler.

"Let us start with the Belle Hire. How have your researches at the servant registry been proceeding, Wheeler?"

"I got five. Three of them are quite happy to go through training for respect—ah that is to say to go through your servant academy. The other two weren't really the sorts. I can't imagine what made them think they'd find work as servants. Fresh from the country, too. I reckon I just snatched them out from under Red Martha's nose. She loves a country fool. They are pretty girls, and they know it. But they liked the offer, so Crats has got them settling in now."

"Good. Do not turn your back to Red Martha. She is vicious. If she looks like she has noticed you, you get word to Crump or one of the lads."

"Yes, Miss."

Tilly smiled. "You are turning out to be a real asset, Wheeler. I want to help as many as possible, but if Red Martha should stab you for your troubles, I will not be pleased."

"Yes, Miss." Wheeler's lips betrayed a stifled little smile.

"Anything else?"

"Some of the street boys brought me a young one. Doesn't want to say where she comes from."

"How old?"

"Five, or maybe six. She's a wee thing, so it is hard to say. Got eyes like an old crone, though, and she doesn't talk much. I reckon she has not had an easy time of things."

Tilly nodded. "What did you do with her?"

"We gave her some work at the servant academy in the kitchen. She can stay in the servants quarters for now. Not sure she'll make a house servant, though."

"Keep me apprised of her progress. Have you the numbers?"

Wheeler handed over some documents. Tilly looked over the accounts for a few minutes. "Very good. You may convey my thanks to Shaw."

Wheeler nodded.

Tilly turned to her brother. "And how are things at the Hell Fire?"

"The income is up about ten percent from this time last year. Part of that is the increase in the cut to the house, part of that is an increased enrolment in the enhanced memberships."

"That is very good news."

"Yes." Frederick pursed his lips. "But I am afraid there may be a problem with one of our enhanced members."

"Indeed?" Tilly knew that Frederick was more troubled than he let on. Enhanced memberships were a delicate matter. On the one hand, the Hell Fire profited from them obscenely well. On the other hand, they suffered from the fundamental tension between the libertine personalities that wished to enrol and the very high degree of discretion required by the nature of the club.

Running a gambling hell that encouraged vice and never closed its doors was one thing. Facilitating every imaginable type of congress and cavorting amongst the aristocracy and the unfathomably wealthy was quite another. No matter how carefully anonymity was protected, a problem with one of the members was a problem for everyone.

Tilly rubbed her temple. "Do you have any biscuits, Frederick?"

"I am sorry. I should have had some brought down."

She smiled affectionately at her brother. "Not to worry. Perhaps we can talk about the Hell later." She knew he would infer that she meant *when we are alone.* Wheeler and Crump were as loyal as anyone working for them could be, but this was not something they needed to know about.

Tilly turned to Crump. "Well then, how are the lads?"

He tilted his head and grinned. "Bit bored, really. And too well fed. Yer spoil them with what yer pay."

"Worth every penny. Are the young ones having any problems with the new delivery schedule?"

"Not at all. Sharp, they are, and lively. Little bastards."

Tilly laughed. She knew very well that Crump had come to love the young mongrels who ran the deliveries and gathered information from the streets almost as though they were his own children—which some of them might be.

"Only thing is," Crump continued, "Shaw did some reckonin', and seems as we may run short. Lot of new folks lookin' to buy."

Not for the first time Tilly wished she were not in the business of growing, importing, and now distributing opium. But it had its uses, legitimate medical uses, and if someone were going to make a fortune off of it, it might as well be her.

Anyway, it was better that someone with morals had control of the trade, for people put all sorts of things in boxes and bottles and sold them. She had heard of one charlatan disguising horse manure as a mummy powder panacea.

And the money generated helped fund the servant academy and the orphanage. But she was conflicted. Opium could carry a person away entirely, and libertarian though she was, Tilly could not see how there was any liberty in being a slave to such a drug. Still it was better that the matter be in the hands of someone who cared about people.

She had started out supplying doctors and apothecaries, but now she had many customers in the upper classes who liked having discreet deliveries.

The problem was that if they could not get it, who knew what desperate things the customers might try? Lord, she really needed a confection. And maybe one of Rutherford's delicious shoulder rubs.

Tilly shook herself and wondered how that thought had come into her head. "Tell Shaw to calculate an appropriate increase in the price. But wait until Friday before you start charging more."

She would get her importer to go to the competitors and buy up a portion of the stock from each. If done quickly, she should be able to acquire another eighth share of the market without extreme expense, before scarcity drove the price up.

"Yes, Miss. Yer not goin' to like it, but there is one other matter."

"What is it?" She badly needed a biscuit.

"Lord Essington is askin' for more."

"Of course he is." Tilly shook her head. The man was hell bent on killing himself, and she did not want to have his death on her hands. He was her best friend's brother in law. But she had little choice but to supply him with weekly deliveries, free of charge. It was the only way to keep him from talking about her brother's wife, who had been compromised by Essington.

In fact, nothing untoward had actually happened, however the matter needed to be hushed up for the sake of appearances, and Essington had a great flapping mouth, but was addicted to opium. Supplying it to him seemed quite a rational solution at the time.

"Only, the thing is, Miss, that he says he knows things, and he'll talk."

Tilly toyed with the idea of giving Essington a stronger mix. No, she did not do such things, even to inconvenient bounders. She was not a monster. She just needed some sugar. She would suck on a chunk from the tea service if there were any—which there was not. Frederick could at least have provided them with tea.

"I see. Well then, give him more. An extra day's worth." She considered for a moment that if he had said that much already, Essington might get incautious and let something slip. "And it would ease my mind if you would take over the deliveries personally, Crump."

"Very good, Miss."

When Wheeler and Crump departed, Frederick confided in Tilly about the problematic member at the club. "It is Lord Screwe." He drew close to her on the stairs as they left the cellar and added *sotto voce*, "He has been boasting in the inner circle that he has procured a slave for his bed sport."

"Good Lord. I wish we had never granted that cur an enhanced membership. I mean, we have almost no rules but one, consent, so it just had to be broken, didn't it? I suppose being thrown out of White's was insufficient. He could go to prison for this. Is the man trying to get the Prince Regent to just give over and strip him of his title?"

"I am not sure that Prinny cares enough about such matters. Justice is not really his fascination." Frederick shrugged sadly. "But in any case, to hear him tell of it, he has her locked up somewhere in his home."

"And the idiot brags about it." Tilly scowled. "That poor girl must be scared out of her wits. We cannot leave her there."

"We also cannot call in the Bow Street Runners."

Tilly waved her hand. "Of course not. I will come up with something, but in the meantime, be a dear and get me some confections."

Frederick kissed her head, then hailed the footman as they entered the parlour.

CHAPTER 4

Rutherford petted Molly's head where it lay in his lap. Her body stretched out indolently on the carriage seat. She had the definite air of a dog who had rapidly grown accustomed to her new lifestyle.

"That is right, little princess. Be at your ease. We are almost at Essington Hall."

He had stopped the carriage several times on the journey to allow Molly to stretch her legs and relieve herself. She was delicate after all. He wondered if some day Tilly would let him look after her. Would she ever be delicate?

She was marvellously resourceful, and more than a little devious—definitely not some vapourish maiden who needed coddling. He admired her for it, but paradoxically could not help wanting to take care of her.

Molly offered him her belly for scratching and he obliged, shaking his head at his own dreamy foolishness. Tilly would marry DeGroen. She could never be his to care for. He could feel a great pit opening beneath him—an abyss of eternal loss which he felt powerless to fight. Molly licked his leg.

"You are my sweet girl, Molly. I know you mean to comfort me. But what I really need is to get a hold of myself and do something, instead of sitting about like a mawkish bacon-brain, waiting for her to marry DeGroen and plunge me into eternal misery."

He resisted the urge to reach for his laudanum and instead toyed again with the idea of using stratagems to win Tilly's hand. Surely she had some weakness. Aldley's suggestion of a feigned abduction was, of course, absurd, but what if Rutherford made her jealous? Could he make her believe that he might marry someone else?

Lady Essington was not a bad candidate, for he had harboured a little calf love for her when a lad. The problem was, she was already married. Of course, affairs with married ladies were not unheard of— particularly amongst noble ladies who had married swine and already provided heirs.

He was not really certain an affair would be sufficient, however. He supposed he could find some quivering blancmange débutante. The trick would be making the courtship seem plausible when the very idea sent him into fits of annoyance and ennui in turns.

He had never met a debutante who did not bore him senseless—well, except Lady Aldley. She had been quite something. And Rutherford's younger sister, Susan, was proving to be more interesting than most, so he supposed he should not dismiss débutantes as a whole. Yet he was convinced that these exceptions merely proved the rule.

But Tilly was utterly brilliant and fascinating. There was no one like her. She was a sparkling gem in the shale pile that was the London ton. It would be difficult to be convincing while courting a tedious little simpleton. Would Tilly even believe it?

His thoughts were interrupted by the carriage turning onto the long stone driveway of Essington Hall.

Rutherford and Molly were conducted through the high-ceilinged hallways of the manor, through arcades spattered with hunting trophies and indifferent paintings of ancestors or men shooting at birds, and cluttered by coarse bronze statues of men and horses, each looking about as brutish as the other. It was decidedly decorated by a disjointed committee—every generation of men tacking on their own bits to make a whole whose only cohesive elements were masculine themes and want of taste.

When Rutherford reached the grand parlour, he was transported into such a different aesthetic that he thought he might not recover from the shock. Floral motifs and fancy embroidery asserted their feminine authority on every available surface. Lady Essington sat on a couch with her needlework, surrounded by a colony of cushions ensigned with enough fancy sewing and ruffles to forcibly evict masculinity from the whole of England, if released into the wild all at once.

She stood to receive him into her matronly refuge from the rest of Essington Hall. Rutherford permitted himself a moment of queasiness, but abandoned any hope of deciding which parts of the manor, the masculine or the feminine, were more virulent. Such an exercise could only lead to madness.

"Mr. Rutherford—it is still *Mr. Rutherford*, is it not? How very good to see you after all this long time. And you have brought your dog, I see."

He smiled. "Indeed it is, Lady Essington. I am quite as enchanted by your beauty as ever. This is Molly. She is in a family way, so I like to keep an eye on her. I hope you will pardon the irregularity."

"Nothing to pardon at all." She bent to scratch Molly's ears, then gestured that they should seat themselves. "She is adorable. So you are not yet the Duke of Bartholmer. No matter. The débutantes are not so near-sighted as that. You must be swarmed at Almack's."

Rutherford shuddered. "I avoid the place like a house of plague. I hope I will not disappoint you, Lady Essington, in confessing that I have no desire to become Bartholmer. My current life is far too much responsibility for a ne'er-do-well like myself, as it is. The heavy mantle of dukedom would be utterly oppressive."

She laughed. "You must call me Lizzy, as when we were young."

He smiled and bowed his head.

"However," she continued, "I do not allow you to be so self-deprecating. It seems to me that only a responsible man would come all this way at a friend's behest, merely to reassure him that his sister is not in dire straits."

"Did Aldley say that was the reason for my visit?"

"Of course not. But despite evidence to the contrary, I am not entirely dull-witted. Nor am I vain enough to believe that you came here to reignite the flame of our youth."

"The thought had crossed my mind." He gave her his best wolfish grin, but could not sustain it when he saw her set her needlepoint down and pick up her fan to wave it frantically in theatrical mimicry of an over-heated débutante. He broke into laughter. "I had forgotten how much fun you are."

"That is easy to do when surrounded by such evidence of flouncy, dull predilections." She gestured around the parlour. "But it is all for show, I assure you." She threw her needlework aside. "I cannot abide fancy sewing in the least. I simply buy these fussy bits here and there, and pretend to have made them myself. Of course, the overall effect is one that Lord Essington cannot tolerate, so he never enters this room." Her face had a determined look.

"I see." Rutherford did see. Her eyes held a sort of steel and pain that had not been apparent at first. She had carved out an existence for herself with a husband that she could not but despise, and patrolled the borders with those more subtle weapons that women forge from bits of lace or ivory. Had Aldley done her a disservice by hauling Lord Essington's miserable, drug addled carcass back from the continent?

"One of the servants covered that screen over there. Monstrous is it not? I gave her a quid as a bonus, for she truly exceeded herself." The serious moment had passed.

"We should reward the faithful servant," Rutherford replied piously. "So where is Lord Essington? Has he contrived to take his wheelchair out for a spot of hunting?"

"Not today. Though I should not put it past him, if he were feeling well. He has become accustomed to it. And he can really get about, when he chooses. Only he no longer has much interest in hunting, unless it be for ices or sweets."

"He is," Rutherford chose his word carefully, "unwell?"

"So he says. He mostly keeps to his chambers, and according to the servants, sleeps a great deal. In fact I believe he could walk with his crutches now, if he took a notion to. But he seems to prefer the chair."

"Has the doctor seen him."

"I asked Dr. Kellerman here, once. He travelled all the way from London, but my husband refused to see him and demanded that he leave and never come back. It was quite a humiliating scene, but I did contrive to meet with the doctor later, to apologize. He told me that he feared Lord Essington was once again under the influence of opium. But I tell you, I do not know how he should get it. He never leaves Essington Hall, these days."

"He must have someone bringing the drug to him."

She shrugged her thin shoulders. "Is it very bad of me that I am indifferent?"

"I should say it is quite understandable. It is not the first time that I find myself questioning whether Aldley should have brought him back at all."

"My brother did tell me that it was your acquaintances in Italy that discovered him, and I thank you."

Rutherford shook his head, incredulous that she should thank him.

She smiled sadly. "You do not believe my thanks sincere, but it is, I assure you. It is very clear that I do not prefer my husband's company, but I am thinking of my son. His father would have frittered away his fortune with debauchery, gambling and utter dereliction of any estate management."

Rutherford only inclined his head in ascent to this indisputable truth.

"As it is we have had to make retrenchments, but here his profligacy is curtailed. And at least his son will not bear the legacy of a father who died in some wretched opium den on the continent. We live a quiet life, free of scandal, and if that requires the constant medication of Lord Essington," she squared her shoulders, "then so be it."

Rutherford shifted uncomfortably. He could certainly understand how Elizabeth had come to be indifferent to her husband's wellbeing. On the other hand he was becoming increasingly conscious of the laudanum bottle tucked into his jacket. "Yes," he said. "I take your point. How old is the little lad now?"

Her face, which had become dark during this confession, lit up suddenly. "Jonathan will be three in May. He is up in the nursery. Would you like to see him? I am sure he would love to meet Molly."

He was a sweet little lad and the apple of Elizabeth's eye. After he had met the little master, Rutherford made his adieus and prepared to leave. He smiled to himself as he stepped out into the cobblestoned courtyard. At least he could report to Aldley that his sister and her child were doing well.

Then Rutherford's heart clenched suddenly. He might never share such a moment with Tilly, never see that gleam of maternal love in her eyes. Did she even like children? He had to confess that he did not know. It was not the sort of topic they discussed.

But he was certain she would be an excellent mother. She had such a good heart and took so many pains about the wellbeing of her friends and family. He ran his hands through his hair and sighed in exasperation. She would drive him mad if he could not make her his own. He rubbed his shoulder.

But before he could settle into a proper bout of self-pity, he was distracted by a familiar face. A man came from around the back where the servants' entrance was, swung onto his horse and rode off. Rutherford instantly disliked the look of him. He was certain he had seen this man before, only he could not recall where. While he searched his memory, his carriage pulled up.

He spoke to his carriage man, as he lifted Molly gently onto the seat. "There is a horseman ahead of us. See if you can catch him."

As they sped off, Rutherford tried to make himself remember who the man was. He could not shake the feeling that his identity was of grave importance.

CHAPTER 5

Tilly watched her brother's house from one of the nondescript carriages she saved for her special business. It was a bit stuffy compared to the refreshingly fragranced regular carriages of her fleet. But a fragrance could betray a person's identity as easily as a face.

She knew that maintaining discretion required some sacrifice—such as the awful black wool ensemble that she wore. It was a rather hideous modified riding habit with a split skirt and strings that would draw it up like a curtain several inches in case she needed to run or to go anywhere that required delicate navigation.

She hoped this would not be necessary, as climbing about in awkward places was not among her talents. However, one planned for undesirable contingencies as best one could. Her companion sat across from her, occasionally dozing.

A black coach pulled up by her brother's door. Tilly watched as Lord Screwe emerged, tapping the ash from a cigar. He knocked on the door with the silver falcon top of his ebony cane.

The doorman opened to him and took his hat and cane as her brother received the loathsome man. Lord Screwe slapped Frederick on the shoulder, then puffed on his cigar while delivering some witticism that Frederick pretended to laugh at. They disappeared inside.

Tilly shook her head as she tapped for the driver to move on. Her task might be more dangerous, but she feared Frederick and Mr. DeGroen had the harder part of the bargain. She could not imagine how they would endure an evening of gambling with such a vile specimen of humanity. Hopefully they would have at least the small satisfaction of beating him into the poorhouse at cards.

When her carriage pulled up several houses from Lord Screwe's abode, Tilly put on a black bonnet with a veil and smiled at the nodding head of Mrs. Carlton, who remained in the carriage as Tilly slipped out into the night.

She looked at her watch. Thirty minutes. Her black clad form disappeared into the shadows as she made her way to the servants' entrance. A female servant met her and wordlessly brought her inside, motioning for Tilly to wait in a closet, while she went to check the stairway and hall.

The tension was stifling, and Tilly could hear her own neck creak as she waited. She looked at her watch. Five precious minutes had passed. The servant returned and beckoned her to follow.

They went up two flights of stairs. At the top the servant whispered, "This floor is unused, except by his lordship. That door at the end of the hall leads to a room with a ladder to the attic. I have unlocked it. I will be on the staircase, dusting. If you hear a sneeze, wait up here, and don't come down until you hear three knocks on the stairs."

"Thank you, Forester."

The servant nodded. "I owe you my position here, Miss, and more besides."

Tilly hurried down the hall. Inside, the room was dim. She found a candle and produced a silver box of matches from her pocket. When she had lit the taper, she gently closed the door and looked around.

The ladder lay on the floor, but there were hooks for it in the ceiling where the trapdoor was. When she had the ladder firmly in place, she took the candle and climbed up, pushed the heavy door open, and stepped up to peer inside.

The attic contained a lot of claptrap, and the shadows cast by the candle conjured gliding spectres, as she turned this way and that, trying to see the woman she knew must be there. There was a pile of blankets in one corner, but it was too far away for the candle to light it properly.

She decided to risk calling out, and in a loud whisper said, "Miss, where are you? I am here to help—"

A heavy blow to the head knocked her off balance, and Tilly fell backwards to the floor below.

CHAPTER 6

The carriage careened too fast around a corner, and Rutherford soothed Molly by stroking her ears. His carriage man kept it on the road, but just. The mysterious man they were chasing was riding like the devil was on his tail. Rutherford supposed that made *him* the devil.

He laughed. Not much truth in it, for he cared too much to be Satan. Molly was feeling anxious, so he could not continue the chase. He tapped the door and the carriage slowed, then came to a stop.

"I think we must let him escape, Elms." Rutherford stepped out of the carriage. "I will walk Molly for a few minutes."

"Very good, Sir."

He lifted Molly out and set her gently down on the roadway. There was a smaller path that turned off the main road nearby. Molly walked with him, happily watering the dandelions and cowslips along the way.

The fresh air cleared his head, and birds were singing cheerfully after an earlier burst of rain. Rutherford wondered about the man. Why was he riding so fast? Was he in a hurry or was he trying to avoid being followed?

It was possible that he had recognized Rutherford and wanted to avoid him. But why? If only Rutherford could remember where he had seen that face.

As he ambled on, he recognized the road to Dunston Hall, the estate of the Viscount Delacroix. From all reports he was a good and decent sort of man, but his younger brother was a rabid dog of a wastrel. He looked over the lay of the road. This must be the spot where Tilly had first encountered him, when he was injured trying to rescue Aldley's wife from Delacroix, the younger.

He had no memory of the rescue, but his time recovering from his injuries were what first put him in close contact with Tilly. He rubbed his shoulder where the scar was. It was well worth having a blade broken off in him, to have had time convalescing in Tilly's care. How quickly she had beguiled him with her cheek, reading him naughty poetry by his bedside.

An ache set into his shoulder and the heart beneath it. Some blades were invisibly thin and cut deep and so quickly, that you hardly felt them until it was too late. That was love. If she married another, how would he ever survive it?

He felt for the laudanum bottle in his pocket, then stopped himself. The lock sprang open in a secret compartment of his mind. Laudanum. Delacroix. The abduction.

"Come Molly, my little love. Let us get back to the carriage." He did not wish to hurry her in her present condition, but he was energized by his realization. He knew who the man was, and he needed to speak to Aldley right away.

CHAPTER 7

When Tilly opened her eyes, she found herself in a heap in a strange room. As her mind and vision cleared, she realized she was in Lord Screwe's upper chamber. A pleasant wood smoke scent tickled her nose, but was followed by a greasier, more acrid olfactory assault. The candle. She cursed and looked about. The candle had lit a small fire in the wooden flooring. There was no water in the room. She cast about for something to put it out. There was a chair in one gloomy corner, and she hastened to retrieve it, pressing the upholstered back into the flame to smother it.

The room went dark. She hoped no one would smell the smoke and come looking. She felt around and found the candle, re-lit it and looked up at the trapdoor. Her head still hurt where she had been struck, but she willed herself not to be angry. The girl must be petrified out of her wits and did not know who Tilly was. She looked at her watch. Ten minutes.

Tilly climbed part way up the ladder, and, avoiding poking her head back into the attic, whispered again. "Look, I know you must be afraid, but I am here to help you. You have been imprisoned by a deplorable piece of filth, and I want to rescue you. Only we must hurry."

A voice came from the gloomy opening. "How do I know you are not in league with that devil?"

"I suppose you do not. But would I really be here if I were his ally? And what sort of woman would help Lord Screwe do this to you?"

"That witch in red, for one." The voice was hot with anger.

Red Martha. Tilly was not the hateful woman in red, but she was apparently the madwoman in black. They were running out of time. "I am not *her*. You must know that." Tilly looked at her watch again. Nine minutes.

"I cannot leave. I am shackled here."

"If I come up to help, do you promise not to hit me again?"

"Yes. Come."

Tilly hurried up the ladder into the attic. When she found the young woman, both her legs and one arm were in irons. A short length of chain tethered her to the wall. Her free arm was bleeding at the wrist, and she could see that the arm shackle was on the floor. That must be what she had swung at Tilly's head.

"You got one of them off."

"My left wrist is smaller, and I bit my flesh so the blood would help me slip it out."

Tilly met the girl's frantic gaze with compassion, then forced herself to focus on the task at hand. "Do you know where he keeps the key?"

"In his pocket." Her face was full of murder.

Good, thought Tilly. Hold onto that emotion. It would probably ensure the woman's survival. "Right. Well, let us hope this works."

Tilly produced a ring with several metal wires hanging off of it like keys, leaned over one leg shackle and begin applying the wires one by one to the lock, just as one of the lads had showed her. She found one that felt right, and left it in position, then produced a longer, thinner wire and inserted it, moving it this way and that. The lock popped. "Thanks to Heaven and a drink to all the saints!" She set to work on the other leg iron.

When she finally freed the woman from the last of her locks, Tilly smiled encouragingly. "Right, now be as quiet as you can, but follow me, and for God's sake, hurry." She darted for the trapdoor.

When they reached the bottom of the ladder the young woman said, "What of my child? He took my little one."

Tilly stopped and looked at her watch. Four minutes. "I promise you, I will find your child. But he is not here."

"She."

"She. Now follow me if you want to get out of here." Tilly ran through the door and did not look back. If the woman did not follow, she could not help her.

They had almost made it to the stairs when Tilly paused. She listened for a sneeze, but heard nothing. She took a deep breath and rushed down. The rescued woman was behind her. When they made the second landing, Forester was there, pretending to dust. She motioned them to wait, and went to check their escape route. She returned in two minutes and led them hurriedly down the remaining stairs, through the servant's passage to the back entrance, then pushed them out the door with a wink.

Tilly almost laughed. Cheeky lass. She pulled the rescued young woman along. "We are not in the clear, yet. My carriage will meet us in one minute, run!"

And they did. The carriage was driving slowly past the house on the street as they emerged from the shadowy lane that connected the road to the back entrance. "Blast!" Tilly pressed a hand to the stitch in her side, then ran again. "We have to catch it!" she called over her shoulder. If they didn't, they would have to wait around in the open until it looped back again, and the young woman was almost naked.

The carriage was not twenty feet ahead of them. Tilly whistled as best she could, but the driver did not hear her. She could not yell for fear of drawing attention, for they were now out of the shadows and in the light of the lamps.

She picked up a stone and hurled it at the carriage. It glanced off the side with a thump. She wished it had winged the blasted dozy driver. Mrs. Carlton poked her head out and saw them. She rapped on the door and the driver halted the coach.

Tilly ran to the door and flung herself inside. She turned to assist the young woman in behind her. The escapee was clad in nothing but a slip. Lash marks, burns and bruises coloured her arms and back. Tilly flattened her lips. She pulled the woman in more roughly than she would have liked.

Panting with exhaustion, she examined the street through the carriage window. Two men were walking down the way, but their backs were to them. Just then Lady Screwe's carriage pulled up at the house. Tilly released a gasp and pulled the curtain closed. They had only narrowly missed being spotted by the monster's wife. Mrs. Carlton wordlessly closed the curtain on her side of the carriage and lit a small lamp.

Tilly handed the shivering young woman a cloak. Even bruised, she was beautiful, with skin the colour of very creamy coffee, and long, thick black hair. Her amber eyes glowed with fearful animation in the light of the flame.

After a few moments of panting Tilly recovered herself. "I would love to make introductions, but I am afraid I did not have occasion to catch our guest's name."

"I am Mrs. Clara Johnson," replied the young woman.

"You may call me Tilly, and this is Mrs. Carlton." They nodded at each other.

"Mrs. Carlton is quite deaf, Mrs. Johnson." Though, Tilly noted, surprisingly capable of hearing a stone striking the carriage. The little fraud.

"You can call me Clara, I reckon, as you have seen me in my undergarments." The woman had stopped shivering, but was now blinking back angry tears. "Will you please help me find my daughter? I do not know where he has taken her, but now that I have escaped, he is sure to hurt her. He is a cruel devil."

"I will find her. But we have to find a place for you. You must stay hidden for the time being, for he is sure to look for you."

Clara wiped her eyes and nodded.

"We have the advantage that he will think you desperate, and look for you on the streets." Tilly smiled and patted Clara's hand. "I will keep you somewhere much nicer, where he will not find you."

Tilly pulled off her bonnet and gave her ear a rub. The black veil was itchy. Tilly looked at the scratchy lace and the blood drained from her face. A large piece of it had torn away. Good Lord, what if Screwe found it? It would not lead directly to her, but it would at least alert him that his enemy was a woman, which he would certainly never have guessed on his own.

She calmed herself. There were a lot of women in London. And he might not even find the piece of veil, after all.

CHAPTER 8

This time, when Rutherford arrived at the Aldleys with Molly in tow, the earl did not seem surprised, but merely shook his head as he rose from the piano forte to greet him with a smile. It was after their dinner, and they had just gone through to enjoy a little music.

Aldley had been singing and accompanying himself, much to the enchantment of her ladyship. It was a picture of marital bliss that made Rutherford wish he were a better man than to feel pangs of jealousy at the sight of his friend's happiness. His head was starting to ache, but he rallied himself and strode across the room to the spot where the countess stood to receive him.

"Lady Aldley, you look positively radiant. I believe nobility agrees with you." Rutherford bowed over the Countess of Aldley's hand. He had not seen her for some time, but she looked genuinely pleased to see him.

"I should never have thought so before." Her green eyes sparkled with mischief. "And my husband has just chastised me for walking such a long distance as a quarter mile. So it would seem that at least one member of the nobility does not *agree with me*."

"Well perhaps, but you must not generalize, Lady Aldley," Rutherford played along, "Aldley is just an especially disagreeable sort."

"I can see," Aldley handed Rutherford a brandy, "that I should never let you two be in the same room if I am in it."

"And when shall you begin calling me Lydia, Mr. Rutherford? *Lady Aldley* seems a bit stuffy for such a good friend." She gave a sidelong glance to her husband and added dryly, "especially as we so narrowly escaped being married to one another."

Aldley huffed and rolled his eyes. "This again. It was an honest mistake that anyone could have made, under the circumstances. But by all means, do not let me spoil your diversion."

Rutherford snorted and ignored his friend, puffing out his chest and addressing Lydia instead. "You are the second lady today to say such a thing. If my week continues thus, I shall have to begin affecting a swagger."

Aldley coughed. "Begin? Oh I see. I had assumed your current swagger was the product of affectation. Do you mean to say that you have been half lame all along? I do beg your pardon, Rutherford. I have misjudged you."

"It would not be the first time. But, however, as it was not five days ago that I bested you with the foils, I should not harp on about my being half lame, if I were you." Rutherford turned a wolfish grin on Lydia. "Have you repented marrying this one, yet?"

Aldley took his wife by the waist. "No, she has not, impertinent buck, so back with you."

"There you have it." Lydia's smile was saucy, but real affection shone in her eyes. "I am too deliriously happy for regrets. You have it on the authority of Bluebeard, himself."

"And except for her persistent refusal to remain locked in her room like a good wife, and only go where I command her to, I also find myself as deliriously happy as is possible for a blood-thirsty tyrant. I am not at all inclined to murder her. So true love works all things out, even for Bluebeards."

Lydia's chuckle turned into a stifled yawn. She squeezed her husband's hand. "Enough banter. I shall leave you two to your tête-à-tête and retire." They bade their good nights, and she waddled from the room.

When she had gone, Rutherford gave Aldley a serious look. "You were probably right to be concerned about Essington. It seems very likely that he is at the opium again. Lizzy declares herself indifferent, however."

"Indeed. Well, I cannot wonder at her indifference."

"Apparently he is more manageable this way. But she does not know where he is getting it from. I do not believe she has inquired too closely, to be frank. However, I discovered something that could be more serious."

"Oh?" Aldley frowned. "There is nothing the matter with Elizabeth, I hope."

"No, no. Not that. But as I was leaving I saw someone, a man riding from Essington Hall on horseback. It took me some time to place where I had seen him before, but I am quite sure now that he is one of the men who assisted Delacroix in the abduction. I am confounded that it took me so long to recall, for normally I never forget a face I have taken the trouble to punch."

Aldley could not laugh at his friend's wit. His face was dark. "Do you think Delacroix could be back in town?"

"I do not know." Rutherford drained his glass. "But if I were you, I should keep an eye on the countess. Delacroix is smoky enough for anything, and I doubt his thug has found Christianity and taken up honest business."

"Your advice conveniently coincides with my own feelings." Aldley shook his head in despair. "But you see how she calls me Bluebeard for even asking her to not over-exert herself. I am not sure how to persuade her to enter her confinement. If only these blasted empire waists were not all the crack, surely modesty would keep her indoors."

Rutherford had to turn his head to conceal his smile. He doubted any such consideration would constrain the countess—or that she would think her condition something that required modesty. "Perhaps if you warned her, she might at least think the better of going about town without you."

"I do not wish to frighten or distress her, especially in her current condition. I believe I shall have to put my foot down and demand she go into confinement."

"I should hate to stand in your shoes, old boy." Rutherford smiled, but he knew he was lying. He would love to be married and expecting a child with Tilly. If his biggest problem were that she would not stay home enough, he could rest content.

Rutherford scratched Molly's ears to keep his hand from feeling for the bottle in his pocket and added, "Before you do something that may cause marital discord, let me see if I can find the man. I lost him on the way into town, but I am sure he was headed for London. London is irresistible for his sort."

"It is also possible that he is the one bringing my brother-in-law opium." Aldley's expression remained dark.

"The thought had crossed my mind. In fact it seems probable." Rutherford scratched his leg to cover the fact that it was twitching.

"You are a good friend, Rutherford. If you find him, I shall owe you a great debt. Only please have a care, and do not get yourself shot and stabbed again."

"I shall do my best." Rutherford smiled. He would not object to a little injury if Tilly would nurse him back to health again.

CHAPTER 9

Tilly sat before her toilette among the wreckage of a half dozen discarded head-dressings. The turban she had chosen was in a muted cerulean blue silk. It paired flatteringly with her golden hair and blue eyes. More importantly, it had gathers and feathers in the right places to disguise the swollen bump on her head where Clara had clouted her with that arm shackle.

"This one will do, Browning." Her lady's maid look relieved and began gathering up the rejected contenders. "Never mind that. Marie can do it, for I must discuss something with her. Will you deliver this for me instead?" She handed the servant a letter.

When Browning left, Marie entered and began tightening the laces on Tilly's corset.

"Not too tight today, Marie." The bruises on her back from the fall were painful. Tilly popped a confection into her mouth and munched inelegantly as she spoke. "I believe you have some news for me."

"Oui, Mademoiselle. I have been over to see Mrs. Ravelsham. She is so desolée! Her brother, Monsieur Delacroix, has returned to London."

MISTRESS OF TWO FORTUNES AND A DUKE

Yes, that would make Tilly very desolée, too. She cursed under her breath. "How does she know he has returned?" Tilly entertained a hope that there was some mistake. "Has he contacted her?"

"He is in hiding, but he has contrived to see her." Marie's brown eyes were wide with concern, and perhaps a trace of admiration.

"See her? Did she receive him?" It must have been while Frederick was away.

Marie twisted her apron, and a look of conflicted torment plagued her mouth.

"Marie, you need not feel disloyal to your former mistress. You know she needs looking after. Recall that I have only ever worked for her good, and she is my sister-in-law." Tilly ate another confection to ward off a headache.

It was a constant struggle dealing with Marie's dull wits and sense of guilt. Her travels back and forth between the two households put her ever in a dilemma between the desires of the old mistress and those of the new. She wondered if the maid agonized half so much when she gossiped about Tilly to Genevieve.

"Oui, Mademoiselle. She received him while your brother was out. The servants brought him in through the back entrance."

"And she is *desolée* because of her brother's straits?"

"Yes. But I think it is more because he is blackmailing her."

"Blackmailing her?!" Tilly almost could not believe it. Almost. The man was a desperate criminal, after all. He was not above abduction, so blackmail was a trifling matter. But his own sister? And Genevieve must also be one of the few members of the ton who would have anything to do with him, even secretly. She shook her head. Tilly, of all people, should really not be surprised at the degree of darkness within humanity.

"Oui, Mademoiselle. He said something very strange." She paused several moments to recall. "It was, em, that he could no longer blackmail Mrs. Beauchamps, or something alike. So Genevieve was all that was left to him. But she did not tell me what he could have to blackmail her with. She is such a sweet, blameless woman. I cannot imagine."

"Mmm." Tilly forbore sharing her thoughts on the topic, but she would hardly call Genevieve *blameless*. Still, most of what Tilly knew was tame enough.

Some people were more susceptible to the fear of exposure, of course. But a criminal like Delacroix was hardly in a position to expose anyone. She could understand why Genevieve would be upset by the threat, however. "You have done well, Marie. I shall do my best to sort things out."

After breakfast, Tilly retired to a sitting room to enjoy a sweet and creamy cup of chocolate. She had just become engrossed in reading the business section of a newspaper, when a servant interrupted to announce the dowager Lady Delacroix, mother to Genevieve and her blackmailing brother.

What a coincidence to receive such a call, just when she had learned that Delacroix was back in town. Tilly was immediately suspicious. She shuffled her papers aside, and rose to receive her ladyship with a curtsey.

"What a lovely surprise, my lady. I do not believe we have seen each other since Genevieve and Frederick's wedding."

"I think you must be right, Miss Ravelsham. But then, one gets so busy, and you have been out of town for such a long time."

"Oh indeed." They both sat, and Tilly rang for tea, which arrived immediately. "But I am so glad you have called. I hope you have been well."

"Yes, I certainly cannot complain of my health. Though it does tax one's nerves worrying about one's children. One never stops, you know."

"Ah yes." Tilly nodded to Lady Delacroix and poured her a cup of tea—weak, as the lady preferred it. "I suppose I shall have to wait to experience the great joys and sorrows of motherhood."

"I am sure you will be an excellent mother." Lady Delacroix's spine was stick straight as she pretended to drink her tea. "You are so naturally caring and compassionate. And so good at arranging family matters."

"Your ladyship is far too kind." Tilly wondered what sort of favour might warrant this degree of flattery.

"In fact, speaking of family, I thought, now that your brother and my daughter are happily wed, it might not be too much to make a little request of you."

Tilly tried to sound surprised. "Whatever can it be? What service might I perform for your ladyship?"

Lady Delacroix flicked her wrist in the air, as if to wave away a trifling bit of dust. "It is a very little thing. But you know that my son, Pascal, has been abroad for his health, ever since that horrible carriage man shot him."

Tilly forced down the little quirk that was forming in the corner of her mouth, and willed her lips into a bland smile at this edited version of history. She nodded for the deluded woman to continue.

Lady Delacroix's face was the model of maternal concern. "It must tear his nerves to shreds to think of coming back to the land where such a terrible thing happened."

"Does Mr. Delacroix have some plans to return to England?" The woman knew he was already in town. Tilly was sure of it. He must have been in contact with Lady Delacroix as well. Tilly wondered what he might have to blackmail his mother with.

The lady's face tightened, then she assumed a smile. "Well, I know of no such plans, but I worry about him being away in these foreign places, you know. I should like to see him settled somewhere nearby, perhaps in the countryside, and starting a family. If the right living should come available, for example. A nice, retired life as a country parson might be just the thing for his health."

Tilly believed she now knew where this conversation was about to turn, and she attempted a circumvention. "Perhaps his brother, Lord Delacroix, might offer the living at Dunston Hall." That is, if, on the last occasion that Lord Delacroix had entertained him, the younger Delacroix had not stolen everything of value in the manor before fleeing the country. Surely Lady Delacroix must know of her younger son's thievery. Tilly suppressed a laugh at the absurdity of putting him forward as a man of God. "That parson that married Genevieve and Frederick is surely almost ready to retire. He looked to be getting on in years."

"Well, I am not certain of the particulars, but it seems *that* living is not available." Lady Delacroix pursed her lips and hid behind her teacup for a moment. "But as you are such a close friend of the Countess of Aldley, I thought you might know of a living through her husband. The earl has so many estates, and I understand that the family seat, itself, has quite a substantial parsonage."

"Your ladyship seems to have the advantage over me, for I know little of the parsonages within Lord Aldley's gift. But, if you believe one may be available, perhaps you should pay Lady Aldley a call, for you have been her acquaintance longer than I." And, Tilly added mentally, I should love to see the reception that you would get, asking Lydia to assist the man who tried to abduct her. Still, it was probable that Lady Delacroix was ignorant of that piece of her son's effrontery.

Lady Delacroix squared her already square shoulders. "I have not seen her for some time. I only thought that perhaps it might be unseemly to pay call all of a sudden, only to ask a favour."

"Quite. I admire your ladyship's thoughtful forbearance." Unlike showing up on Tilly's doorstep, asking for a favour. On the other hand, Lady Delacroix was Tilly's relation, not Lydia's. It would be selfish of Tilly to fob Lady Delacroix off on her friend.

"Will you, then, enquire on Pascal—on my son's behalf?" A crack in Lady Delacroix's armour showed a brief glance of what lay beneath. True maternal preoccupation—the worn and weathered heart that will always believe in the child she once knew, that will suffer every deprivation and humiliation to protect and care for that child, even if he is a nasty, filthy, hateful criminal who would rob and blackmail his own family.

"I will mention it to Lady Aldley when I see her next. But I must confess that I believe there is little reason for optimism." For, if Delacroix should show his face anywhere near Lord Aldley, the miscreant would most likely meet his God before he ever had a chance to represent Him.

"Oh thank you, Miss Ravelsham. We must take these opportunities, even if prospects do not look bright. One never knows what might turn up." The lady seemed genuinely optimistic.

It occurred to Tilly, as she listened to Lady Delacroix's peculiar brand of deluded audacity, that it would have amused her to no end, a year ago. But something within Tilly had changed, and she now found this character at turns pathetically broken and irritatingly enabling, but never terribly diverting.

Perhaps it was Tilly's countervailing need to protect her own loved ones. After all Delacroix had very nearly violated Lydia. Perhaps Tilly had been sobered by her feelings of guilt that Lydia had once been seriously injured, in part because Tilly had failed to protect her, opting instead to amuse herself by sporting with the bad characters of the Delacroix family. Or was it some of Rutherford's broodiness that was rubbing off on Tilly? She did not know what, but something had changed her.

When Lady Delacroix left, at last, Tilly was faced with a dilemma. She needed to call on Lydia, as she wished to give the Aldleys the earliest possible warning that Delacroix was back in town, but she also should check on Mrs. Johnson—Clara.

It seemed likely that Clara was feeling quite nervous in her new environment, especially as it was crucial that she not go out of doors, and she would naturally wish to look for her child. Still, Tilly could trust the people running the servant academy to make the new inmate feel welcome and to watch over her. It had been either the academy, or the *Academy*, as she euphemistically called the Belle Hire.

She grimaced. Screwe was now on the blacklist at the Belle Hire, but it seemed unlikely that a woman who had so recently been violated and terrorized would wish to hide in a brothel, anyway, no matter how kind and charming the company. And it was the sort of place a person like Screwe would go looking for his escaped victim. He was no doubt working his way through all the brothels in London.

Or would he leave well enough alone? Would he think it better not to do anything that might corroborate his victim's story, should she choose to tell it to a magistrate? She shook her head. Wishful thinking. Screwe expected to behave however he liked with impunity, and he liked power and suffering. He would never let his victim go without a chase, without inflicting whatever punishment he could.

Tilly drummed her fingers on the ebony table. But Clara was safe now. Lydia might not be. It would have to be Lydia first. She had, after all, not seen Lydia since returning from Amsterdam, and hardly at all even since Lydia's homecoming from her honeymoon. It would be good to see her friend. She only wished she had better news to bear.

When she arrived at the grand Aldley home, she was shown into a parlour with a great fireplace and a table full of sweets. It was like a fairytale. Tilly wondered, as she selected a delicacy from the table, if a witch might suddenly appear and try to roast her in the fire for cheekily eating sweets that did not belong to her.

She munched on the confection defiantly, and waited for Lydia to join her. Some time elapsed before Tilly's repose was interrupted, not by the arrival of Lydia, but by the entry of Lord Aldley.

"Miss Ravelsham, it is good to see you. I only wish you had arrived ten minutes ago, for Lydia has just left, despite my strenuous objections."

"Left? She is not yet in her confinement, then?"

"No." The earl's face betrayed his feelings on the topic. "And I have not yet been able to persuade her to do so. I had not thought of it before, but perhaps you might hold some sway. Can you not suggest it to her, Miss Ravelsham? You would be doing us both a great favour, though only one of us might know it."

"I suppose I might, if I ever get to see her." Tilly laughed and shook her head. "Do you know where she has gone, my lord?"

"Where else? Off to another meeting with her *business partner*." His lip curled in distaste. "She will not let me accompany her, either. You will think me a tiresome worrier, but I cannot help being concerned that something will happen to her. She is always tripping about in parts of town that I wish she would never set a foot in."

"While I understand your lordship's concern, I do not think straying a hairsbreadth from Knight's Bridge is so very hazardous. But I shall have a word with her, I promise." Tilly poised her hand over a confection with a delicious looking glazed cherry on top. "May I?"

"Oh, yes, of course. How uncivil of me. Lydia loves to eat sweets now that—now that we are expecting."

"I can understand that." Tilly smiled broadly and munched down the confection in two bites. "Do not trouble yourself ringing for tea, my lord. I shall be on my way again shortly, for I have quite a lot to do today. But," she licked the sugar off her fingers, "before I go, I have some rather awful news. Your lordship might want to be seated."

CHAPTER 10

*R*utherford waited as Smythe made adjustments to his attire, perfecting his azure neckcloth, and giving his brick red jacket a final brush. When this visual marvel was completed, Rutherford bent down to pet Molly, to the visible irritation of Smythe. "You be a good little princess, Molly. I cannot take you with me, but you shall be well attended to while I am gone." She licked his hand and rolled over to expose her growing belly.

When he straightened, the strange pains in his body worsened. His shoulder ached, his leg twitched, and his stomach was cramping. His laudanum bottle was now empty, and he needed more. He thought he might call on his doctor to see if he had any, before he met Frobisher in the sport club.

As he rode in the carriage, he contemplated his most recent distraction from Tilly. He had not yet come up with an idea of how to track down Delacroix's henchman. He had thought of going to Bow Street, but it seemed pointless when he had so little information and a description that half the men in London would answer to. Besides, he had no offence to report. What had happened to Lady Aldley last season had been quite successfully hushed up, and so could not be laid at the feet of those responsible.

No, he would have to find the nasty character himself. But the shadowy side of London was a massive and labyrinthine place. He had no idea where to start, except, perhaps, with the horse. The man had ridden a large chestnut mare, with a white diamond on its forehead and a white stocking on its right hind foot. And it was fast. There could not be so very many horses of that description in London. Perhaps he could hire someone to look for it. Or perhaps it had been stolen—after all it was odd to see a cheap ruffian riding an expensive mount.

His stomach twisted in another cramp, and a cold sweat broke on his brow. Perhaps he should have stayed home and called for the doctor. But no, Rutherford was not a weakling, and he had things to do about town. His carriage pulled up to Doctor Kellerman's home, and he alighted with difficulty, his leg twitching stupidly.

"Wait here, Elms. I shan't be long."

Dr. Kellerman came to him into the small parlour promptly. "Mr. Rutherford! Very good to see you, but you should have sent for me. True, you look peaked and sallow, if you do not mind my saying so—though it may just be the colour of your shirt."

"I do not mind. It is just this blasted pain." Rutherford rubbed his shoulder. "It seems to never go away. And my body has such queer tremblings and pains. Do you not have more laudanum you can give me?"

"Laudanum? You are still taking it? Have you had some recent injury?"

Only to my heart, Rutherford thought. "It is just my shoulder never stops aching."

"Well, I am afraid I cannot help you for I am fresh out myself. I know of a trustworthy apothecary who mixes up batches. He is not too far away."

He wrote out the direction for Rutherford, and as he handed over the paper, he said, "But Mr. Rutherford, I think you must stop taking the laudanum."

"It is the only thing for the pain," Rutherford snapped. Could Kellerman not see he needed medicine?

"I believe the shoulder pain will subside in time. The other symptoms you describe are from the body's growing need for the drug. Over use can cause great health problems."

"I am only using it as necessary. It is medicine given me by a doctor."

"And I tell you, as *your* doctor, that if you do not wean yourself off of it you will go into a decline that shall best you. I have seen it happen to healthy young men."

Rutherford had no more time for lectures. "Thank you for your time, Dr. Kellerman. I have appointments to attend, so I am afraid I cannot stay longer."

Dr. Kellerman looked sad. "I hope if your condition persists, you will summon me."

Rutherford hardly heard the doctor as he quitted the parlour.

CHAPTER 11

When Tilly arrived at the servant academy, she looked around at the improvements. All the peeling wall papers and crumbling plaster in the main hall, dining room and parlour had been cleared away and replaced with plain, unfinished wooden boards. It was not polished or fancy, but clean and practical, and had cost a fraction of the estimate she had been given for the plaster work and wall paper.

She preferred to spend the money on rescuing the dispossessed from the predators of London. The servants had already gone about decorating the freshened walls with the few paintings that Frederick had donated to the cause, and the carpets and tables were all back in place. Tilly was pleased.

The woman who ran the servant academy for Tilly entered and greeted her warmly. "Miss Ravelsham, I am glad you are come."

"Hello, Dawking. I see the improvements have been quite a success. Have you started with the sleeping quarters?"

"That will be next week. It is fortunate that we have some extra spaces to shift people into while their rooms are improved."

Tilly smiled. "So I suppose my timing with the new guest is not the best, then."

The woman shook her head. "Not at all. I believe, as she would have it, your timing was none too soon, Miss."

"Indeed."

"But we also have the new urchin, so we are a bit pressed for space. However, three of our students will be leaving next week to go to placements, so with a few cots squeezed in here and there, it shall go off without a hitch."

"How is the new urchin? Has she told you anything of herself, yet?"

"No. She is a quiet little thing, but she is always watching, and is a fast learner. She won't even tell us her name. We just call her Sweep, because she was as filthy as a chimney sweep when we found her. To be honest, she seems to prefer a dirty face above all things."

"I am mostly come to see Clara, but would you at least introduce me to the child?"

Sweep was industriously peeling potatoes in the kitchen. Her face, as Dawking had foretold, was covered in dirt. And she seemed quite unwilling when Dawking sent her to wash it, before introducing her to Tilly.

"Hello, Sweep." Tilly examined the child when she returned from washing up. She was a tiny thing, with black hair and skinny limbs that were all lines and angles under her black servant's garb. In contrast to the smudged face, the little girl's frock was remarkably clean.

"Hello, Miss." The child bobbed a curtsey. "Mistress Dawking says I am to thank you for taking me in."

"I am very glad that you have a place here. You may thank me by attending your lessons and learning as much as you can." Tilly remarked how seriously the child's dark eyes looked at her—they had an amber halo around the rim.

She could see why Wheeler had called them crone-like. They were vaguely disturbing, set in the face of a child. And what a face it was, with delicate bones and creamy skin tinted slightly amber. It seemed strangely familiar, but Tilly could not place it.

"That I shall, Miss. And I am already learning such a great lot, that Levi says I shall replace her soon." Sweep smiled impishly.

Tilly smiled back. The little girl was charming and she would grow up to be remarkably handsome. Tilly thanked heaven that her people had got to her before someone like Red Martha did. Then Tilly had a sudden revelation about why the girl's face was so familiar. "Sweep, have you met the new guest?"

"The secret guest, what keeps to her room, and no one is to know about?"

Tilly nodded, trying not to laugh at the obvious failure to preserve secrecy the child innocently displayed.

"No, Miss."

"I am just going to go visit her. Perhaps you would like to make her acquaintance?"

"I should like that, Miss. But then again, these potatoes won't peel themselves." The earnestness of Sweep's face as she said this made Tilly laugh.

Tilly turned to Dawking. "I thought you said she was a quiet little thing."

Dawking was trying very hard not to laugh herself, as she said to Sweep, "I am sure Levi will still have work for you, when you get back."

Tilly found herself glad for the improvements as she walked down the academy halls to the servant's quarters. Everything smelled less dank, but she knew the rooms were still dingy. She hoped Clara's spirits were not too oppressed.

When Clara opened the door to the tiny chamber she had been settled in, she looked apprehensive and her eyes were shadowed. But she smiled at Tilly.

"Miss Ravelsham. I have been wishing to thank you. And I am so grateful that you have come to see me. Have you any news of my—"

"Mama!" Sweep dashed past Tilly's skirts and into Clara's arms.

"Oh my darling! My baby!" Clara cried.

"I see my suspicion was correct." Tilly hated that she was a little teary-eyed at this sight. The emotion of the mother and child was quite understandable, but in Tilly it was mere sentimental foolishness.

She waited several moments while the two hugged and sobbed and marvelled that they had found one another. Then Tilly decided that it was the wrong time for her to talk to Clara. "Clara, I will leave you with your daughter. I think you and I should speak another time."

The woman, who was openly bawling, only nodded and said, through trembling, snotty lips, "How can I thank you? You have given me back my life and my heart."

Tilly was once again struck by the tremendous power of motherhood over women. Then she chided herself for comparing the Delacroix offspring to Sweep, who was growing on Tilly. There was little doubt that Clara would do anything for her child. She had almost remained in Lord Screwe's lair because of Sweep, after all. But *her* child was fundamentally good, even if a bit dirt-encrusted.

Tilly shook her head to dispel her mawkishness. She still had to go down to the warehouse and consult with Shaw. "You can thank me by healing up, taking care of Sweep, and thinking about what you would like to do with the rest of your life."

Clara wiped her eyes with the back of her hand. "What I *want* to do?"

"Yes, mama," Sweep piped in. "Miss Ravelsham helps people be safe and happy and *gainfully employed*. Just ask Mistress Dawking."

Mistress Dawking had already crept away from the scene of so many tears.

"Is that so?" asked Clara of Sweep, then turned to Tilly. "I do not wonder at it. You have already rescued me and my child, Miss Ravelsham. We are already safe and happy, thanks to you."

"Well then, all that remains is the *gainfully employed* bit." Tilly returned the smiles of the two beaming faces. "Think about it, and I will assist you, if I can."

CHAPTER 12

Rutherford cursed his shaking leg as he debarked from the barouche in an unpleasant warehouse area, near the river. If only the blasted apothecary had some laudanum to sell, but alas he was out too, and directed Rutherford to the warehouse where the apothecary bought his supply. He suggested that Rutherford send a servant, but that would be too much delay.

The owners, the apothecary assured, not only sold pure opium, but also mixed up a good, reliable formula—though perhaps not quite as good as his own—and delivered it to certain households. He indicated that they might also set up a delivery schedule for Rutherford. He had mentally scoffed, for surely he did not need a delivery schedule. Only he was a bit sick just at the moment, and he needed some medicine.

He was thinking the better of it now, for he should prefer never to return to this place, which stank quite dreadfully. He supposed he could send a servant, but delivery would certainly be more convenient.

His was the only vehicle about that could reasonably be called a carriage, and the street's denizens went to and fro in a shadowy, indistinct existence. Rutherford was glad he had brought his family sword, which he thought gave him an air of distinction down at the sport club. He was now dreadfully late for his fencing appointment with Frobisher, but it could not be helped.

There was a small hut attached to the larger building, which he assumed served as the *office* for the warehouse. An evil sort of greasy film coated the door, but he nonetheless reached out his cane and knocked on this inauspicious portal.

A decent looking man in spectacles displayed an ink-stained hand as he opened the door to Rutherford and gave him a looking over. "Good evening, sir. I believe your business may be conducted on the other side of that door down there." He indicated a small door in the side of the warehouse that Rutherford had missed before. There were several unsavoury looking youngsters hanging about it in the shadows.

"And how do you know what my business is, sir?" Rutherford tried not to betray his disturbance at having been so summarily sized up by this total stranger.

"I have developed an eye for it, sir."

Rutherford pulled out a kerchief and mopped his face. "I am come to get some medicine," he said. "I am not well, you see, but my doctor has run out, and so has the apothecary to whom he referred me. So I am come to enquire here."

"I am not surprised." The man rubbed an eye, knocked his spectacles askew, then straightened them. "There is a shortage in town. I believe it will be temporary, but it has driven the price up."

"I am not concerned about the price, but I should prefer to have it delivered." And to never set foot in this smoky little corner of London again. "And I should also prefer," he gave a meaningful glance at the lads around the other shadowy door, "to do my business with you."

"I am expecting company for a business meeting, and I do not handle sales." The man pinned Rutherford with a steel-eyed gaze as if to penetrate his stupidity and make him understand. "I do not have any laudanum in my office."

For the first time in his life, Rutherford wished he were a duke, so that he might pull rank on this disobliging man. But all he had at the moment was money. "I am willing to pay an extra fee."

The man made to close the door. Rutherford did not wish to be fobbed off on the pack of hungry jackals around the other door. He pushed past the man into the little hut, aware of how rude it was, but unwilling to be put off. "You must assist me, I dema—" The protest died on his lips as his mouth gaped open and he watched Tilly enter the little office from a back door. "My God. Tilly."

"Mr. Rutherford." Tilly looked at first displeased, and then compassionate. "You look unwell. Please sit down."

Rutherford collapsed into a wooden chair. "This must be some horrible dream."

"I am very pleased to see you too, Mr. Rutherford." The levity in Tilly's voice sounded forced.

CHAPTER 13

Tilly stood in the cramped office of her opium warehouse and stared at Rutherford. She had avoided seeing the worst of what her drugs could do, but she had seen enough to know what she was looking at. Her heart clenched as she watched him cover his face with his hands and shake. This was her stallion, and she was poisoning him—not just figuratively but literally.

Was she really, as the admiring Sweep had said, a person who helped people to be safe and happy? It seemed that she was, in fact, a devil, who ensnared people and took away their happiness and security in exchange for slavery. She was no better than the slave traders she abhorred. No better than Screwe. She had never felt so low in all her life.

Tilly gave her manager, Shaw, a look, and he quietly stepped outside.

"Oh, Willi—" *William* just did not sound right. It somehow seemed less intimate than his last name. "Rutherford." She reached out to lay a hand on his back, but withdrew quickly.. Her touch was like the laudanum, a temporary comfort that disguised an insidious corrosion. She did not deserve to touch him.

He looked up at her. "Tilly, how do you come to be in such a place as this?"

She could not hide her guilt. "I could ask the same of you, but I know the answer. Oh, you must listen to me, and give up this horrible habit. It will kill you."

"But how come you to be here?" Through his sweat and shaking, a glimmer of clarity was forming in his eyes.

"I wish I could say I am come to rescue you. But I will not conceal the truth from you. I own this warehouse. I was here to meet with Mr. Shaw, my accountant and manager. I am to blame for your condition." Her voice trailed off.

"Then I suppose you can arrange to get me more of the medicine. True I am dying, Tilly." He looked at her pathetically.

"But I would be giving you poison. It is not medicine for you, Rutherford. Seeing you here, I cannot justify myself any longer. The way I am selling it, it is not medicine at all."

Rutherford laughed hoarsely, then winced and pressed his hand to his stomach. "Do you know, I think Aldley is rubbing off on me. At the moment I do not much care what you are selling. In fact I find myself strangely thankful that you deal in opium. But I suffered a moment of shock just now when I heard that you were *in trade*."

Tilly laughed sadly. She reached out to him and stroked his head.

He leaned into her hand. "Ah my angel, how I love you. I never meant to be like this."

"I know it." She wrapped her arms around his shoulders and kissed his head. "I know you have never been anything but brave and good. I have never deserved you."

"How can you say that? I live for you. True, I do not care that you own this enterprise—though I wish you were not so directly involved." He paused for another spasm of pain. "Darling, can you not get me some laudanum, just a little, so that we may speak without my convulsing every five minutes?"

Tilly was torn. Her instinct was to deny him any more of the poison, but she hated to see him in such suffering. She straightened her spine. "I will get you a small dose, if you agree to wean yourself off of it."

"Agreed." His smile was too ready.

She sighed and went to the door to speak to Shaw. In a few minutes she had a bottle of laudanum, from which she dropped a light dose into a half mug of cold tea.

He drank it immediately and thanked her.

"It will not end your discomfort entirely, but it will stave off the worst for a while. Remember your promise, Rutherford. It will be a painful process, but you must be strong and fight through it." She looked down in sadness. "I will have the lads bring you a supply, but it will be diminishing every week. You must promise me that you will pace it out to last the whole week, and not take extra and then go searching after more."

"I shall." His breathing was already slowing, and he was shaking less.

She stroked his hair. "You will get the better of this, my stallion."

"It would be easier if I knew you would be mine. I love you, Tilly. I think it is the torment of seeing you slip away from me and knowing you will soon join with another man that has driven me to this." His face was open and full of an anguish that the laudanum could not address.

She fought the desire to kiss him, to strip off all of his clothes and bring him to ecstasy. It was probably not possible at the moment, and it was not what he needed. He needed the love of a good woman, not the passion of a poisoner. She heaved a despairing sigh.

"No," he said. "Forgive me for saying that. It was unmanly of me to blame my weakness on you." He stood and enfolded her in his arms. "I love you so. And this is not your fault."

She knew very well that it was. But for once in her mouthy little life, words failed her, and she pressed her face into his chest in desperation. She could feel the inevitable creeping up on her. She could not hold on to him, or she would destroy him. But she loved him.

The realisation terrified her. She had to fight back the tears forming in her startled eyes. She loved him like no one else in this world, and if she wished to save him, she had to let him go.

Their moment was interrupted by the sound of someone unfastening the door latch. They released each other and stood apart instinctively, just as the office door opened, and Crump stepped inside.

"Begging your pardon, Miss. Only there has been a terrible accide—"

Rutherford lunged for the man. Tilly only restrained him from attacking by throwing herself in front of Crump. "Do not! He is not who you think he is!"

"I *think* he is one of the two men who tried to assist in the abduction of a woman who is a close friend of both of us." Rutherford reached for his sword. "Pray, tell me why I should not flay the bastard here and now?"

Crump's body clenched, but then his gaze dropped to the ground in sad concession.

"Because he has changed. He works for me now." Tilly reached out to stay Rutherford's sword hand. "And because to injure him you will have to injure me."

Beads of sweat glistened on Rutherford's forehead as he stared intently at Crump, who lifted his head to return the gaze, not in anger, but in sadness.

"Please sit down Mr. Rutherford. All will be explained." She tried to smile consolingly at him.

He turned and looked at her peculiarly. "Right, I shall sit down." He took his chair. "But it is only a coward who lets a woman be his shield."

Tilly suppressed a strong impulse to roll her eyes and scoff. "We could equally question the valour of jumping to take a sword to an unarmed man, before one even knows all the circumstances. Discretion is certainly not the better part of such conduct."

Rutherford sulked.

Crump cleared his throat. "I see some explainin' is called for. Only it might be better if yer could wait on it. It is yer friend, Miss, the countess. She has taken a bad fall."

"What have you done to her?!" Rutherford was on his feet again, and Tilly had to push him back down.

"Crump has done nothing to her. I had him watching over Lady Aldley because I got word that Delacroix was back in town."

"Delacroix? Well that is like setting the wolf to keep watch over the lambs. Why did you not warn her?"

"I tried to. I told Lord Aldley, but he informed me that Lydia had already left on some errands, so I got word to Crump right away. And before you get your back up again," she put a steadying hand on Rutherford's shoulder, "let me remind you that Crump was *protecting* Lady Aldley."

"If I might continue, Miss."

Tilly nodded.

"Delacroix came after her, I made for him and she scampered off. I thought she had got away, but she fell badly. I let Delacroix escape and I attended her, but she would not wake. I got her to the, uh," his gaze flicked briefly to Rutherford, "*Academy*, as it was the closest place I could take her. Then I fetched the doctor. He is with her now, and I made off to fetch yer."

"So she is at the academy? We must get her home right away. It is fine enough for the students, but no place for the countess."

"Em, no Miss. Not the academy. The *Academy*."

"Hang on a minute—is he speaking of a *brothel?*" Rutherford shook his head and sought Tilly's eyes with his own. "Who *are* you, really?"

Tilly only shrugged. "That will also have to wait. We must go to her. Unless, of course, your moral delicacy will prevent you from ever entering such a place." Tilly arched an incredulous brow.

"Not at all, I assure you." Rutherford's face was flinty.

Tilly carefully tucked her turban under the wide-brimmed bonnet that she used to hide her face and wished that she could hide her *everything*. "I do not suppose," she sighed, "that either of you has a biscuit?"

CHAPTER 14

The inside of the Belle Hire was spotless. Several of the students from Tilly's servant academy had found placements there, but only the best and most discreet. Some were constrained by a sense of dignity that they could not reconcile with working in a brothel, but for many the allure of higher wages and very stable employment was sufficient inducement.

As she walked up the servant staircase to the upper rooms, Tilly hoped the high standards for cleanliness, quality and discretion might possibly conceal from Lydia that she was convalescing in a bawdy house.

Lydia and Tilly shared many secrets, and Lydia was no prude, but Tilly felt the countess was not quite ready to know all of Tilly's covert dealings. She only really wanted to help the women who worked at the brothel, but would Lydia understand Tilly's motives? She could not bear losing Lydia's friendship, but more importantly, Tilly did not wish to derange her friend's nerves any more than they must already be. The countess was with child, after all.

That should have been sufficient reason for Lydia to stay at home, but the countess was headstrong and loved her secret business dealings as much as Tilly loved her own. Lydia owned a shop for hair pomades and accoutrements, however. It was not quite the same thing.

On the other hand, Lydia had promised her husband that she would control the enterprise from a distance and not be personally involved with the shop. Clearly Lord Aldley had not known that Lydia's *meeting with her business partner* would be at the shop in question.

Lydia, too, was hiding things. Tilly hoped that this fact might persuade Lydia not to judge her too harshly.

When Tilly entered the chamber, a robust fire blazed in the hearth. The flames threw a cherry amber glow on Lydia's face and lit up the highlights in her copper hair. She was sleeping, breathing normally. Tilly sat herself on the indigo velvet cushion of the bedside chair and held Lydia's hand.

"If Delacroix has harmed you, or your babe, I shall kill him," she whispered.

She sat and quietly watched her friend for a quarter hour, and then rose to light tapers around the room. The doctor would arrive again soon and would need light.

"Where am I?" came a sleepy voice behind her.

Tilly's heart leapt with joy and she turned to see Lydia awake and smiling. "You are awake!"

"Well, Tilly. It is very good to see you. However, it seems that whenever I wake up in a strange place, you appear before me." She grinned with mischief. "I suppose I should be thankful Mr. Rutherford is not here with you."

Tilly embraced Lydia gently. "Oh, he is here. But I made him wait in the parlour. There was not really any place in the chamber for us to do indecent things while you slept, you see."

"Same old Tilly. True it is good to see you."

Tilly's face turned serious. "The doctor will arrive soon to examine you. How are you feeling?"

"Very refreshed, to tell the truth. I do not believe I have slept this well in a long time. This bed is terribly comfortable."

"So, you do not feel altered? And you remember everything?"

Lydia's face clouded. "Yes. Yes, I remember. But the joy of seeing you drove it from my mind." She shook her head. "Delacroix is back."

"I know. I heard. I called at Aldley House to tell you, but you had already left."

Lydia looked troubled. "Thomas will be so cross if he finds out I was down at the store." Then her face lit up suddenly. "It is doing so very well, Tilly, and business just keeps growing."

Tilly smiled at her friend's excitement. She had just been accosted by a horrid man and had taken a bad fall trying to escape, but she was all a dither about her business. "I am very glad to hear it. And I shan't tell Lord Aldley you were down at the shop, but we probably do need to tell him about Delacroix's affront."

Lydia scowled. "He walks sort of half bent over now, you know. Delacroix, I mean. And he is very gaunt. I have never seen anyone so altered in such a short time. He looks older too. He would be positively Gothic, if he were not so pathetic. I was not running from him, you know. The little worm was trying to blackmail me. Imagine. He claimed the child I was carrying was probably his. I told him that such a belief betokened a rather poor grasp of the subject matter involved."

Tilly laughed. "This was a kinder reply than he deserved."

Lydia scoffed. "And then the sad little beast suggested that Thomas himself was the bastard child of Lady Aldley and Beauchamps. He called our babe a *bastardly gullion*. I was about to plant him a facer, but then I saw he had that henchman with him. The one who pulled me off my horse in the park."

"Ah. Really." Tilly tried to keep her face neutral.

"Indeed. I should like to drag them both before a magistrate. But anyway, the henchman is a great, hulking beast, and I ran when I saw him. Then I fainted, which is humiliating. It happens now and again if I exert myself, or my nerves are too agitated." She rubbed her belly and grinned. "I suppose the little one did not much care for being jounced around."

"Probably not." Tilly smiled at Lydia's maternal happiness. "Your husband begged me to persuade you to enter your confinement. I think it may be time, my dear friend. Only think what might have happened to the baby."

Lydia sighed. "Yes, yes. Everyone is so terribly prudent. But I had already decided to do so, before all this happened. True, my back pains me all of the time now. And it is almost impossible to conceal, even with a cape and an empire waist. I just wanted to check on the store once more before I was incarcerated."

"I am glad to hear you shall be an obedient little inmate. And you know I shall come visit you in gaol."

"You are very good. But I should expect nothing less from the woman who marries compromised débutantes off to rich relatives and redeems criminals to give them work."

Tilly blanched. Her friend did not know the half of it. Lydia knew that Tilly was trying to help Wheeler, who had once done Lydia a very bad turn while working for Lydia's rival. But Lydia did not know Wheeler was working for Tilly. And Tilly could not tell her friend about Crump yet. Not when Lydia might be so delicate. It could wait until the doctor pronounced her well, and she had been returned home.

Tilly forced a bright smile. "Perhaps I should make a professional service of it and hang out a shingle next to your shop. *Miss Ravelsham's Bleach, Starch and Press—Reputation Cleaners.*"

"Too long. How about *Five-a-penny Faradiddles and Frauds?*"

Tilly tapped her lips pensively. "I shall allow that you have a natural talent for jingles and shingles. But as usual, you do not charge enough."

CHAPTER 15

*R*utherford sat in the neat, warm parlour of the Belle Hire and pretended to read a paper. He surreptitiously eyed Crump, who stood near the fire. It seemed he would not be seated, but always stood at attention, and it irked Rutherford.

On the other hand, it would have vexed him doubly so, if the man had put on airs and seated himself, as though he were a gentleman and not some cheaply hired reprobate servant. Rutherford supposed the principal problem was that he detested the sight of the yahoo.

It was also possible that he was just cross as two sticks. He might not hate the man so, if Tilly had not betrayed them all by taking him into her employ. What sort of person was she? Did Rutherford know her at all? And yet he was utterly fascinated by her. Her shady dealings, though he could not approve of them in any official way, made him long for her even more.

His shoulder was aching. He could no longer deny that the pain was an artefact of some other affliction—love for Tilly or for this blasted drug.

Even as he had the thought, his hand felt the pocket where the loathsome bottle was hidden, its evil vapours churning inside, whispering sweet lies to him. He had to best this illness.

And he had decided that he would take Tilly up on her offer. As much as it pained him to be so pedestrian and weak, she had probably seen many such cases. Surely she knew the secret to curing him. It was also possible that being in a weakened state was the way to Tilly's heart.

He rubbed his shoulder and smiled faintly, not sure whether to mock this mad hope, or to indulge it.

Tilly entered the room.

Rutherford stood. "How is she?"

Tilly smiled and his heart fluttered. God help him. They seated themselves close beside each other on a low-backed couch, as Tilly reported, "I believe she will be well. It seems she only fainted because she was exerting herself—at least that is how she has it. But I have been talking with her, and she seems herself."

"Did she fall? Did she hit her head?"

"I saw no injury to her head. She fainted while running away—unfortunately because she saw Crump and believed him to be working with Delacroix."

Rutherford's face twisted. "Her surmise was not unreasonable. You do not know where his allegiance lies either."

"Oh, but I do." She smiled and patted his hand. "But it is sweet of you to worry so. On the other hand, I should ask Crump to clear out before she sees him. She does not need further agitation."

Rutherford's frustrated sigh was his only answer.

"The doctor is examining her now," Tilly continued. "I have ordered a chair to bring her downstairs and out to the carriage. Assuming the doctor permits it, we should return her to Aldley House as soon as may be."

Rutherford winced to think of his friend's mental state. "Yes, Aldley must be beside himself. I am sure she is never out without him this late."

"I have already sent him word that she is well and should be home shortly. But I doubt his anxiety will be quelled until she is safely at his side."

Rutherford smiled, "And then, if I know him at all, he shall never leave her unattended again, until the child comes, and for some time after."

"It speaks well of him that he cares for her so dearly." Tilly turned away quickly, but Rutherford had seen the mist in her eyes.

He reached out his hand, and tipped Tilly's chin back to face him. Her periwinkle blue eyes shone so full of her heart. He knew he could never give up on her. Not even if she had this other, unseemly side.

For what else had he been looking for but a woman with whom he would never be bored? He could feel his body responding to her, to that look of heart-filled longing that she could not conceal.

He leaned his head to her ear and whispered, "Yes, it does speak well of him. His heart is so true, and it is truly hers. No matter what great risks she takes with her own happiness, with the happiness of both of them, he will never stop loving her more than he loves his own life."

CHAPTER 16

Tilly felt the sudden need to flee from the Belle Hire, from the magnetic love of Rutherford, from the body and the heart and sweet mouth that drew her in and weakened her resolve to do what she must do.

He was so close to her, whispering in her ear. It was all she could do not to drag him upstairs to one of the rooms. She stood suddenly, aware that she was panting.

She could see that he was sweating and pale, still craving laudanum. And yet his eyes fixed on her, and his penetrating stare was victorious.

"Whatever is the matter, Tilly?" He smiled rakishly. "Are you unwell?"

"I am well enough." She returned his gaze and lifted her chin. "Only I must go give Crump instructions and get the servants to take the chair up for Lydia."

"Indeed." Rutherford played his finger across his beautiful lips, making Tilly want to kiss them. "We should not risk her trying to come down on her own."

"No." Tilly tried to control her breathing. She left the room to attend to the chair and to save her own sanity.

They arrived at the Aldley home shortly after nine o'clock and had their cargo carefully unloaded into the parlour.

"Am I permitted to stand now?" Lydia was petulant. "Or must I suffer myself to be carried around like some Chinese empress for the rest of my life?" She did not wait for a reply and stood.

Lord Aldley forgot that anyone was there and rushed to embrace his wife. "Darling! I have been so worried. Thank God you are home. Are you all right?"

"I am very well, thank you. A little irritated that Mr. Delacroix is back in town."

Aldley paled. "Yes. Wait—did he approach you? I will kill him!"

"Calm yourself." Lydia walked over to the fire to warm her hands. "I would prefer my child's father not to be tried for murder. Besides, it seems unlikely you would even recognize him if you saw him. He is so altered. He has become a foetid little hunchback from a Gothic novel."

"I am glad you are well, but I cannot stand by and allow a common criminal to accost my wife—particularly while she is carrying our babe. Has this man not one grain of decency?" Lord Aldley took up the fire poker and assaulted the log in the fireplace.

"In fact, I believe it was our child that interested him." Lydia stepped back from the fierce blaze and ensconced herself on her favourite chaise longue. "He seems to think he might extract money from us by threatening to reveal the paternity not only of the child, but of you, if you can imagine."

There was a deadly gleam in Aldley's eye. "He did not dare suggest..."

Tilly did not scruple but to interrupt glibly. "Audacity is a Delacroix trait, it would seem."

"Oh, he dared," continued Lydia. "The little lump of pig dung called our child a *bastardly gullion*."

Aldley's fists clenched. "He dares insult my child and accost my wife. He shall not get away with this."

"I was about to draw his cork," she smiled like she would have greatly enjoyed punching the villain, "but then his henchman chased me off."

Rutherford gave Tilly a pointed look. Lydia was lying down. Tilly supposed it was as good a time as any. She cleared her throat. "Yes, well about that."

Everyone turned to look at her. Tilly swallowed. "You see, Mr. Crump no longer works for Delacroix. He has reformed his ways and now works for me, guarding my warehouses and such."

Lydia's eyes narrowed and her lips flattened. She looked at Tilly like a cat doused with water.

"And how, pray tell," Aldley's voice was cold and only kept from sounding menacing by an obvious exertion of will, "did *Mr. Crump* come to accost my wife?"

"He did not accost her." Tilly raised a palm, as though the gesture might calm the earl. "After I called on your lordship, and discovered that Lydia was out, I asked Mr. Crump to watch over her, from a distance. When he saw Delacroix approach her, he went after him. Only Lydia misunderstood Crump's intentions and ran away. Which is when she fainted."

"You have done it again," accused Lydia. "You have put your blasted redemption schemes ahead of the happiness and wellbeing of your friends."

"I did not think you would ever find out." Tilly looked desperately at her friend. "True, Mr. Crump genuinely has changed, and he is very sorry for his role in Delacroix's attempt at abducting you. And I was thinking of your safety, more than your happiness. It was thoughtless of me to put him on the task of guarding you. *Thoughtless*, and this is all my fault, I will warrant you. But I only did it because Mr. Crump is very good at guarding and knows what Delacroix looks like. When I heard Delacroix was in town, I was so worried for you."

Lydia did not relent, but shook her head and stared at Tilly.

Tilly turned to Aldley. "Lord Aldley, will you not take my part?" She was desperate. "You know I was concerned, and so were you, my lord."

The earl did not look very inclined to support her. "If you knew where Lydia was, why did you not simply tell me, so I could protect her, instead of sending some yahoo?"

She looked from Aldley to Lydia, whose expression was tense. Tilly would not reveal to Lord Aldley that Lydia had been down to her shop. Tilly could not betray her friend's confidence, even to defend herself in this ridiculous situation. "It did not occur to me where she might be until after I left you, my lord."

Lydia's face relaxed. She released a breath she had been holding. "Very well, Tilly. There is no harm done. In fact," she wriggled into the blanket behind her on the chaise longue, "I had a rather good time of it. I have always wanted to see your brothel."

Tilly blanched. This situation was not going well. She decided to play innocent, for as long as that lasted. "Whatever can you mean?" But if Lydia knew about her brothel, why in God's name did she not keep her mouth shut about it in front of Aldley? It was as though she were intentionally setting the cat among the pigeons.

"I mean the house of ill repute in which I convalesced after my faint." Lydia was beaming. "I am only disappointed that I did not get to see a bird of paradise."

Rutherford shook with silent laughter. Tilly could kick him, the traitor.

A look of horror crept into Aldley's face. "Do I rightly understand what I am hearing, Miss Ravelsham? Surely I do not, for it *sounds* as though you brought my wife, the *countess*, into a common bawdy house."

Tilly lifted her chin with wounded pride. "It is not a common bawdy house. It is quite uncommon, I assure you." Her voice trailed off. "And only ever so slightly bawdy."

"Well, there you are then." Lydia had such a gleeful look of enjoyment on her face that Tilly wished to steal the pillow upon which the countess smugly rested and beat her about the head with it.

Lydia turned to her husband, whose features were contorted with the effort of suppressing his rage. "I am famished, thank you for asking, darling. Will you have a servant bring me some biscuits and a tisane." Then she addressed Tilly with a smirk, "Would you like to join me, Tilly?"

She was still miffed with Lydia's so casually revealing her secrets. On the other hand, *biscuits*. Tilly had not had time for so much as one bonbon down at the Belle Hire. "Yes, thank you, Lydia. That would be just the thing."

CHAPTER 17

When Tilly went to call upon her brother, she was bone-weary. Her day had not been much longer than usual, for she was accustomed to keeping herself occupied. It was not even all the trying to protect secrets, and rescuing, and dealing, at every turn, with more people in need of help.

The thing that really drained her was having her friends turn on her in accusation, when Tilly's secrets were only exposed in the first place because her need to help Lydia quickly had made her incautious. When they discovered her unusual enterprises, they did not seek to understand. They were not grateful for the risks she had taken to aid them, but instead, leapt to judge her.

She supposed Lydia might be forgiven for disapproving of Crump, as she was still frightened of him. He had assaulted her once, though not with an intention of hurting her, just with a sort of desperate indifference as to what Delacroix might plan to do to her.

He had acted very wrongly, and Crump knew it. He was, unlike Delacroix, regretful. And like so many others Tilly had encountered, his misconduct was driven by desperate circumstances.

Yes, Lydia might be pardoned for her fear and mistrust, particularly as she did not seem to disapprove of being placed in a brothel to recover. This showed that her mind was more open than most. In fact she had seemed rather scintillated. But Aldley's face had been a study in angry disapproval.

She understood he was worried about Lydia, especially now that Delacroix was creeping about the city, following and harassing his wife. But Tilly could not accept his immediately assuming an air of superiority, as if his wife would catch some moral disease by being in such a place, and completely ignoring the fact that her removal there had been dictated by necessity.

Had he thanked Tilly for saving his wife and unborn child from harm, for trying to protect them? No, he had not. He had looked down on Tilly, and had not even asked where his wife had been when she was accosted, that she might be most expediently removed to a brothel.

In retrospect, that was probably why Lydia had let the cat out of the bag about the Belle Hire. She was trying to distract her husband from asking any questions about her own conduct.

It was a shameless betrayal. Lydia should not have promised Aldley to stay away from her little shop, unless it was a promise she would keep. And now Lydia's need to hide this bit of trivial nonsense from her husband had also become Tilly's problem.

Tilly did not see why she should always be the one to carry the burden of other peoples' secrets, to make constant sacrifices and assume undeserved blame, in order to prop up other peoples' relationships. And she had expected better from her friends.

Frederick and Mr. DeGroen entered the parlour and immediately made for Tilly's side.

"Come now, Tiddlywinks. Why does your sweet little face look so sour?" DeGroen eyed the half-empty dish of bonbons beside her. "It cannot be for want of sugar, I see."

"Yes, Tiddly." Frederick jounced her elbow several times, to make her hand fly about madly, as had been his amusement since they were children. "What has happened now?"

"My friends have turned on me." She knew she was pouting, and she popped another sweetie in her mouth, then spoke around it. "They know about the brothel, and Rutherford knows about the opium warehouse, and it is all only because I risked exposure by trying to help them. But now they think I am a bad woman for my troubles."

"But you *are* a bad woman." DeGroen's smile was rakish. "It is one of your very best features."

Tilly rewarded him with a bland curl of the lips. "Thank you, John. You are not a bad man at all, despite appearances."

He patted her arm. "Why not tell us what happened?"

When she finished reciting her tale of woe, the bonbon dish was empty, and she felt a little better.

"I know it is hard, my dear sister." Frederick shrugged. "But then, you have always been a bit misunderstood."

"But I am not used to it from Lydia. And she sacrificed me to save her own stupid little marital secret. Aldley would have easily forgiven her for it. It is such a nothing."

"I suppose the question is, will *you* forgive *her*."

Tilly sighed. "Probably." She rudely mopped bits of sugar out of the dish and licked her fingers. "You know how terribly stupid I am."

"I know you are feeling judged and betrayed, but remember, they cannot really hurt you." DeGroen picked up the bowl with a look of distaste and placed it out of her reach on the mantel. "They cannot expose you without exposing themselves. They will keep your secret. We may hope that in time they get used to it."

"We may hope." Tilly looked glum.

"And what of Mr. Rutherford?" DeGroen lowered his lids and peered out from beneath his lashes. "Has he abandoned you as a fallen woman?"

"Of course not." Tilly was disgusted and despised herself, as Rutherford would not despise her, for what she had done to him. "He is even more taken with my defects than you are, dearest fiancé."

Frederick and DeGroen chuckled.

She tried to share in the light humour. "So why are you two not out causing trouble at Almack's? Or have they finally revoked your memberships?"

"Hardly," Frederick scoffed. "Despite their pretences, that set cannot resist the smell of money. And new money is like blood to a hound's nose. What society lady can abstain from an opportunity to enrich herself while still flattering her own sense of superiority? Thank God I am a married man now." He tilted his head at DeGroen. "But they haven't given up on him yet, though he is betrothed. Relentless leaches."

"It is too much to be endured. I shall be glad to leave that part of my life behind when we marry." DeGroen moved close and kissed Tilly's head. "Then I shall not have to suffer the endless incursions of the *dégoûtantes*. The little chits get more audacious every year."

Frederick shrugged. "It is your fault for being so angelically handsome."

"And," Tilly smirked, "so devilishly rich."

DeGroen pretended to preen. "I am sure you shall rid me of that curse, soon enough. For what else is a wife for, if not to run her husband into poverty with her love of high stakes and lady's fancies?"

Tilly was formulating a pert reply when the servant announced Lord Screwe.

"Ruddy hell," she hissed and flew into her chair, taking up her dusty fancy sewing.

They all stood as the viscount entered and made their greetings. Frederick formally introduced Tilly, which, though unavoidable, was supremely irritating to her. Tilly exerted extreme facial control as she seated herself again, and became a dull young maiden with nothing in her head but her next stitch.

"Charming to see you, my lord," Frederick drawled. "To what do we owe this great pleasure?"

Screwe's oily gaze slid about the room, looking for anything it might exploit or colonize with its unwholesome extromission. Tilly bowed her head to her needlework and shifted to move it closer to the candlelight, and to turn her ear to the gentlemen's conversation.

"I should think you would recall." Screwe's voice was nasally, and his breathing whistled and wheezed in his lungs like the screeching of distant rats scampering through derelict catacombs. "I owe you a debt." He placed a fold of notes in Frederick's hand, then added in a louder voice, "And I *always* repay my debts."

Tilly mulled this over. This was a vulgar thing to speak of, and it was a generally accepted fact that Screwe did *not* always repay his debts. It was one of the major infractions that got him kicked out of White's. Was this comment meant as a threat? Did he blame her brother for the loss of his slave? Had he puzzled things out that far? The thought was disconcerting, and she tried to keep her fear for Frederick from registering on her face as she strangled an innocent violet with her ill-aimed embroidery yarn.

"Why thank you, my lord." Frederick inclined his head. "I admit it had entirely escaped my mind. And it is most obliging of your lordship to deliver the purse personally." He smiled at his own word play and rang the bell. "Will you not stay for some brandy, my lord?"

"Indeed I shall." His evil gaze cast a shadow in Tilly's direction. "Perhaps we should go to the study, so we can have a manly talk. I cannot abide all these coloured yarns and needles."

Tilly could not abide them either, but the note of misogyny in Screwe's voice was unmistakable.

"Indeed. It is fortunate that Mrs. Ravelsham is from home this evening, then." Frederick turned to Tilly. "Will you excuse us, my dear sister?"

Tilly pretended to rouse herself from the dreamy torpor of needlework. "Oh, yes, brother." She yawned. "Indeed, I find myself quite tired. I believe I shall retire."

As she left them to make her way upstairs to the room that her brother had assigned to her permanent use, she could feel Screwe's filthy eyes following her. She was not sorry to be leaving them, but she wished she, Frederick and DeGroen had had a chance for a proper chat. And she also wished she could be certain that Screwe did not suspect them of some involvement in the rescue of Clara.

But she was most worried about Rutherford. She would wait until the *manly talkers* were properly foxed, then sneak out the servants' entrance to see him. Her brother and DeGroen were quite familiar with this arrangement. They would have to manage Screwe on their own.

CHAPTER 18

Rutherford paced across the jewel-toned Persian carpets of his study. He stared at the patterns and discerned stories from them, as he had done when still a lad, amusing himself while his father attended to papers. The designs were opulent and convoluted, and could be interpreted multiple ways. They had always beguiled him. It seemed that his fascination with complication had started before he ever met Tilly.

Smythe stood in attendance, watching as though mesmerized by a pendulum, as Rutherford walked back and forth. Rutherford sat finally. His leg twitched. He gestured to Smythe for a brandy.

"That will be all, Smythe. You may go rest." There was no need for the faithful servant to be sleepless, just because his master was. Smythe had a way of expressing his deep worry, without losing his perfectly composed London butler face. But Rutherford could not attend to Smythe's worries. He had too much else to think about.

He pushed against the bottle in his pocket. Tilly had told him he could have one more dose tonight. He looked at the long clock. In fifty-five minutes he could take it, not before. She said she would deliver more tomorrow, with a schedule. And the week after that, too. He was meant to take weaker doses each day. She wanted him well, she said.

She was right, of course. But it was vastly irritating to be ordered around that way. He felt the bottle again. No. He knew his irritation was part of the illness. The cold sweat was starting to creep up his spine. Fifty-four minutes.

Letters lay unread on his desk, he had not had time to attend to them today. Well, he would have had more time, if he had not been distracted by his pursuit of laudanum. He also owed Frobisher an apology for completely failing to appear for their fencing appointment and not even sending so much as a note of excuse. He did that first, hoping that his hand was not so altered by tremors that Frobisher would be alarmed.

When he was finished, he looked at the clock. Forty-four minutes. He swallowed and turned to the pile of letters. One caught his eye. It was addressed from his Uncle Emmet, the Duke of Bartholmer.

Dear William,

I know it has been some time since we have seen one another, but I should like to invite you to come visit me at Blackwood. But perhaps I should explain myself.

There is probably nothing that makes a man more honestly consider his choices in life than does the prospect of losing his life. I have always been a Corinthian, confident in the strength of my arm and my constitution, but disease is no respecter of men.

My doctor has advised me to set straight what I would, for I have not long. He has tried every treatment, but the worm that afflicts continues to gnaw and grow.

I shall spare you the unhappy details, but as you are the closest thing I have to a son, and as you shall inherit all I have, not just the entail, upon my death, I should like to see you in my last days.

Will you indulge a dying man's wish, and come see me as soon as you should be at leisure to do so?

Until then I remain, as ever,

Your devoted uncle,

Emmet.

Rutherford shook his head. He had known of his uncle's disease, but had hoped it might be cured. He did not know his uncle well, but the man had always been kind to him when he was a child. Rutherford had never understood why he did not marry to continue the line. It was reckoned to be the one thing a duke could be expected to do. But, after the death of his first wife in childbirth, Bartholmer became a recluse and flatly refused to entertain the notion of remarrying.

His uncle must have been violently in love with his first wife. It was the only explanation that made sense to Rutherford. It would never have made sense to him before he met Tilly. The pre-Tillian Rutherford would, if he had thought upon the matter at all, simply have assumed that Bartholmer did not wish to marry because he was enjoying his liberty and bachelor amusements.

But now Rutherford knew what it was to love a woman more than anything or anyone. He did not like to contemplate what he might do if she were to die birthing his child. He shuddered, as much from the horror of the thought as from the tremors of his illness.

Thirty-nine minutes. His stomach was cramping. He took out the bottle, set it on the desk and stared at it. Then he roused himself and stuffed it back in his pocket.

Rutherford took up his pen again and wrote a reply to his uncle, assuring him that he would come see him as soon as might be, and that he should expect him in the coming days. His second letter completed, he set his pen aside again. Twenty minutes.

He was making remarkable progress for being so wretchedly ill. He congratulated himself by finishing his drink and pouring another. He sorted through a few more letters. Read some, threw others aside. There was nothing more requiring his immediate attention. He drummed his fingers on the rosewood desktop. Nine minutes.

His legs were both twitching, and his stomach was a misery. It was only nine minutes. Surely it would not hurt to take his dose nine minutes off the mark, one way or the other. Somehow the bottle was in his hand again. He discovered that he neither knew how that little bottle of poison had got into his hand, nor how it had got so out of hand. But he could not laugh at his own wit. Seven minutes.

He pulled out a sheet of paper and began composing a list:

1. *Get Tilly to marry me*

2. *Visit my uncle*

3. *Take more exercise*

4. *Sort out Delacroix*

5. *Become a grandfather to a dozen little champion pointer puppies*

He cursed himself and put down his pen. How could he have forgotten Molly? He had returned home and settled himself into a rut of craving after this poison, without a thought to his beloved little princess.

Five minutes. He tore himself out of his chair and wandered shakily down the hallways to the room where the dogs were. Molly and Mack greeted him with barks and leaps and slobber.

"Careful now, Molly." He petted them both, and wished he had more hands, for they seemed to transmute into four dogs as they dashed and gambolled about him. "Have you forgotten you are an expectant mother?" He chuckled. "You are as bad as Lady Aldley."

"I imagine her ladyship would find the comparison amusing. But do not let Aldley hear you say it."

His face glistened with sweat as he looked up to see Tilly standing in the doorway, wearing the widow's weeds, broad black bonnet, and veil that she always wore when she sneaked into his house at night.

"Tilly."

"How are you faring, my darling stallion?" She removed her bonnet and veil to reveal her glossy golden curls and periwinkle blue eyes.

He stared at her a moment, his heart fluttering, then laughed bitterly. "I feel like hell has vomited me up onto an ant hill and pissed on me. How do you do?" He inclined his head in a mocking gesture of gentle deference.

She removed a watch from her pocket and smiled sweetly at him. "I do very well, now that I know your resolve has taken you over the first hurdle."

"Hurdle?"

"It is now two minutes past the appointed hour for your next dose. And you have not yet taken it. You are so strong. I know you can do this." Her voice was full of warmth.

Was it his illness or wishful thinking that made him hear the resonant tones of love in it?

"It is not a hurdle." Rutherford walked over to her. "It is an internment in hell." He looked at her watch.

He could smell her faint magnolia and vanilla scent, and he longed to bury his face in her hair.

Just as she said, it was two minutes past—now three minutes. He was gripped by a craving to take his poison. But instead he took Tilly by her waist and turned her to face him, crushing his mouth against hers. She still tasted of biscuits. Rutherford could feel the heat rising in his blood. He dipped down and hoisted up her skirt, working his palms past the silk shift to massage her luscious bare buttocks.

"Mmm. My hot little angel. How I love you. You drive me wild, even now."

Tilly was breathing heavily. Her nipples were hardening. He could feel her desire. Why did she resist his love? He pressed his growing erection against her abdomen.

She gasped and whispered, "Oh, how I want you inside of me."

This would normally be all the invitation he needed, but just then a leg tremor and a series of excruciating cramps in Rutherford's stomach doubled him over. He sat down on the floor.

Mack and Molly licked at his hands and face, and Tilly shooed them away gently, taking his hand.

He hated and he loved the look of deep pain and pity on Tilly's face as he fumbled for the bottle and his brandy flask, poured the dose into the cap of the flask and tipped some brandy into it. "I love you, my angel. I will best this." He swallowed the cocktail.

"By the way," he said, lying down flat and scratching Molly's ear, as the drug diffused through his wretched carcass. "My bitch is pregnant."

CHAPTER 19

*A*s Rutherford dozed on the floor, Tilly petted the dogs. It was fairly obvious that Molly was expecting. "Congratulations, Molly. I am sure your puppies will be as beautiful as you."

She wanted to stay, to have her way with Rutherford when he recovered from the initial torpor of the drug. It had been a stressful day, and her body was hungry. But she also wished to unburden herself to him. She needed to feel assured that he did not, as her other friends had done, judge her for her less conventional businesses.

Why was this so important to her? Oh yes, because she was an idiot who had permitted herself to fall in love with her paramour. She needed him to understand her, to believe her good, despite appearances.

On the other hand, those were her needs. What Rutherford needed was for her to be strong for him, and not to further ensnare his heart while he was sick and vulnerable. It was, after all, sort of her fault that he was so dependent on laudanum. She was supplying a fair sized part of the London market, and the pain he was seeking to smother was her own doing. Tilly's heart sunk as she was reminded of how toxic her influence was.

She should never have started the affair. But she would never have guessed that a sport-loving buck like Rutherford would have such a vulnerable heart.

And, if she were honest, Rutherford's was not the only vulnerable heart. But she could not act upon her love. One of them had to be sensible. And if Rutherford knew that she returned his love, it would only add to his torment. She gave the dogs a final scratch. She should not be there when he awakened.

Tilly extracted the piece of paper with the dosing schedule on it and set it beside Rutherford. The first few days would be the hardest, but she believed in him. She made for the door.

"Where are you going?" Rutherford roused himself and sat up. His eyes had a sleepy, dilated quality that changed the hazel almost to brown.

"I thought I should leave you." She looked down.

"Are you ashamed of me, Tilly?" His words were soaked in a real, but pleasantly diffused anxiety.

"No." Tilly met his eyes. "Never. I am very proud of you, in fact. The first day is the hardest." She swallowed. "Are you ashamed of me?"

He sighed dreamily. "You mean because you deal in opium and game pullets? No, not ashamed. Fascinated, to be completely truthful. But I do fear for your wellbeing and your reputation. And I wish you would sell out your interests in these ventures."

"If I sold out, some smoky piece of pig filth like Screwe would take over."

"Do you know Lord Screwe?" Rutherford looked bewildered.

"I know of him." She sighed. "And I was recently made acquainted with the man. He makes my skin crawl."

Rutherford nodded. "You are not alone in that. No one really likes the man. His membership at White's has been revoked."

"I know. You might as well know that I also run a hell fire club—from a discreet distance."

"Of course you do." Rutherford chuckled. "You are an angel out of your element, my love. And you are so utterly perfect for me that I hate to ask you to change—"

"Then do not." Her voice was serious.

"But I do not want to lose you. And the games you are playing are dangerous. Some of the people you associate with are dangerous, and your reputation would be ruined if it ever got out. You saw how Aldley reacted, and he is your friend."

"Is he? I believe he may never recover from having his wife exposed to a brothel." Her voice was bitter. "He blames me for it, but in truth, it is easier for him to be angry at me for removing Lydia from harm's way, than to hold Lydia to account for putting herself there."

"No doubt. Using Crump to protect her was a flourish of genius, however." His sardonic drawl was back.

"I used the means I had at my disposal to protect her, and all anyone can focus on are the superficial flaws of the means." She crossed her arms over her chest. "No one seems to grasp that Lydia might have been seriously harmed, or abducted again, were it not for the measures I took."

"I grasp it." He stood up and took her in his arms. "I truly do think you are a marvel. And I am sorry Aldley reacted as he did, but I think he may get over it. He is in a difficult position with his wife, at the moment, but he is not an entirely unjust person. Only you have had your amusement now. Is it not time to give up these mischievous ventures?"

"You misunderstand my intentions entirely." It was just like a man to assume a silly motive for anything a woman did. "It is not for the purpose of amusement or mischief that I run these businesses. It is for the purpose of good."

Rutherford's eyebrow quirked. "Oh really? I had no idea God's work could be so profitable."

Tilly scoffed. "God's work. Who does God's work? If you mean the work of the church, you should ask how all of its trappings of worship came to be encrusted in jewels, then, if its work is not profitable. But I do not claim any holy calling. I merely grew tired of waiting for someone else to do the right thing, so I took it upon myself."

"The right thing is selling poison and bodies? You have an unusual sense of ethics."

Tilly was suddenly tired. She drew Rutherford over to a low, fur-bedecked couch and sat. "The right thing is setting up these ventures so that people have a choice about their life and a chance to better it. Do you not see? I always ask the people we find to choose between training for more *respectable* work and training to become a courtesan or peculiar."

"There is some training involved, is there?"

"You have no idea. But the point is, if I simply turned a blind eye, like every other society woman, and let things go as they have done since the first city drew in the first penniless chit from the countryside, there would never be any hope of anything other than exploitation."

"Clearly you have been reading that rubbish from France. But can you honestly say that you do not exploit these women?"

"The women working at the Belle Hire have chosen to work there. They work in a safe, clean environment, receive better remuneration than most in their vocation, and have access to a trust for when they are beyond working years. If they were working on the street, or for someone like Red Martha, they would never live long enough to bother considering a future after they could no longer work."

Rutherford did not ask who Red Martha was, and this did not shock Tilly. She did not think him prone to consorting with prostitutes, but he could scarcely avoid hearing of Red Martha. Gentleman often spoke about such things when they thought women were not listening.

She continued. "And the proceeds from the Belle Hire and my other enterprises go to supporting the servant academy and orphanage, and giving employment and some decent accommodation to children on the street. It is a firm rule that children are protected from the people who *mistreat* them."

Rutherford's face showed his disgust. "I have heard of such things, but I assumed it was exceptional."

She could not stop herself from gritting her teeth at this convenient dismissal, which was all too common among his class. "The exploitation of the vulnerable has never been the exception where it is permitted to thrive by a hypocritical, squeamish society. I count every child that I have saved from Red Martha, or her like, as my reward for taking the risks that so worry you."

"You are quite the revolutionary." He smiled condescendingly. "Very well, but can you not give up the drug trade? I know how this craving takes a man over." His face darkened. "Surely being around such desperate people puts you in peril."

She waved her hand dismissively. "It is not to be thought of, in the context of the greater good."

"Then consider its effects. Can you not see how people become enslaved?" His expression showed his own self-consciousness.

Tilly sighed more heavily than she wished. "Yes. But at least they had some choice in the matter, unlike the very real oppression of people into slavery."

He looked uncomfortable. "I think you may be making excuses for yourself. And anyway, slavery is simply inevitable."

"You would not look at it that way if it were you, or someone you loved who was being bought and sold like chattel, being made to work without pay at whatever the master might wish, and being beaten at the master's whim. And worse things besides."

He huffed. "Not everyone treats their slaves so badly."

She pursed her lips and tilted her head. "And how do you treat yours, sir?"

He looked away and picked a single dog hair, out of the hundreds, off of his pantaloons. "I do not have slaves, as well you know."

"I know you own sugar cane plantations and rum production in the West Indies."

"That is not the same."

"True. It is worse. Here at home you mount the high horse of not owning slaves directly, which is in any case illegal in England. But you only relegate the moral responsibility for their treatment to the colonies, to some distant manager, far away from your notice." Tilly could feel her anger rising. A part of her knew that she was, unfairly, blaming Rutherford for the crimes of all of England, which, she feared, would never be laid at the proper feet.

Rutherford shook his head and laughed. "I do not believe I ever conceived in all my life that I should someday be subjected to moral strictures from a woman who profits from prostitution, poisoning, and incorrigible gambling fiends."

Tilly squared her shoulders. "As I have explained, this is all for the greater good."

"Only take care you do not turn into the very evil you are trying to thwart. And anyway, I do not see how someone who cannot stop eating bonbons and biscuits for more than fifteen minutes at a stretch can reprimand *me* for owning sugar plantations."

Tilly felt the blood drain from her face and then rush back in. He had the right of it, and she knew it, but it was not pleasant to be confronted with her own hypocrisy. "I am working toward procuring a plantation and liberating the erstwhile slaves. They shall work for wages."

"But in the meantime, you continue to eat the sugar produced by slaves. Tilly, I know you mean well, but can you not give up your schemes to save everyone? They are pointless. The world is how it is. You should think of yourself."

"I do not know how to give up caring for people who are suffering and vulnerable." Tilly sounded miserable.

"Then at least stop selling this noxious drug."

"But it has legitimate medical purposes." Her voice trailed off weakly.

"And if I told you I was just taking it *medicinally*, would you accept that?"

"No. Certainly not."

"Then let us speak plainly and have a right understanding. You are not selling it *medicinally*, either."

"But it funds so many other projects."

"If I could demonstrate all the good I was doing with the proceeds of my sugar plantations, would you then turn a blind eye to the slavery?"

She would not. But it was not precisely the same thing. Still, he had a definite point, and she had never been comfortable with the destructive power of opium. "Very well. If you will free your slaves, and pay fair wages to those who wish to stay, I shall find a way of getting out of the opium trade."

Rutherford thought about it for a few moments. "And will you also give up eating sugar which is made with slave labour?" His grin held a playful sort of malice. "You are asking me to give up laudanum, after all."

Tilly was sure he did not believe she could do it. "But laudanum will kill you." She unconsciously pressed her fingertips to her temples. "Sugar is the only thing that rids me of my headaches."

Rutherford tilted his head. "And what of my cramps and spasms and profuse sweating? I might equally say that laudanum is the only cure for those."

Tilly did not like it, but she was willing to agree to anything, if it would keep Rutherford on his program of weaning. "Very well, although you know it is a nonsensical comparison."

In fact, the whole conversation was nonsensical. She was supposed to be setting Rutherford free, not getting further entangled with him by making reciprocal agreements.

He was sitting close to her and he kissed her then. His lips were so soft and so teasing, but so strong. All of her rational faculties were overcome in a flood of love and wanting.

"You know," he said huskily, "I can think of an excellent way to seal this bargain."

And Tilly could think of one too, but she dared not. He was so vulnerable, continuing to exploit his tender heart for her own gratification would be cruel. And her own tender heart also needed guarding.

She tore herself away and stood, trying to keep the dreadful wave of love that flooded over her from seeping into her voice. "As tempting as you are, my stallion, I must go. This cannot be good for your recovery."

"I think it will be excellent for my recovery." He stood and re-entangled her, pressing his erection against her again. "And getting more exercise is on my list of things to accomplish this week."

"Then may I suggest a more traditional form of sword play." She wriggled out of his grasp and bolted for the door, grabbing her bonnet and calling, "Do not forget to follow the schedule. I shall make one for my sugar tomorrow, though the very thought pains me."

Her heart pounded and she felt the loss of him so deeply that she wept as she left through the servants' entrance.

He had not proposed to her this time. He always proposed to her when they met clandestinely. Was he becoming inured to the idea of merely having her as a mistress? Had he given up on fighting her marriage to DeGroen? Or worse, was he tiring of their affair?

She wanted to turn back, to tell him that she loved him, to tell him she had changed her mind. But nothing had changed. Still, it was walking against a hurricane to leave him. It was as though a cord at her waist was pulled taut. And every step she took away from him was excruciating.

CHAPTER 20

When Tilly entered the breakfast room at Frederick's home the next morning, she was relieved to see that Genevieve had not yet emerged from her chambers. Frederick and DeGroen turned from closely examining the new wallpapers, as Tilly entered.

"Good morning, my dear." Mr. DeGroen pecked her cheek.

Frederick kissed her forehead, adding, "If any morning can be good, when it begins with such a spectacle as *that*."

"Genevieve's new wallpapers have been installed, I see." Tilly examined the red and gold dragon pattern. "It seems the penchant for new wallpapers runs in the family. But these are not so very bad, brother."

"They are, in fact, perfect for an oriental-themed house of ill-repute." Frederick scowled.

"Not to demean houses of ill repute in any way." Mr. DeGroen was equanimous.

"No, of course not." Tilly joined in the game. "However, I will allow that it is a bit much to face before one has broken fast."

"By themselves, they might be endured. But she has ordered Doric columns for the doorway, Tilly. *Doric ruddy columns.* And a collection of *authentic* ancient Grecian urns, a set of miniatures of all the great Roman statues, and God knows what else." Frederick pressed a finger into one temple, and gestured frantically with the other hand to encompass the entire parlour. "This is all to be strewn about our breakfast room just as though an ancient Mediterranean god cast up his accounts on the pagoda of some Chinese emperor."

"You see, Tiddly." DeGroen was enjoying Frederick's torment. "Our Frederick is an artist. He has a delicate constitution where aesthetics are involved."

Tilly patted Frederick's arm. "I know it is true, my dear, suffering brother. However, there are simple solutions to your predicament."

Frederick looked hopeful. "What would you propose?"

Tilly seated herself at the table, and her fingers twitched at the plate of bonbons by her water glass. She had eaten her sweetie upon rising and could not have any more until afternoon tea. She poured herself a cup of sugarless tea instead. "You are only looking at the situation from your own perspective and not from hers. The central problem is not a tragically ill-advised love for what one might euphemistically call *improvements*. It is that she is bored and has nothing with which to amuse herself but spending your money as conspicuously as possible."

Frederick shrugged. "And?"

"So you must either give her free rein to do it somewhere else. For example, by buying her a massive house and letting her redecorate it into perpetuity, as she is possessed by this or that evil spirit of fashionable tastelessness. Or..." Tilly raised her eyebrows at him and gave him a pointed look.

He shook his head at her. "Well, do not leave me hanging. What is this alternative that is less likely to drive me into the poor house?"

Tilly laughed. "As if that were possible." She sipped her tea maddeningly slowly, then added, "Or you could give her a child."

"There you have it, Freddy!" DeGroen slapped Frederick's shoulder and laughed. "You can always rely on your sister for the most sensible advice. True," he turned to Tilly, "I do not know what we should do without you to do all the difficult thinking. Give her a child! Why did we not think of that?"

Frederick frowned at her. "You know I should very much like a child."

"As should I." DeGroen winked. "And I suspect I shall beat you to it, Frederick." He sat down at the table and ate a sausage with his fingers, drawling, "Whatever is taking you so long, old boy?"

"I believe it might be arranged, Frederick." She smiled at her brother sadly, as though he were a slightly slow puppy tying to learn a trick. "I am somewhat surprised that you have not sorted it out yourself."

Frederick pulled a face at her. But then he came to her side and gave her a sweet smile while he jounced her elbow. "But you always sort things out so well, Tiddly."

She sighed. "I will look into it." She loved them both, but why must she always fix everyone else's problems? Frederick had essentially all the same connections as she did. She wanted a ruddy bonbon. "Will someone take this sodding dish of sweets away!"

Frederick stared at her as though she were a woman possessed, and DeGroen gave him a look of alarm, but removed the dish to the hallway without comment. Then he dashed back in and said, "The missus is coming!"

Tilly shook her head, as the two men seated themselves more theatrically than she thought possible, and pretended, most pointedly, to be having a normal breakfast conversation. They all stood as Frederick's wife entered.

"Good morning, Mathilde." Genevieve kissed at Tilly's cheeks and missed twice, like a true daughter of France. "I hope you slept well."

"Yes, thank you. How was your card party at the Beauchamps' last night?" Tilly remarked that Genevieve's eyes were shadowed.

"It went terribly late, but it was quite diverting." Genevieve's voice had the practised lightness that was uniform among the ton. "The lady of the house plays rather high, but I do not think I quite sent her to the poorhouse."

"Ah, well." Tilly crinkled her eyes. "There is always next time."

Genevieve giggled.

"I see you have been making improvements." Tilly could not resist tweaking her brother's nose.

Genevieve beamed. "I saw the wall paper and just fell in love with it." She turned to her husband. "How do you like it, Frederick, my love?"

"It is," he blinked, "so emphatically oriental that your friends will all be mad with jealousy." He then stuffed his teacup in his mouth.

After breakfast, Genevieve pulled Tilly into her sitting room. "Do not go just yet, sister. I should like a longer visit with you."

Tilly had a sense of foreboding that she was about to be treated to more of other peoples' troubles.

She sat in one of the newly upholstered Mandarin red chairs, and admired the elegant counter-point they made to the delicate lilac plaster in the walls. She could not even have a biscuit.

Genevieve took up her needlework as a matter of course, and Tilly waited for her to begin.

"I believe," Genevieve said after she had pulled a few stitches through, "that my mother came to visit you the other day, did she not?"

"Indeed. She seemed to be of the impression that your brother, Mr. Delacroix, might be induced to return to England if the right gifts were offered to him."

Genevieve's lips flattened. "Well, *perhaps* she has not had news of it, but I can assure you that he is already in England. In London, in fact."

"Forgive me for saying it," observed Tilly, "but you do not sound especially happy about this fact."

"I should have been." She stabbed at her fancy sewing. "However, when I received him—I did so on the quiet you see, and you must not tell Frederick, for he cannot abide my brother—Pascal did not scruple but to threaten me with vicious gossip."

"Oh indeed?"

"Yes, well, you are among the very few who are aware of a misunderstanding that occurred last year—the incident involving the Viscount Essington." She straightened her spine primly.

Tilly smiled reassuringly at Genevieve. "But you are a married woman now. That is all water under the bridge."

"Only my brother is threatening to tell anyone who will listen!" Genevieve blurted out, throwing aside her sewing. She stood and paced the room.

"How could he possibly know about the incident with Essington?"

Genevieve put the knuckle of a fist to her mouth. "I am a great fool and told him about it myself. He was there at Dunston when Frederick and I got married. I do not know why I told him. Only he was still bed-ridden from being shot, and we have always shared secrets. I never believed he would be such a foul beast as to use them against me."

"Calm yourself." Tilly stood and guided her distraught sister-in-law back to her virulent red chair. "I know it is very hard when our relatives disappoint us. But perhaps you have had some occasion to observe that Mr. Delacroix's manners are not always what they ought to be." Tilly winced at her own understatement, but a little diplomacy was in order.

"Yes. I knew he had treated other people badly." Genevieve shook her head in disbelief. "But I never thought he would turn on his own sister."

Tilly nodded patiently at this calm confession of selfish indifference. "But now you do know. My brother will protect you, Genevieve. He will not allow anyone to speak ill of you unchallenged, and Mr. Delacroix must know that he cannot prove whatever he thinks he knows about that night. Your brother's threats are empty."

She sighed. "Do you think so?"

"Indeed." Tilly tilted her head and asked, "What did he demand of you?"

She looked reluctant to reply. "What do you mean?"

"I think we both know he did not show up on your doorstep to threaten you merely for his own amusement."

Genevieve stood again and walked to the mantel to fondle a particularly saccharine Wedgwood figurine of two children. "Yes, you have the right of it. He was aiming to blackmail me. He asked for a monkey to start."

"Five hundred pounds?" Tilly gave a faint whistle. "I hope you did not give him any money."

Genevieve kept her face turned away. "I had a hundred pounds of pin money handy. I gave it to him."

Tilly shook her head. "If you feed a stray cat, it will keep coming back."

"It is not a comparison favourable to my brother, but I cannot contradict you." She laughed bitterly. "I have already seen him skulking about the park when I go for an outing with friends. And I am sure I saw him in the shadows at the Beauchamps'. Then as I returned home from the card party last night, he approached me again. He said that as he could no longer get anything out of Beauchamps' wife, he should require two monkeys from me. He had the audacity to reckon that I owed him nine hundred pounds."

Out of Beauchamps' wife? The former Lady Aldley? No doubt Delacroix wished to blackmail her too, with what he knew of her past scandalous tryst with Beauchamps, before she married Aldley's father.

Tilly suppressed a bitter laugh. Now that the lady was married to Beauchamps, there was not much to blackmail her with. Their history had slowly become public knowledge, and the lady had given up pretences to high social standing when she married a merely knighted gentleman. In the end, she proved to be much more romantic than anyone would have thought. And, if personality counted for anything, she was definitely not susceptible to blackmail.

"You must listen to me, Genevieve. He will not stop there. If you pay him, you show him you fear his words, which you should not. And he will always come back for more. In your heart, I think you know this of him."

Genevieve nodded sadly.

"So you must tell your husband of your mistake." Tilly smiled encouragingly. "I know Frederick. He will forgive you, my dear. And you must never receive Delacroix again. It is hard, I understand, but you see how things are. Whatever there once was between you, he has changed into a ravening beast who will only try to take advantage of your vulnerability. You must cut him off."

"But what will Mama say?" Genevieve looked apprehensive.

"I imagine she will not like it. But she is only your mother. Frederick is your husband and master." Tilly winced internally at using this tactic. "Simply inform Lady Delacroix that you must be ruled by your husband's edicts. I know Frederick is not a tyrant, but it is a line of reasoning your mother will surely understand."

Genevieve pursed her lips and looked like she were devising a plan. "I suppose it would help if I were to give her a grandchild."

"Yes." She smiled at her sister-in-law. Tilly was really growing fond of the little minx. "That would be wonderful news for us all. And I suppose it might help shut your brother's gossiping mouth."

She doubted this last piece of optimism. But it had been long enough since the incident with Essington that, even if Delacroix made insinuations, no one would believe the child was sired by anyone but Frederick.

"Perhaps..." Genevieve looked uncomfortable and cleared her throat. "Perhaps you might suggest the notion to Frederick. I am not certain he is keen to have a child."

Oh, but he *was* keen. Genevieve seemed so vulnerable that it gave Tilly pause. Only a desperate woman would admit what Genevieve was hinting at. When Tilly had arranged the marriage to her brother, she had not thought Genevieve to be an especially romantic type. Quite the contrary, she had thought the girl to be delightfully ruthless and calculating, and all but incapable of love.

But Tilly could now see that there was a heart hidden behind all the fan-fluttering, upper class posturing and mercenary fortune-hunting. She was not, as Tilly had thought before, just bored. She wanted a child to love, and, unless Tilly was very mistaken, the girl might even be a little bit in love with Frederick. Tilly sighed. A girl in love with her husband. Once again Tilly had made a proper mingle-mangle of things.

She remarked upon the mortified look on Genevieve's face and realized she had waited too long to reply. Tilly reached out to pat her sister-in-law's arm. "Forgive me. I was caught in my own thoughts. I think what you are describing is quite normal."

"Really?" The word came out with the release of the breath that Genevieve had been holding.

"Well, yes. I am not an expert, of course, but I have read books that suggest some young husbands need a little encouragement."

Genevieve's face brightened with hope. "Oh, you do not know how relieved I am to hear it."

Tilly could imagine. And if she were one to learn from her mistakes, Tilly would not even entertain a notion of doing what she was now contemplating. Her interference had already caused enough trouble. *Enough* trouble. She would stop right now. Not intervene any further. She looked at Genevieve's desperately vulnerable face. Ah well, in for a penny, in for a pound.

Tilly's eyes crinkled sweetly as she said, "Let me see what kind of reading material I can find on the subject."

Before she left, she popped into Frederick's study, where he was sitting with DeGroen. They had their heads together admiring Frederick's latest work. It was a painting from memory of dancers at the Moulin Rouge. There were no definable lines. It was a flurry of gaudy colour, motion and sexual energy—very unlike the fine detail work of his architectural renderings. Frederick often experimented with styles.

Tilly admired the painting. "It is beautiful, Frederick. Breathtaking and transporting."

Frederick shook his head, unable to accept praise. "I am a mere hack. You should see what some artists in France are getting up to. Amazing stuff. Truly visionary."

Tilly was too accustomed to Frederick's natural auto-criticism to argue with him. "Have you shown it to Mama?"

Frederick smiled a little sideways smile. He knew how their mother was, but could not help adoring her. "She has been working on *a series of sketches*, at the moment, and is too absorbed."

Their mother was always working on a series of sketches, as this theme or that preoccupied her, though she rarely showed her work. Tilly knew Frederick was right. She shared a roof with her parents and yet seldom saw her mother when she was under the spell of her art.

Nor did she see much of her father in these periods, for he was under the spell of his wife. He would sit in her art room and fetch her things, make her take food by standing at her side and feeding her by hand. Or, when there was nothing else to do, he would sit and sip wine or brandy while he watched her work in rapt adoration.

They were both so single-minded that they scarcely had time for their children or their own financial affairs. Growing up in such a household was like living in a kingdom under a spell. Tilly and Frederick had been raised by servants, and if they had not taken matters into their own hands, the family fortune would by now be in serious decline.

Tilly shook her head. "Ah yes, a series of sketches. Well, one must have some novelty in life."

Frederick took her hand and squeezed it. "Do not judge her so, Tilly. She is a true artist, brimming with such passion and sensibility that she may do without the fashionable distractions that divert society. She sees so deeply that a single leaf or shadow on the window pane holds for her myriad possibilities of beauty and meaning."

"I shall allow that she is a luminary, brother." It was true.

When Tilly had become engaged to DeGroen, her mother formed a sudden obsession with turning out her daughter. She frantically designed and picked fabrics for a hundred beautiful dresses for Tilly's trousseau. And Tilly's wedding dress was the crowning glory.

It would probably be the envy of every duchess in the land, but that was little consolation to Tilly. "But *you* must allow that she is not much of a mother."

"But we get on well enough." Frederick jounced her elbow. "Do we not, Tiddly?"

"I should say you do," agreed DeGroen with a look of love in his eyes. "And at least your parents do not take issue with every little thing you do."

"And yours are very hard on you, DeGroen, though you do not deserve it." Frederick looked sympathetic. "I have never seen such relentless criticism."

"My marrying you is the only thing they approve of, Tilly." DeGroen gave her a look that conveyed a shared joke.

"I am flattered, to be sure." She assumed a bland ingénue smile. "They are, if officious, at least excellent judges of character."

All three laughed for several moments, then Tilly continued, "But speaking of parental misconduct, I would have a word about your future fatherhood, Frederick."

CHAPTER 21

Tilly returned to her own home by noon, which was late by her standards. She felt as though she would collapse from exhaustion and fell upon her ration of two bonbons and a biscuit. It would be another two hours before she could have more, but for now she was slightly restored.

Her servants prudently waited until she had consumed her sugar ration, before they approached her with the news.

"We have been broken into, Miss."

"What?!" Was there no end to the parade of troubles and bad news?

"Last night Miss. We are still checking inventory, but it seems as if nothing was taken. However every room what didn't have someone sleeping in it was gone through. Made a right mess of things. Even your room, Miss, and your mother's art room. The missus is right beside herself. Mr. Ravelsham has been attending to her all morning."

Tilly merely rolled her eyes at this. "Oh yes. Well, they will console one another. But nothing is missing, you say?"

"No, Miss. Not even your jewels, nor the silver, even all the wine in the cellar."

"They searched the wine cellar?"

"Indeed."

Tilly's mind began to turn over immediately. This was certainly Screwe's doing. It was a relief that Frederick and DeGroen had stayed home last night, or Frederick's house might have been searched as well. There was not much to hide, but she did not fancy anyone discovering the secret meeting room in the wine cellar. It could be taken as a mere eccentricity, but it could also generate suspicion. She walked to the parlour with a window facing the street and peered out.

It was a quiet neighbourhood, with a broad avenue down which the occasional carriage travelled. A few parties enjoyed leisurely walks in the park across the street. No one looked out of place. At first. Then Tilly noticed a man standing alone in the park in the shadow of a great tree. She sensed him, before she saw him. There was something unusually cold about that shadow, and it was as though she could feel his gaze slithering over her.

It was not possible. He could not see her against the glare of the window's glazing. And yet, she could make out that he was watching the house. He must have watched her arrive home. She shuddered. She could not perceive much detail of the man, but she was certain it was Screwe. She stepped back from the window.

She had to be more cautious about where she went, if Screwe was watching her. He did not know of her many other enterprises. But if he discovered them, and he became aware that she had stolen away his slave, he would certainly try to ruin her, even if it cast further shade upon his own reputation. She needed to get some of the lads to guard Frederick's house, discreetly. And she needed to get a message to him, to put him on his guard.

She wanted more sugar. Tilly tapped her fingers to her lips and walked to her study. She quickly wrote a note to her brother. Frederick could send word to Crump at the warehouse, tell him what happened and that guards were required for her house and Frederick's. He should also send guards to the servant academy.

"And when you leave," she instructed the servant as she gave him the letter, "make certain you are not followed. In particular, there is a well dressed, quality gentleman across the street, with a silver falcon head on his cane. Do not let him see you leave. You will know him if you see him, for all the hairs will stand up on your arms. So go the back way. If you believe you are pursued, go somewhere else, like the market square, and get lost there. Do not go to my brother unless you are certain you are not followed."

"Yes, Miss." The servant's face did not betray the least disturbance at these unusual instructions.

"Then go to Bow Street, for we should report this burglary."

"Yes, Miss."

Tilly collapsed into a slouch in the desk chair. "And will you ask someone to bring me a cup of tea?" She grimaced sullenly. "With no sugar."

CHAPTER 22

Rutherford loaded Molly and Mack into his barouche and seated himself for the trip to Blackwood Manor. He did not feel in any condition for travelling, but refused to permit himself further wallowing in self-pity. And besides, he did not know how long his uncle would remain in this world.

He should have made a greater effort to get to know Bartholmer. He had told himself that the man was a recluse and preferred to be alone. But the truth was that, as usual, Rutherford was being selfish. He was enjoying his youth and wealth and saw no reason to trouble himself about an ageing uncle whose title he had no wish to inherit, and who had sealed himself off like a hermit, far from the amusements of town.

On the other hand, there was no doubt some good sport to be had at Blackwood, and getting exercise was on his list of things to do. Rutherford hoped it would distract him from the discomfort of weaning off of laudanum.

He scratched Molly's ears and idly stared out the carriage window, looking enviously at other people's equipage.

Rutherford perked up when they entered Tilly's neighbourhood. He always asked the driver to take this longer route, as it was easier for the man to navigate these broad streets and minimal traffic, and as it afforded Rutherford a view of the scenic park.

But the true reason was that it allowed him to moon about around Tilly's domicile and perhaps catch a glimpse of her, which he rarely did. But still, it gave him pleasure to gaze upon her home and dream about her in a more domestic context. Stolen moments in the dark, no matter how pleasurable, were not truly satisfying. They were no longer enough for him, if they ever had been. In fact, they had started to carry a sort of guilty sadness with them.

A smart carriage was waiting near the park and he recognized the colours. It was Lord Screwe's coach. This was odd to Rutherford, for an amble in the park was not Lord Screwe's sort of amusement. And one rarely saw him out before dinner time, for he was a creature of night time diversions. Then he saw Screwe himself, staring straight out of the park in the direction of Tilly's house.

Right at that moment, Tilly's carriage rolled up, and she disembarked. Rutherford's heart fluttered. He made to wave, but of course she would not see him in his carriage. She seemed preoccupied and walked straight into the house without looking about her.

He smiled. Someday she would be in his house. They would take breakfast together and talk about current events, or play whist to while away an afternoon. He shook his head. His illness was making a bore of him. Even his fantasies were becoming dull.

Rutherford turned away as she disappeared through the door. He saw that Lord Screwe had moved into the shade of a tree, but was still staring. The hairs stood up on Rutherford's spine. Was Screwe watching Tilly? He gritted his teeth. Well, he had planned to start regular sword practice. Why not start with Screwe? No one would miss that piece of filth.

As his carriage rolled past the park, a spasm of pain gripped him. He clasped his hand to his stomach. Mack licked his other hand and looked up at him with the sorrowful, pouched eyes of a bloodhound. Rutherford smiled at her weakly, then lay down on his side and propped his head on the carriage blanket. He would look into Screwe later. For now he would try to sleep and wait as long as he could to take his next dose, so that he might take it closer to his arrival.

Rutherford preferred not to show up at his uncle's soaked in cold sweat and looking like he too was near to death.

CHAPTER 23

Tilly sat in an overstuffed indigo chair, sipping her third joyless cup of bitter tea and wishing her headache would recede. She did not desire to read any more letters, for her eyes were sore. She rubbed the lump on her head. The swelling had at least gone down. Perhaps tomorrow she might be able to set aside the turbans.

The last letter in the pile was from Lydia. Tilly had a sense of foreboding. What if Lydia were writing to inform Tilly that she was ending the acquaintance? Tilly felt blue devilled at the very thought of it. She had picked a horrid time to stop eating sugar, and Rutherford was a ruddy bastard for extracting the promise from her.

She winced and picked up the letter from the table beside her chair.

Dearest Tilly,

I am now in my confinement, much to the relief of Thomas, though he cannot stop clucking about me like a hen with one chick. I am no longer home to anyone, except family, for I am so big that even my empire waists cannot conceal it. It really was scandalous of me to refuse entering confinement until so late.

But I find there is a mischief maker inside of me that enjoys taking advantage of the great liberties I may indulge in as a countess. I digress, however. I meant to point out that I should happily receive you, if you were to come visit me in my gaol as you said you would.

I admit, however, that I do not hold out much hope that you should do so, after the miserable way I treated you when you were last here. Forgive me, my dearest friend. I should never have let it slip that you own a brothel. I shall also blame that on the little mischief maker side of me. And Thomas' high horse was hardly justified. It is not as if most of the men in our acquaintance do not visit brothels, so I see no call for this hypocrisy.

I suppose you will remind me now, as of old, that hypocrisy is simply a crucial part of surviving in the ton. But I shall not allow it to govern my friendships.

I have since explained to Thomas that I was accosted by Delacroix while visiting the shop. He was not happy about this, but I made it clear that my need to keep the truth from him was what put me in danger.

I also told him that we should apologize to you for acting so affronted when we should have been thanking you for rescuing me, which we entirely neglected to do. Let me remedy that oversight now. Thank you, dearest Tilly, for always watching over me, even when I am behaving badly.

Knowing you, you will not be terribly surprised at the news I have to convey. But I must confess to being shocked to discover that, not satisfied with accosting me in public, Mr. Delacroix actually had the audacity to call on Thomas at our home. The scoundrel is lucky to have escaped with his life, for he insinuated to Thomas that he had best pay five hundred pounds, or risk public exposure as a bastard and a cuckold. Can you imagine?

I am very relieved that Thomas did not call him out, though I should not have minded seeing the bounder shot for his misery.

Ah, but I see that Thomas is returned from visiting his mother. So I shall end this letter here and hope that we may discuss things further in person, if you have forgiven me for crying rope on you.

Until then, I remain always, your intolerably bad friend,

Lydia

Tilly was at first relieved that the letter was an apology, and not a termination to the acquaintance. But then she became anxious again, as she mulled over the lengths to which Delacroix was willing to go in his desperation to extort money from Aldley.

Lydia was quite mistaken if she thought this news would not surprise Tilly, for such an intrusion was alarmingly risky. So far Delacroix had only gone so far as to menace the women of his acquaintance like the coward that he was. Provoking an earl in his own home was downright reckless.

She wondered if she should have also warned Frederick about Delacroix. But then, she supposed he would be warned when Genevieve told him of her meeting with the dirty dish.

She returned to the parlour to see if Screwe was still spying on her house. He was no longer visible in the park or anywhere on the street. His principal business was probably to make her know that he was watching her. Otherwise, why would he not just put someone else up to it?

Then it occurred to her that someone, indeed, might have been given that duty. She would have to be very careful and evasive from now on. And no more visits to see Rutherford under the guise of staying with her brother.

This made her sad, but at least it would assist her in her resolve to free him. She rubbed her throbbing temple and looked at the clock. Another hour before she could have a biscuit. She returned to her pile of letters.

CHAPTER 24

The torpor of the dose had worn off and the tremors had subsided by the time Rutherford's carriage rounded the bend and Blackwood Park came into view. They had been driving beside the vast forests of the estate for some time, but now the expanse of grass and clusters of trees enclosing meadows opened up, and the sombre arboreal depth was tempered with a brighter, more optimistic verdure.

Rutherford knew, rather than saw, that the grounds were bedecked with little patches of wild strawberry plants, which would be laden with plump, sweet and tart little berries in summer. He smiled at the private knowledge. It was wondrous how the child-memory opened, unbidden, like a hidden treasure chest to bring joy to the man long removed in time.

As they turned into the drive, Rutherford admired the long promenade of ancient, noble black oaks that watched over the way to the great manor. The grandeur of this guard of honour was softened by the presence of geese and peacocks, indolently lolling around, shitting and looking pleased with their fat and feathers.

He was not received at the door by the master, but was conveyed to his uncle's chambers by a very grand looking butler with a worried face.

"William, my boy." Bartholmer's face was thin, and his lips were cracked as he smiled and greeted Rutherford from his bed. His hair was no longer the deep lustrous black of his youth and had instead surrendered to its fate as an indifferent grey mass. But his eyes still had a twinkle in them.

"Uncle. I am come." Rutherford's words choked in a flood of feeling. Why had he not come to visit his uncle sooner? Why had he selfishly permitted himself to believe that his uncle's reclusiveness excused Rutherford from familial duty? He took a breath and steadied himself. The last thing a dying man needed was visits from people made maudlin by their guilt. "It is so good to see you."

They clasped hands.

"Would you be so kind as to hand me that tumbler?"

Rutherford complied, and his uncle took a long drink.

"Barley water. Forgive me for having nothing better to offer, at the moment." Bartholmer grinned. "I am no longer permitted the comfort of brandy, nor even strong tea. My doctor rules with an inflexible despotism."

Rutherford permitted himself a chuckle. "I should imagine he has your best interests in mind."

"I suppose. He has kept me alive this long, beyond all reasonable expectation." Bartholmer flapped his hand downward to set aside the topic. "In any case, the servants will bring proper refreshments for you shortly."

"Do not think on it. It was not such a long journey, and it would be perverse for me to glut myself in front of you while you sip barley water."

"Hah!" The old man shook his head. "Watching others enjoy their meat is one of the few pleasures left to me. That and a delightful young lady who comes to read to me in the evenings to help me sleep. Lovely voice. Very sweet."

Rutherford wondered who this woman might be, but did not detect any passion in his uncle's words. At least he might hope she was not some hanger-on looking to exploit his uncle's weakness and marry advantageously.

"Ah." His uncle shook his head. "I see the look on your face. There is no romance in the air to threaten your inheritance, not to worry."

"I hope you do not think—" Rutherford was mortified that he had given this impression.

His uncle lifted a finger pre-emptively. "As we have not seen each other for so many years, I shall forgive you for thinking me soft in the head. However, I must protect Miss Colling's reputation and assert that there is not the faintest hint of what you fear."

"It pains me to confess it, uncle, but I believe my mind instantly went to the worst possibility only to escape my own guilt. For here is this young woman, who is no relation to you, attending to you so kindly, spending her own vision reading to you by candlelight in your dark hours. Whereas, in all these years I could not be troubled to come visit my own uncle. I flinch at the comparison."

He chuckled. "You are so serious. Just like your father."

"I do not deserve the praise or the simile. Among my friends I am not reckoned to be a serious character."

"All the better." Bartholmer raised a grizzled brow. "True, you must not torture yourself, William. I did not seek out your company either, and a better uncle would have done so when you lost your parents. I told myself you would be better off in the care of your aunt, for I was no company for a child. I have lived as a crusty old hermit by choice—

though now I can see that may have been a bad choice. That is why I would most earnestly talk to you now."

Just then the servants entered and began to move furniture about, to make room for a table. As they cleared away boxes and bottles from a low table at the foot of the earl's bed, Rutherford's eye alighted on a familiar bottle. It called to him. He clenched his fists and averted his gaze. It disgusted him how far this evil worm had worked its way into his soul.

When he was seated at a table laden with all manner of dishes Rutherford watched guiltily as his uncle ate gruel. He put aside his own feelings and asked, "So which are your favourites, Uncle, that I might enjoy them on your behalf?"

The old man laughed. "I see you are still the cheeky one. But very well, some of those oysters to start, then that red soup with the fresh bread. Then you must have some of the roasted pork and the poached fish, and white cake with dried fruit and sweetened cream."

As Rutherford obliged him, his uncle watched and delightedly slurped his gruel. At least the food was excellent, even if Rutherford were forced by circumstances to eat more of it than he was accustomed to. He was not, for example, terribly fond of puddings. But it was the least he could do for his uncle.

"I must say, my gruel has never tasted better." His uncle tapped a crisp white serviette to his lips. "Now as to the reason I have summoned you all this way... I suppose I should get down to business. I shall have to rest soon."

Rutherford inclined his head. "Very well. How may I ease your mind, Uncle?"

"I believe I may ease yours. The estate, as you know, consists of an entail, which passes to you by law. You shall be the next Duke of Bartholmer, not to worry." He laughed and his breath rattled in his lungs. "There is not any olive branch about to sprout up unexpectedly in Miss Colling's garden.

Rutherford shook his head. "I believe you, Uncle. My mind is quite at ease. And indeed, I must confess that I view the possibility of becoming a duke with no small degree of apprehension."

"You will get used to it. And you will be a better duke than I, for I am sure a handsome young rake like you has a great deal of practice siring progeny." He cackled again.

"Practice, yes. But at the moment the only line I lay claim to is a future brood of champion pointers."

"Delightful! I wish I should be able to see them."

"You may meet their mother later, if your doctor will permit it, for I have brought her with me."

"I should be delighted! But back to your inheritance. It is also my intention to leave you the rest of my estate."

Rutherford felt uncomfortable. He did not need the money, and he was not a greedy man. He was growing fonder of his uncle by the minute, and would happily trade the inheritance to keep the old duke in this mortal world a few more years. He swallowed. "I do not deserve this kindness. You must have some instruction you wish to give me. Tell me what office you would lay upon me."

"Only this, that you will try as best you can to add to the fortune, instead of frittering it away. It is what will support the family seat when bad decisions are made by some future beefwit descendent of yours—and believe me, they inevitably visit a few generations of every family."

"I hope you are wrong, but your words have the ring of truth, I am afraid."

His uncle took a long drink of barley water, then continued. "The fortune is large. I should prefer to see it go to good use than to covering idiotic gambling debts. And some of it shall be made over to a trust to the benefit and maintenance of the family seat in bad times. But the bulk will be in your hands. However, I have been thinking of the people whom I have most relied upon in these past difficult years. The servants, my steward and, most recently, Miss Colling."

Rutherford nodded and leaned in. "You should like me to do something for them."

"There is already a trust for the servants and steward, to provide an annuity when they are beyond working years. I hope you will administer it justly. But now I do not wish to attempt redrafting my will at this late date. Can I rely on your good character to provide protection and a reasonable living for Miss Colling? She is clever and would make an excellent governess, for example."

"I shall be sure to look out for her wellbeing, and provide for her generously, Uncle."

"And will you keep on the servants?"

"Of course. I see no reason why they should not stay employed here. They know the running of the household and the estate farms. I shall, in particular, be very desirous to have a reliable steward. However, if I feel the need to dismiss anyone simply because I do not need them, I shall be certain to set them up a reasonable annuity and give them good references. Would that suffice?"

"Yes, yes. Only you may not dismiss the butler, Sandes. He comes with the house, I am afraid."

"I should not dream of going against your wishes, then." Rutherford laughed. "Though it will make my own butler unhappy. He is not just my butler, but also my personal valet and general worrier. He is rather possessive."

"Yes, they can become almost officious, can they not?" The old man's eyes were drooping. "I am sorry, my nephew. But it is time for me to rest." He gestured to a novel that sat on the windowsill. "Will you indulge an old man and read to me from that book over there? Miss Colling always leaves off at the best parts. She says if she leaves me in suspense I shall live longer." He laughed.

Rutherford's heart clenched. He so *wanted* this man to live longer. He picked up the book. "It would be my great honour to read to you, and I shall try to benefit from Miss Colling's example and leave you tottering on the most excruciating point of suspense I can find."

CHAPTER 25

As Tilly seated herself in the Aldley parlour, she remarked that the table of sweets was no more to be seen. It was at the same time a disappointment and a relief.

She stood as Lord Aldley entered. They greeted one another awkwardly.

"Miss Ravelsham. Thank you for waiting upon me." His smile seemed nervous.

"It was my pleasure, Lord Aldley, but why can I not see Lydia directly? She is not unwell, I hope." She had seemed healthy at their last meeting, but things could change quickly with a pregnancy.

"No." He huffed and swallowed. "She is doing well, but the labour has started." He put out a hand to restrain Tilly from running to see Lydia.

Tilly was animated with nervous energy. "I must go to her, my lord. Has she not asked for me?"

"Of course you shall see her. And it is early yet. Only I must speak with you first. It is subject matter that I do not wish to distress my wife with at this time."

Tilly allowed herself to be seated. Lord Aldley sat across from her.

"What is it you wish to discuss, my lord?"

"First, I am aware that I must apologize."

Tilly shook her head, "There is no need, my lord. I understand why you reacted as you did when last we spoke. I hope Lydia has clarified matters since."

"She has, but please indulge me. I have been quite anxious to apologize to you since I discovered how much I am in your debt for your foresight on that day. I am grievously sorry for having misjudged you."

"I accept your apology, my lord. It puts my mind at ease, and it shall all be forgotten. May I go see Lydia now?"

"In a moment, if you please." He drew a breath and his demeanour was strained. "One of the reasons I am now so thankful for your foresight in sending this Mr. Crump to watch for Delacroix—his being one of the few people of his caste who would recognize Delacroix on sight—is that I now understand just how desperate the man has become."

"Yes, Lydia wrote me of the little turd's not scrupling but to harass your lordship in your own home. I admit, I had thought him too much of a coward."

"Indeed." Lord Aldley did not look pleased. "I am not a violent man, Miss Ravelsham, but I believe I could have torn him to pieces in that moment. I could tolerate him hurling whatever insult he would at me, but to try to tarnish my wife and unborn child, to threaten their well-being with black lies, and to do so under my own roof... True, I do not know how I restrained myself."

Tilly nodded. "I should like to strangle him myself. I can only imagine what your lordship must have felt in that moment. But surely measures have been taken, and that horrid creature will not gain access to your property again."

"Not precisely, no. But let me explain. Now that I know how desperate this man is, I understand what a great danger Lydia was in when Mr. Crump intervened—hence my thankfulness for your foresight. He may have had designs worse than blackmail, in short."

"Anything is possible with such a man."

"Which leads me to believe that he will keep accosting us until he is dead or imprisoned." Aldley's face revealed that the former would be his preference.

"If I may say so, my lord, even an earl should not risk his own liberty by committing murder, however much I understand the temptation."

"That is why I wanted to tell you of my other plan, and see if it meets with your approval. Lydia tells me you have just the sort of mind for stratagems."

"That is unkind of her to say." Tilly laughed. Lydia did not know the half of it. "But I suppose I can no longer conceal a certain predilection for intrigue."

Aldley smiled and shook his head. "I shall have to overlook your unusual business dealings. In fact I shall pretend I do not know about them at all—I am quite practised at this skill, I assure you. As punishment for being of noble birth, one must bear the acquaintance of other nobility. They are a colourful lot."

Tilly inclined her head in deference to this observation.

He continued. "But let me explain what I have in mind, and you can, perhaps, share with me your thoughts."

When Aldley had finished explaining his plan, Tilly was finally permitted to see Lydia. The room was dim and two servants stood by the bedside, fanning the countess, whose hair was loose and clung to her damp face in strands here and there.

"Oh, Tilly you are come!" Lydia's smile was radiant, juxtaposed against her tired face.

"I was not expecting that your babe would come today." She moved to her friend's side and kissed her cheek. "But I am overjoyed to be here for all the excitement."

Lydia's laugh was ragged. "I should not call it excitement. More like a tedium broken only by horrible pain and a great mess, if what I have read is at all accurate."

"You shall pull though, my dear, brave friend. And I shall stay with you as long as you will permit me."

"Oh, I am so glad to hear you say it, for my parents are on an outing and will not be back in town until tomorrow. The babe is coming a little earlier than we thought. Doctor Gant says it is quite within the expected time, but one cannot predict too nicely."

"You have brought Dr. Gant into town?"

"Yes, I felt more comfortable with him. We have set him up in a guest house nearby. He said it was too early for him to be needed, but he will return in a few hours." Her face suddenly went white and clenched into a grimace of pain, as her legs bent in sympathy.

Tilly took her hand. "You may squeeze my hand." She gasped along with Lydia. Tilly underestimated how strong Lydia's grip was. Clearly the countess' hands had not weakened much during their hiatus from riding and climbing trees.

It seemed like forever before Lydia's face relaxed. "Oh blast. That was a bad one. The doctor tells me they will become more frequent closer to the time. I am sorry. I hope I did not break your hand."

Tilly rubbed it and smiled consolingly at Lydia, "Do not trouble yourself about it. But do you not want your husband here with you? He has stronger hands."

"No. I have banished him. I do not wish him to see me like this. And you do not know him. He would only fret and pace and drive away my peace with his worrying."

Tilly nodded. "I can well imagine it. He loves you so." She wondered if she would want Rutherford to be there when she bore their child. A hand instinctively went to her stomach. Where had that thought come from? She was, after all, marrying Mr. DeGroen. Surely once they married, Rutherford would give her up entirely.

"Why do you look so sad, Tilly?"

Tilly slapped on a smile and lied. "I am not sad, just feeling sorry for Lord Aldley. He does worry a great deal about you. I am sure that his coddling gets irksome at times, but keeping him away is a little like forbidding a lad to look at the tree before Christmas."

Lydia laughed. "You will not persuade me. And I may be as big as a tree, but I am not nearly as pretty to look at."

Tilly smiled slyly. "The analogy was bad. Your gift is much better than anything under the tree."

"It is certainly the largest parcel, or so it feels." Lydia grimaced again and cried out, writhing on the bed for several moments.

It was terrible to watch her friend so in pain, and be unable to assist. There was a cloth on the bedside table. Tilly took it up and wiped her friend's face. "That was rather soon, was it not?"

"Yes." Lydia's breath was ragged. "I hope Ole Maeb arrives ere long."

"Ole Maeb? Is she not the house servant that saved you from your childhood fever?"

"Just the one. I am so glad longevity runs in her family. I am terribly fond of her, and she must be here for the birthing. I trust her more than Dr. Gant."

"Yes, I can imagine she would be a comfort."

"She has assisted many births in her time. She promised me an herbal drink to soothe the cramps."

An herbal drink. It sounded much safer than laudanum. Tilly

wondered how Rutherford was getting on with his weaning. Her own weaning was progressing. She had not thought of sugar since she had arrived in Lydia's chamber, which was an improvement. She supposed distraction was a crucial element in these early days.

Lydia smiled and waved at her. "Have you gone into some ecstatic state? Or are you thinking about Rutherford again?"

Tilly laughed nervously. Was she that transparent? "To be honest I was thinking about the fact that I have not thought of bonbons or biscuits since I have come to you."

Lydia shook her head. "I am uncertain if I should question if you are truly Tilly, or whether I should be flattered that my sugar-loving friend finds my company sufficiently sweet."

"I think we may rule out the former question, for who else but your best friend would endure your pert remarks? And, although you are terribly sweet, it is more probable that you merely provide distraction in your current interesting condition."

"And do you require distraction?"

"I am trying to give up eating sugar."

"Whatever for?"

"I shall spare you the details, but suffice it to say that Mr. Rutherford has extracted the promise from me."

"Rutherford?" Lydia's surprised mouth gradually formed into a sly smile. "And how did Mr. Rutherford *extract* such a promise? Have you decided to accept him, after all?"

Tilly could not keep her sadness from slipping out in a sigh. "No. There has been no alteration of the sort. We are as we ever were."

Lydia shook her head. "Poor Mr. Rutherford. But I pity *you* even more, my dearest friend. You are allowing your stubbornness to override your happiness."

Tilly was spared from having to formulate a reply to a truth so basic that it defied argument, for Ole Maeb just then entered. She brought Lydia her drink, and as they chatted amongst themselves, Tilly contemplated her situation.

Lydia had one thing wrong. It was not Tilly's stubbornness that was the issue, really, though she had a sufficient supply of that. It was her role as the person who fixed things for everyone else. But she had never considered why it might be that she was willing to sacrifice her own happiness for the happiness of others. She had never expected to fall in love with Mr. Rutherford.

He was meant to be a beautiful and charming diversion. And he was that, but like a fool, she had let him work his way into her heart with his roguish smiles and maddeningly attractive juxtaposition of such strength and such tenderness. It was heartrending to watch a man who could lift Tilly as though she were a feather and best most of the ton at foils or fist-a-cuffs, gently minister to his pregnant dog and watch over the little canine as though she were a child.

She loved him, she needed him, but she could never offer him what he needed, so long as she was entangled with Mr. DeGroen. It spiralled around and around in her mind and drove her to distraction.

Lydia gasped again, almost a screech this time. Tilly took Lydia's hand again, as a wave of pain moved perceptibly through her friend's body.

"Permit me, my lady. I must check you." Old Maeb was lifting the sheet.

Lydia merely nodded and waved her permission, her body still clenched in pain.

"Well now, the little one is eager." Ole Maeb grinned. "You are in the birthing, my lady."

Tilly knew not what she should do. She tried to assume an unconcerned smile and not clench her teeth as her hand made crackling noises in Lydia's grip. "How wonderful."

CHAPTER 26

While Bartholmer napped, Rutherford went to check on Mack and Molly, who were happily gambolling about the grounds, worrying the peacocks and so affronting the geese that the birds chased after the surprised dogs. Rutherford laughed and called them to him. Mack arrived first, for Molly could only waddle along.

He was torn. He had only planned to stay the afternoon and then return in the evening to London, but his uncle had pleaded with him to stay, at least for the night. He petted the two drooling dogs as they came to him. Perhaps he should take a little exercise in the forest, while his body was still calmed by the last laudanum dose.

"Shall you come along, Molly? Are you not too tired, my little princess?" He did not wish to over-tax the expectant mother, but she seemed very game, and he did not have the heart to refuse her.

The air was cool in the shade of the trees, and spiced with the mysterious perfume of life and death that swirled and festered beneath the canopy of leaves. The path was smooth from the compacting of many generations of feet, and Rutherford was struck by a notion of taking his place among the ancient procession. He wondered how Tilly would like being a duchess. He laughed and shook his head. She would be a *force majeure*. What intrigues might she then get up to?

On the other hand, as much as he loved her strange predilection for bettering the *beau monde* by dabbling in the *demimonde*, all he really wanted to do was whisk her away from all that. He wished to spend the rest of his days in her company, preferably alone, and with regular attendance to the delightful task of getting her pregnant. It was, perhaps, a wallow in the mundane, but it was his dream.

Then a thought suddenly occurred to him. Would Tilly not very much like to be a duchess? Would not marrying her own fortune to Rutherford's plus the substantial estate he would come into from his uncle be as good as marrying DeGroen? She once told him that marriage concerned only wealth and status, not love. But what if she could have both? Would she not abandon this preposterous engagement to DeGroen, whom, Rutherford was certain, she did not love?

His hopeful musings were interrupted by a deliciously familiar scent. Cinnamon. As he walked down the path this smell was joined by the other sweet notes of freshly baked biscuits. Odd. He realized that his pace had quickened, and he turned to see where the dogs might be.

Molly was lagging behind, and Mack was with her, licking her ears and looking concerned.

Rutherford turned back immediately. Molly was barely waddling along, and her breath was laboured. When he reached her, she flopped down on the ground and looked miserable.

He cursed himself. "Oh, my poor little princess, I am so sorry. How thoughtless of me." He picked her up gently and cradled her in his arms as he walked further along the path. Surely if he could smell baking, there must be some domicile nearby where Molly could have a nap by the fire.

His need was answered as he rounded the next bend and found a cosy little cottage with a small garden. He pushed through the unlatched wooden gate and followed a neat little path of crushed seashells, punctuated here and there with potted flowers, and little roughly carved figurines of mythical sea creatures.

The door to the cottage was painted white and sat in a neat frame of nautical blue. There was no one to be seen in the yard, but a pie and a couple dozen biscuits were cooling on the windowsill. Rutherford knocked with his Hessian-clad foot, so as not to lose his grasp on Molly.

No one answered. He knocked again, then went to peer in the window. He could see no one inside, but there was a fire on the hearth. Shifting Molly to one arm, he tried the door, and it turned. He hated intruding, but his concern for Molly overrode all sense of propriety and he entered the neat little home, carefully setting his burden down near the fire. Mack sat beside her, soberly taking up the watch.

Rutherford cast about for something to make her more comfortable. There was a cot in the corner, tidily made up with layers of quilts. He thought about it, but discarded the idea of taking one to make a bed for Molly. Instead he removed his own jacket and repositioned her upon it. She whined and looked up at him as he petted her head.

He was becoming truly worried. It was too early for her to deliver, but she was far enough along that any complication could pose a serious risk. He rubbed her belly gently, and she made a plaintive moan that stopped him immediately. There must be something seriously wrong. He felt her nose. It was wet. That was good. He spied an empty pot hanging on the wall, and went to fill it from the water barrel he had seen outside.

When he returned into the house, he held out the pot to offer her a drink. She only sniffed it, then laid her head back down, her eyes glassy.

"Very well, little princess. You just rest now." His eyes grew misty. This could not be happening to his beloved Molly.

She whined again and her body convulsed. He winced in sympathy. She must be dying. Tears welled in Rutherford's his eyes, as stroked her ears gently. He suddenly detected a very organic smell. Rutherford looked down expecting to see that Molly had soiled the floor, but instead a squinting, furry little face appeared to hang out of her backside. She gave another shudder and the whole puppy plopped onto the floor.

Rutherford laughed. "Oh thank God. They are just coming early." Molly moved her head down, bit the umbilical cord off, and began to lick the slimy little squirming lump clean. And then another long shudder came. "Oh, good girl Molly!" Tears of relief streamed down his face. "My wonderful, wonderful girl." Another little glistening blob of fur appeared.

As he was watching Molly attend to this second little furry gift, a woman's voice came from behind him.

"Do not do anything foolish or I shall shoot you. Stand up and state your business."

CHAPTER 27

Lydia had been pushing for what seemed like hours. Tilly checked her watch. Yes, it had been two hours. Ole Maeb remained cheerful and assured them both that everything was proceeding normally.

"The head is cresting just right, my lady. All is as it should be." Ole Maeb had an unsinkable energy, especially for someone of her advanced years.

Tilly thought she might like to procure some of the woman's concoctions. Perhaps the old herbalist had something to help with her sugar cravings.

"The head is roughly the size of an oak's trunk." Lydia gasped. "I should not have eaten so well." She strained and bore down.

Tilly had never before witnessed a birthing. Some of the ladies at the Belle Hire had delivered children, and Tilly made certain they were well attended and as comfortable as was possible under the circumstances. She peeked again at the mass of blood and other mysterious fluids on the sheets, and at Lydia's straining body. She forced herself to maintain a pleasant smile.

Perhaps *comfortable* was the wrong word. But in any case, she had never troubled herself to actually attend a birthing. Certainly the mothers could not want her there. And after today, she hoped she should never attend another. Well, that was not entirely true, for she did, at times, dreamily wish to have a child with Mr. Rutherford, and she supposed there was no way to avoid being present for the birthing of one's own babe.

She looked at Ole Maeb hopefully for a brief moment. No. If Ole Maeb had any such potion she would be rich as the devil—or perhaps burned at the stake as one of his consorts. Tilly suspected that the men who ran the world, and burned *witches*, took a secret, misogynistic pleasure in the pain women suffered in childbirth.

Where had that thought come from? She laughed at herself. She was not even the one delivering the baby, and the process was turning her into a man-hater.

Lydia screeched and the whole head of the babe was out.

"Well done, my lady! The head is out. Your work is almost done, for the head is the biggest part."

"I believe I had apprehended that much," Lydia gasped. "For, even in the kingdom of Brobdingnag there must not be a larger object." She panted for a few more minutes, then pushed out her baby to the waiting arms of Ole Maeb, and to the great relief of Tilly.

"Congratulations, my lady. A beautiful baby girl."

Lydia was crying. Tilly had never seen her cry before. She felt uncomfortable when she realized that she was also crying. The whole affair had been so draining.

When the final bits of messy work had been done by Ole Maeb—involving a knife, but Tilly averted her gaze—and the babe had been cleaned and handed to her eager mother, Tilly finally sat down and massaged her hand.

"She is beautiful, Lydia." Tilly watched the look of rapt love spread over her friend's face and entire body. All the pain of a few moments ago was completely washed away in a sea of forgetfulness. "Should we let the earl in?"

Lydia stirred herself and looked up mistily at Tilly before her face settled into a look of shock. "Oh no! Not yet. I look a fright. I must at least wash and have my hair brushed."

The servants were already removing the blood-soaked upper bedding and placing swaths of fabric over the stains on the lower sheet.

"It is a bit soon yet." Ole Maeb wiped the tears from her eyes.

Tilly, who had been oblivious before, suddenly realised how much this happy event meant to the elderly servant. She truly loved Lydia, and the new baby was more important in her eyes than any princess of the realm.

Ole Maeb sniffled. "She has not yet delivered the afterbirth."

Tilly almost fainted at this mention of more delivery. She did not think she could endure it. But Lydia received the comment serenely, smiling and nodding at Ole Maeb. Then she returned to happily cooing at her daughter as though there were no one else in the world.

Watching this vignette of maternal complacence, Tilly understood the great universal fascination with the theme of *mother and child*, pervasive in the world's art. It preceded the Catholic obsession with Mary, which only built upon it. Its origin was from time out of mind, and it presented Tilly with a mystery she could not comprehend. She only viewed it from the outside as a curiosity under glass, or as a delicacy appeared to a child with her nose pressed against a sweetshop window.

Tilly shook her head to dispel such thoughts, slouching back and groaning. "Afterbirth, eh? I believe I shall require a drink."

Lydia bestirred herself from admiring her baby and chuckled. "Oh, poor Tilly! Has this ordeal been too exhausting for you?"

CHAPTER 28

Rutherford rose slowly and turned to face the woman who had a hunting rifle pointed at him. His jaw dropped. She was unbelievably beautiful. She was tall and willowy, with luscious black curls, perfect ivory skin, beautifully curved ruby lips, and penetrating blue eyes. Except for the eyes, and the fact that she pointed a gun at his heart, she was beautiful in a way completely opposite to Tilly.

He smiled wolfishly at her. "Truly, madam, I am sorry for the intrusion, but is it really necessary to point a gun at me?"

She looked suspiciously at him. "You are a gentleman?"

"Despite recent evidence to the contrary," he drawled, "yes, I am."

Just then Molly whined, and Rutherford squatted back down to attend her. Another puppy had appeared. The others were already settling in by her nipples.

"What is your business here?" The woman's voice wavered at the sight of the puppies.

Rutherford did not turn, but petted Molly to soothe her and replied snappishly, "What does it look like my business is?"

"It looks like your business is invading other peoples' homes."

Rutherford huffed. Why was this woman so fearful of him? What ill-intentioned person brings puppies along to assist them in their crimes? "I apologize for the intrusion. My only excuse is that my pointer here began birthing her pups, as you see. I needed to get her somewhere warm and secure. They are early."

She paused before replying. "Truly? And no one sent you here?"

"No, I found my own way while taking a walk in my uncle's forests. Who would have sent me?" The young lady—and she did speak like a lady—clearly had some enemy.

"Your uncle?"

"Bartholmer." He noted that she had ignored his question.

There was a pause. "If you are his grace's nephew, what is your name?"

Rutherford turned to look up at her incredulously. "I am not sure I wish to make your acquaintance, though I suppose under the circumstances it is unavoidable. But my *name* is Rutherford. What is your name, pray, if it is not *impudent* of me to ask?"

She relaxed and lowered the gun's barrel to the floor. "My apologies, Mr. Rutherford. I am Mrs. Colling. I rent this cottage from your uncle."

Rutherford laughed then. "So you are Mrs. Colling." He was sure his uncle had called her *Miss Colling*. "My uncle spoke of you. Though the impression he gave was certainly much more bookish and much less gun-wielding. And, if I may add," Rutherford gave her a sceptical look, "he omitted to mention how beautiful you are."

She rolled her eyes. "Oh, I know that look. Because of my face, I must be after your uncle's money and title, I suppose."

Rutherford found her forthright way of speaking refreshing, but that did not mean she wasn't a fortune hunter. "Are you?"

"No, I am not." Her beautiful lips pressed flat, but could not entirely lose their curve. "His grace is a kind and lonely old man who is terribly sick. I read to him because it gives him some comfort, which also comforts me. That is all."

Rutherford conceded to himself that her voice had the sound of offended honesty. "You will forgive me for being suspicious on this point, but one wonders why a beautiful young lady might hide herself out in the forests of the countryside, instead of enjoying the amusements of London."

"And trying to find a husband? I am a widow, sir. Your uncle and I have this much in common: for our separate reasons, we have no wish to remarry."

This revelation shocked Rutherford. What an utter waste. So *Miss* Colling was a widow, eh? There was a lot more to this story. But the arrival of another puppy turned his attention back to Molly.

Mrs. Colling left again, and a few minutes later was beside him with rags and a bucket. "Do not let her eat too much of the afterbirth. It will make her sick."

Rutherford shuddered and grimaced with distaste.

She laughed at him.

CHAPTER 29

Tilly was exhausted when she arrived home that evening. She ordered dinner in her chamber and flopped down on the Danzig down that transformed her bed into a cloud. Then, as she stared at the various batik images quilted into cryptic pictorial stories on the top panels, Tilly dissolved into self-pity.

Lydia's baby was born. Both the parents were ecstatically happy. So why was Tilly so dispirited? She did share in their joy—truly. Only the perfection of the moment, their happiness and love was like a persistent little tap all around Tilly's outer shell, and the mournful echo within proclaimed her empty. She could no longer deny it. Her plans to marry Mr. DeGroen could not make her happy, and they were certainly making the man she loved miserable.

She did love Mr. DeGroen dearly—almost as she loved her own brother. But it was a friendship that could never be what the earl and countess shared. Tilly and Mr. DeGroen would never conceive a child together. Not that Tilly had been especially mad about having babies, but of late she was becoming increasingly aware of a desire to have *Mr. Rutherford's* baby. It was maddening folly. When, within the schedule of all her machinations, shady businesses and rescues, did she have time for a child?

A rap came on the door. Tilly thought it was her dinner tray, but her brother's voice summoned her to lift her leaden limbs and propel herself out to see him.

"What is it now?" She knew she sounded peevish, but she could not be bothered to slap on a smile for anyone.

Frederick did not even register her crossness and spoke directly. "I have been down to the servant academy to check on things. Mrs. Johnson and her child are gone."

Tilly snapped out of her melancholia immediately. "What?! I thought they were being guarded."

"Crump thinks they slipped out."

"Has Screwe been around?"

"No. There was a smoky looking lad hanging about. Crump sent him on his way. But Screwe has not been seen."

"Ruddy hell." Tilly began to think where they might have gone, but the truth was she could not think her way out of that labyrinth. This was London. They could be anywhere. She pressed a hand against her mouth. "We must pray that he has not found them."

"I questioned everyone about, and no one saw the two leave. They did not have many things, but what they had is also gone—some clothing and a reading primer that the teacher gave Sweep."

"That is good." Tilly sunk into thought. "Yes, they must have left." It was decidedly better than if they had been taken by Screwe or someone working for him. Still they were in danger and without any protection.

"There is more, Tilly." Frederick looked serious. "Forester showed up at the academy looking for a place to stay and assistance to find a new placement."

"Forester?" Tilly felt the blood drain from her face.

"It seems Lord Screwe dismissed her for no cause at all this morning. Just like that." Frederick snapped his fingers.

"Good Lord. He must have sorted out that she had something to do with Clara's escape. But his butler knows Forester was trained in the academy. Do you think Screwe has puzzled out the connection to us?"

"I hope not. His surmises may not have got that far. Screwe also fired several other servants—upstairs servants all. So perhaps he has not narrowed it down to Forester, in particular."

"Perhaps." Tilly held onto the little hope. Then an idea struck her. "Do you think Clara saw Forester, heard of her dismissal and panicked? She could have believed that if Screwe knew Forester had helped free her, he would be hard on the servant's heels to come and search the academy for Clara."

"Quite possibly. But in any case, we must find her and Sweep. I asked Crump to put the lads on alert."

"Good. My God, that poor woman. She hardly had a chance to recover from her last ordeal." Tilly passed a hand over her face. "And if he finds her, things will be so much worse."

"Did you know that she was training to dress hair with Miss Grey?"

"Indeed? No, I have not been back to the academy, and I have been too busy to get updates. That is the profession she chose?"

"She is apparently already trained and is quite adept. With all the business the Belle Hire gives her, Miss Grey was only too happy for the assistance."

Tilly smiled wanly. "That is good news. Now if we can just find her—

but wait! Has anyone looked at the Belle Hire? If she knows the place, she might have sought refuge there."

She resisted the urge to slap on a black veil and dash out to the Belle Hire. It was maddening, but she could not just go wherever she pleased now. Screwe could have eyes on her, and the last thing she needed was his knowing that she owned the Belle Hire. She certainly did not want him to poke around the place, if, indeed, Clara had fled there.

"I shall have a message sent to Crats," said Frederick, with a concerned look at Tilly. "But please do not venture to go there yourself, even in disguise. It is too risky."

Tilly sighed. "Very well. But I have picked a dreadfully bad week to stop eating sugar."

CHAPTER 30

Rutherford hoped the ravages of the cravings did not show, as he walked beside Mrs. Colling along the forested path back to Blackwood Manor. And yet, they were not so very bad, this time. Or, they were bad enough, but Rutherford found them easier to ignore at the moment, for his heart was so full.

Mrs. Colling had fashioned a great sling for Rutherford to carry Molly and the pups in, so they would be only minimally disturbed by the removal back to the manor. He reached in to stroke the sleepy mass of fur and tails and pet Molly's head. They were so beautiful, his little furry family.

There was also an extra spring in Mack's step as he walked beside Rutherford. The hound forbore wandering around and sniffing things, as was his habit. Instead he held vigil by the sling, never straying far from Rutherford's side. Rutherford was impressed by his dedication.

"This is a marvellous contraption, Mrs. Colling." Rutherford stared in rapt adoration at his brood.

"The sling you mean?" She was grinning at the sight of him.

He knew he looked foolish, but he did not care. "Yes. You are quite the genius for having contrived it. I should never have thought of it."

"I suppose that is because you are strong. Strong men always elect to do things with their muscles first. Whereas frail young ladies are wont to resort to their wits."

He detected that there was a thorn of a slight hidden in the nosegay of that compliment, but Rutherford was feeling too happy to let it tweak his nose. Eight little puppies. He petted Molly again. What a good little mama she was.

"I should never call you frail, however." Rutherford recalled, as she must also, that, not an hour ago, she had pointed a rifle at his heart. If he were not in love with Tilly, he might be in some serious peril.

"These things are all in proportion." She shrugged philosophically. "But I should add that I cannot take credit for the invention of this sling. As a girl, I often observed farm workers' wives carrying their babes thus. I imagine peasant women have been doing it for hundreds of years, or thousands."

So she had been raised on an estate then. What was a gently raised beauty doing out living rough in the countryside? Rutherford thought the better of asking, and merely chuckled. "This is further evidence of your feminine mind. If you were a man, you would be sure to take credit for it, regardless."

Mrs. Colling's expression betrayed that she did not disagree with him.

When they arrived at Blackwood, Rutherford was advised that the duke was awake and was asking for him. He excused himself to take a half dose of his poison.

He thought if he could reduce the size of the doses and increase their frequency, he could manage the cravings tolerably and reduce the sleepiness caused by the drug. He thought Tilly would not disapprove of this modification, as his overall consumption did not exceed her prescription.

Molly and the pups were transferred into a basket, which Sandes lined with a pillow and some folded flannel. The way the proper butler could not help smiling at the furry, squirming balls made Rutherford like him very well. He should never dream of demoting Sandes. Smythe would have to live with it.

Mrs. Colling elected to wait in the parlour. Rutherford was ushered in, basket in hand, to see Bartholmer, who had been impatiently ringing the bell to summon someone to fetch his nephew, and "To be sure to bring the pups!"

The old duke greeted Rutherford, then patted a spot on the bed beside him. "Put that basket down over here so I may take a look at them."

A great, child-like grin spread over his face as he petted Molly and the pups. "So this is Molly." He scratched her ear. "You are a pretty little pointer, aren't you?" Then he turned to behold Rutherford, who could scarcely keep the emotion from his face. "Oh don't get all weepy, my boy. But would you be so kind as to open the curtains. I should like to see the little champions better."

Rutherford obliged, and Bartholmer picked up the pups, one by one, examined them and gave them a little kiss—as though he were blessing his grandchildren. Rutherford approved.

This scene of benediction was interrupted by a rasping cough.

Rutherford was alarmed and moved quickly to Bartholmer's side. "Uncle, what is the matter? Can I fetch something for you?"

The old man shook his head, and it became clear that he was not suffering some sort of fit, but laughing. When he recovered himself, he said, "I thought these were supposed to be champion pointers."

Rutherford looked affronted. "They are. They shall be. I could have ransomed the prince for the price I paid in stud fees."

The old man laughed again, then let out a long sigh of amusement. "I think you may have bought a pig in a poke, William. Look at these ears." He held up one puppy, and affectionately played with his long, floppy ears. His uncle then pointed to another pup. "The colouration on that one is a bit suspect, too."

Rutherford took the disparaged puppy from his uncle and looked at the ears, then cuddled the little darling to his chest. "There is nothing wrong with his ears. He is perfect."

Bartholmer's smile was crooked. "Indeed he is. They are all beautiful. But I should not depend upon selling them as champion pointers."

Rutherford was horrified. "Sell them? Of course not." Still, his uncle had a point. He looked down at Mack who sat at his heel, looking, Rutherford thought, particularly pleased with himself. A suspicion formed in his mind. "Well, it does not matter whether they are champions or not. I have plenty of room for twice so many dogs at my estate."

"And you may fill Blackwood with as many pups as you like. I always thought those self-complacent peacocks could use a little worrying." His uncle was cuddling the puppy whose colouration he had earlier maligned. "I shall stare down from heaven and smile."

The thought made Rutherford both happy and deeply sad. "I should hope you would be around for long enough to take on one of Molly's pups."

It went against his instinct to offer any of the pups to anyone else. But the obvious joy they gave his uncle made Rutherford think that the duke loved them almost as much as he did. He thought he could part with one, if it would give the man some happiness. If only he were well enough to take Rutherford up on the offer.

His uncle smiled. "We shall see how my health stands, when the little nippers come to be weaned."

The puppy at Rutherford's chest seemed to object to any such idea as weaning, and began to whine for his mother. When all the whelps were safely tucked in and nursing, Bartholmer turned his attention to Rutherford. "So you met Miss Colling, I understand."

"Indeed." It seemed the duke's servants kept him well informed. He wondered if he should disclose that the lady had levelled a gun at him, but thought it might disturb the ailing man. "But she informs me that she is *Mrs.* Colling."

His uncle waved his hand as if that little detail did not matter. "She is quite a stunner, is she not?" The uncle did not even pretend to make this comment sound offhanded.

"The Widow Colling is unarguably handsome." He thought he should nip this line of thought in the bud. "If my heart were not otherwise engaged, I might be in some trouble."

Bartholmer furrowed his brows. "Are you betrothed?"

"No." Rutherford sighed. "But not for lack of trying."

"She has refused you, then? Or her parents disapprove?"

Rutherford had never met her parents, but from the titbits he had gleaned from Tilly, they were entirely negligent as guardians and hardly attended to her at all. "It is, unfortunately, the former. But I have not given up."

"Well, far be it from me to dissuade you from your faithfulness to one woman. It is certainly a predicament I can relate to." He smiled at the memory. "My own wife refused me the first several times I proposed. She was magnificent."

"That is just how I feel about T—about my love. She is unequalled among women."

"But if she will not have you... Will you not consider another?"

"Never."

"And yet," the old man tapped his fingertips on his lips, "you have put

Miss Colling in a rather difficult position, what with your visit to her home and your meander through the woods."

"*Mrs.* Colling. According to her own testimony, she is a widow, Uncle." Rutherford rolled his eyes. "So I believe we may dispense with the *Miss Colling* designation. And however frail the dignity of a woman who does not give you her real name, as a widow, I believe her reputation may withstand being seen walking with me and my dogs. No one need know that we were alone in the cabin together."

"Perhaps. But you should consider her under my protection, William. So you must not toy with her."

"Toy with her?" Rutherford laughed. He wondered how much the duke knew about this young woman's real story. Rutherford was certain that she had one, and that it was probably scandalous. "I should as soon toy with a highwayman! If there is a woman who does not need protecting, it is she."

CHAPTER 31

It had been two days, and Tilly's agents could get no intelligence regarding Clara and Sweep. It seemed to her that this was good news, for if her network of urchins could find nothing out, a lord like Screwe, however corrupt and connected to the evils of London, would surely fare no better.

She had begun making inquiries into how to dispose of her opium business. It was not as simple as selling everything. She wanted to preserve the livelihoods of those working for her and she did not want the business to fall into the hands of the unscrupulous.

Then she realized that she *was* the unscrupulous, at least in absolute terms. But there were much worse characters, and she was trying to make up for her lapse in ethics. Her past indifference certainly did not give her leave for the fresh sin of passing the business on to a nastier profiteering fiend than herself.

Her head spun over such thoughts. It blue-devilled her and made her wish for a biscuit. But she was down to one per day, and she had eaten her ration when she awoke. Her headaches were now subsiding. She only got a faint one when she stayed up too late. Tilly was forced to concede that, much like Rutherford's symptoms, her headaches had been caused, rather than cured, by all her sugar.

The comparison vexed her, but it was time that she accepted the truth. She was dependant upon biscuits and sweeties. She pursed her lips unhappily.

She might be the only person in all of England to confess this weakness, but she would do so. If she could not give up this little overindulgence, how could she ask Rutherford to claw his way through the hell of weaning himself off laudanum?

She wondered how he was doing. She had procured a supply of the dried herbs used in the infusion that Ole Maeb gave Lydia for the birthing. The aged herbalist had confirmed that it should alleviate, but not eliminate the ordeal of quitting laudanum.

Tilly had been so busy that she had not seen him in days, and anyway, she was not supposed to see him. Wasn't that the plan? But she had an excuse to see him now, if only she did not fear she were being watched by Screwe's henchmen.

And it would be nice to chat with Rutherford. Who did she think she was fooling? She wanted more than a chat. Yet what she wanted most was to see that he was well. Perhaps they could encourage each other. He might be pleased to know of her progress in giving up sweets.

But would her presence make things worse for him? Her heart throbbed. Why could she not rid herself of this pining after what could not be? Rutherford would not be happy in an affair. He wanted a wife, and Tilly was to marry another.

Her fingers twitched with the memory of gliding them along his smooth skin and enjoying the lithe curves of his muscles. Giving up sugar was child's play. Giving up Rutherford seemed impossible. If only she didn't care so deeply for him, her life would be blissfully simple.

Blissfully simple? Hah!

She stood up, abruptly. "Right! Enough ruminating. I shall go see Lydia and her new babe. That will take my mind off the mayhem of my life."

When Tilly arrived at the Aldley house, she was shown into Lydia's chambers, where the countess was happily ensconced upon a chaise longue, the new love of her life asleep on her shoulder.

Tilly paused in the doorway and felt wretched for the pang of jealousy that tore through her. Was she jealous of the child that now had all of her best friend's heart, or jealous of the friend who would evermore possess the heart of this child? Either way, Tilly was an awful person for envying a happiness that was almost holy. She entered and they exchanged their greetings.

"Is she not a perfect little angel?" Serene contentment illuminated Lydia's features, as she showed the sleeping infant to Tilly.

"She is very… pink." Tilly shook her head. What a stupid thing to say. "Just like a little blossom." She hoped it sounded convincing.

"Oh, but you are such a bad liar. She has a ruddy complexion, but all the experts assure me that it may go away in time. I really cannot complain, for she must have got it from my side. My mother says I was a very red-faced little thing right up until I took my first communion."

"Who knew that the blood of Christ was so efficacious." Tilly could not help herself.

"Hah! Irreligious little goblin. Have you ever even taken communion, or does the wafer catch fire as soon as it hits your tongue?"

Tilly tilted her head and arranged her lips in an expression of philosophical resignation. "Well, yes sometimes, but only if I forget to pay the tithe upfront."

Lydia played along and assumed an air of mock piety. "If only the

Church of England had indulgences, you could defer payment on the wages of your sins."

"Would that be an interest-free deferral, do you think?" But Tilly's smirk soon soured. "Bah! This is enough holy talk. Even in jest it reminds me too much of Grandfather Fowler's speeches."

"And how is your future grandfather-in-law?"

"Still alive."

"Tilly! You must not say such things, or I shall have to take measures to protect my daughter from your corrupting influence." Lydia pretended to cover the one exposed ear of her daughter.

Tilly gave her friend a nonchalant look. "I imagine the nursery might be lined with lead, easily enough. You could pop her in there, when I come to call."

"Ah, but I never relegate my babe to the nursery. Unless we are entertaining, she is always here with me, if she is not being fed. So you must learn to behave yourself."

"That I never shall." Tilly grinned. "And anyway, I am the only obstacle between you and the maddening tedium of maternal incarceration. Prisoners cannot be too choosy about their visitors. But to answer your question, the old geezer is as puritanical as ever. However he gives every appearance of being ready to confer a large settlement on his grandson, and make him the heir, finally. I believe he has already begun redrafting the will, so he must be satisfied that Mr. DeGroen is of sufficiently good character."

Lydia had a strange look on her face. "And so you shall marry your own massive settlement with a prince's fortune. And it is certain—you have not changed your mind?"

"My mind is unwavering," Tilly lied.

"I had hoped," confessed Lydia, "that Mr. Rutherford might turn your head. True I have nothing against Mr. DeGroen, but it is so clear to me how much Rutherford loves you. It shall break his heart when you marry another."

Tilly knew that it would also break her own heart, but she had been over it in her head, and there was just no way out of things. DeGroen's inheritance was precariously perched on the long engagement followed by marriage, along with proving his *moral character*. If only the puritan grandfather knew how things really were, he would die of an apoplexy. But that would do DeGroen no good, as the old man was yet to make over everything to his grandson. No, these were the terms dictated by Grandfather Fowler, and there was no way around it.

"To be honest, Lydia, Mr. Rutherford *has* turned my head. But I am not free to follow my own inclinations."

Lydia's face lit up with hope. "But of course you are! It is a lady's prerogative to break off an engagement, after all."

Tilly sighed. She would like to explain it, but there were just some things that were private and it was not her right to share them, even to explain to her friend that she was not a heartless, money-grubbing fiend in petticoats. "It would not be without severe consequences. I cannot do it. And Rutherford is better off without me."

"Oh, how can you say so!" Lydia looked distressed. "You are wonderful. More fun than any young woman I have ever met, which is perfect for Rutherford. And Rutherford is perfect for you. He loves a little intrigue and irreverence, and does not, like three quarters of the ton, expect women to be dull and stupid. And you must concede he is as handsome as anything."

Tilly could not take much more of this line of talk, so she changed the subject abruptly. "And what of Lord Essington? Have you heard any news of him? Rutherford mentioned that your husband was concerned the bounder was up to something."

"Do not think I have missed remarking that you are changing the subject, but yes, I have heard a little something, and I believe it involves you."

Tilly cursed herself for not bringing up some other topic, any other topic. "Me? I cannot imagine how."

"Can you not? Tilly, I am your friend. It bothers me that you do not take me into your confidence, but I have come to a surmise and I should like you to answer me directly."

Tilly lifted a brow. "I see you take very quickly to being a countess. You certainly have adopted the requisite imperiousness."

Lydia merely proved Tilly's point by lifting a finger to cut off the objection and continuing, "I admit that we were rather too hard on you about the brothel, and I am thankful that you have forgiven me for my indiscretion. But, honestly, Tilly, this is beyond the pale. In short, you must stop selling Lord Essington opium."

"I am not selling Lord Essington opium." It was true. No money had exchanged hands. But how had Lydia found out about it?

"Oh, indeed?" Lydia squinted into Tilly's face, trying to scry out of its contours some indication of whether or not she told the truth. "Then why do you look guilty?"

"If you are registering some troubled expression on my face, it is not guilt, but shock. Whatever has led you to accuse me of selling your brother-in-law opium?"

"I will tell you," said Lydia, not persuaded in the least by Tilly's dissembling. "After the baby was born, Thomas was more willing to discuss the distressing events involving Mr. Delacroix. He told me that he first feared Delacroix's return when Rutherford spotted Crump leaving Essington Hall."

"Indeed." Tilly swallowed. This was not good. "What was Rutherford doing at Essington Hall?"

"Thomas sent him to check on his sister, but do not change the subject. At the time he and Rutherford believed Crump to be still in the employ of Delacroix. We have since learned that you are his new master."

"And yet, I do not watch him every minute of the day. I will have a word with him about associating with turds like Essington. Will that do?"

"No, it will not." Lydia gave her a look of supreme disdain for such a trifling attempt to deceive her intellect. "Now, Thomas has not yet made the connection between the fact that Essington is somehow getting a supply of opium delivered to him, and the fact that Crump is your man. Or if he has, he has decided not to mention his suspicions to me."

"You see? He is not suspicious, though he is so fastidious a person."

Lydia raised a hand. "I know you, Tilly. I know, as my husband does not, that you made some sort of deal with Essington to buy his silence about the unescorted carriage ride he took with your sister-in-law, before you married her off to your brother."

"I had no need to make a bargain. Why should he wish to say anything about it at all? He is a bounder, but he is not a gossip. He gives every indication of holding common morality in contempt."

Lydia shook her head in complete dismissal of this reasoning. "You have your fingers in a lot of pies. That is just how you are, and I find it charming. It does not bother me in the least that you deal in opium."

Tilly would not allow herself to be relieved until she heard the equivocation that she knew was coming.

"However," continued Lydia. "Thomas is trying very hard to keep Essington away from the drug, for the sake of Lady Essington and the child."

Tilly sighed. "You have no idea how opium takes a person over, Lydia.

Lord Essington would get that drug one way or another. If he is having it regularly delivered, it will keep him out of London, and out of trouble."

"Except for the trouble of destroying his health."

"I will not debate that point. But you have seen a little of the man's character, and your husband knows it only too well. Do you think he would not have his way and get the opium, no matter what?"

Lydia huffed and gave a dissatisfied look. "I suppose you are right about that. But it is unseemly to have my own best friend delivering the poison to him."

"Very unseemly. So unseemly that it only *seems* that way to one person, notably you."

"It cannot be long until Thomas makes the connection, Tilly. And he is less broad-minded than I am."

"Well, put your mind at ease. If I *were* supplying it to your brother-in-law, which I by no means concede, I should certainly be thinking, at this point, of getting out of the trade." She was willing to let Lydia think it was because she feared detection.

Lydia looked relieved. "That is more than I could ask for. At least I will not have the pain of knowing that the noxious substance is coming from your hand."

Tilly shrugged at her friend's being so easily appeased with this cold comfort. It certainly would not solve anything.

It was hard for Tilly to believe, but it appeared that neither Lydia nor her husband had recognized Rutherford's dependency on laudanum, probably because he behaved like a gentleman. So many people held onto the foolish prejudice that vice was always obvious in the conduct and the features of the vicious.

"But Essington is a selfish brute," Tilly could not resist adding, "because that is who he is, not because of opium." And Rutherford, despite his dependency, was a good man. The drug could ruin that, to be sure, but it did not have the power to improve anyone's character. "Denying Lord Essington opium, even if such an effort succeeds, will not make him a better person, husband or father. Your husband should be prepared for that."

"If only there were some way of weaning him off, without having him turn into a completely rabid savage."

Her friend's wish floated about Tilly's cranium like a tiny dandelion seed carried by the winds of desperate fancy, before dropping into her head and poking her brain. That was it! That was what she would do with her opium business. She would not merely sell off her interest to someone yet worse than she was. She would hold onto it and use it as a base for a sanatorium to treat those who were addicted, to gradually wean them off, and to help them regain their nerves.

She sprang up and kissed her friend loudly on both cheeks. "Lydia, my dearest friend, you are brilliant!"

Lydia looked very surprised and unconsciously clutched her baby closer, as she watched her mad friend dash for the door. "Where are you going?"

"I am going to see Rutherford!"

Lydia's face brightened. "That is wonderful. But you know he is out of town to see his Uncle Bartholmer."

"Then I shall go to him there."

"But you have not been invited!" she called to the disappearing back of her friend.

As she skipped down the hall, Tilly heard Lydia add, in a disappointed voice, "And I have not told you of the name we selected for the babe."

But Tilly was too excited to stop. Baby names could wait. She had to share her news with Rutherford.

CHAPTER 32

Rutherford inhaled the fragrance of his uncle's roses and stroked Molly's silky ears. He thought the new mother deserved an outing after having been pent up inside with the pups, so he had brought the whole litter out into the rose garden for a frolic, while *Mrs. Colling* read to Bartholmer.

That whole *Miss Colling* business had only been his uncle not hearing her correctly when she introduced herself, apparently. After that, she said, she did not feel equal to correcting a duke. It seemed plausible enough, and at least it meant she had not deceived the duke about her name. But Rutherford suspected there was a lot more to her story than she was letting on. Still, so long as she was not actively misrepresenting herself to his uncle, Rutherford supposed her intrigues were none of his concern.

And yet, he could not deny his curiosity about a woman who levelled guns at strangers and lived on her own in a cottage in the woods. There was no question that with her looks, she could marry advantageously. There was certainly no need to put herself on the shelf and live in poverty, just because she was a widow. If her vivacity was any indication, he did not think she was especially pining for her dead husband, either.

He shook his head. There was no reason to be brooding about it. His own oddly motivated woman kept his mind sufficiently occupied, without borrowing someone else's. He picked up the puppy that resembled Mack and rubbed his long ears. "How do you do, little Mick? Are the other pups treating you well? Do not let them tease you about your ears. Did I ever tell you the story of how your papa helped to save my life?"

"Rutherford?" A head peeked around the hedge. "I thought I heard your voice."

He blinked. It was Tilly. His heart surged with joy. He had been missing her, wishing she could be with him to meet his uncle, see Blackwood, meet the puppies. And now she was before him. She walked over to his blanket, Mrs. Carlton in tow, and plopped herself down next to him.

Tilly was beaming as she petted one of the pups. "Molly had her puppies? Already? How exciting! And look at them. They are adorable."

"Indeed." His voice was hoarse. "I have to agree. But what are you doing here? I mean, I am overjoyed to see you, truly. But I did not expect you. Do you know my uncle?"

"No. And I am glad I heard your voice before I made it to the front door, for you have spared me the embarrassment of calling at a grand house where I have no business calling." She laughed merrily enough to belie her professed scruple about imposing her company upon the household. "This is your uncle's estate, is it? I had no idea you had such rich relatives."

Rutherford smiled as he contemplated what effect his next words might have. "My uncle is the Duke Bartholmer." He watched her face.

"Oh!" said Tilly with affected consternation. "Then it is a very good thing I found you out here first, before I had a chance to expose myself and my ignorance."

He had hoped she would be more impressed, and perhaps make some further enquiry that would permit him a delicate way of revealing his own prospect of holding the title. But what of it? It was a beautiful day, her eyes were merry and her smile was as devilishly adorable as ever. He was happy. And he would make his own opportunity to reveal his future prospects. "So, I am overjoyed to see you, but whatever could have brought you all this way? Did you come to spy out your future home?"

She looked puzzled. "My future home?"

At that moment, Mrs. Colling came around the edge of the hedge carrying a large basket. She stopped suddenly. "Oh! I did not realize you had guests." She did not sound pleased. She turned her face awkwardly away from Tilly as she placed the basket on the blanket. "Your uncle sent me with some victuals for you. But there is certainly enough for three."

Rutherford looked at Tilly. She did not look pleased either. She was trying to get a better view of Mrs. Colling, who made to dash away as quickly as she had come.

Unworthy as the thought was, Rutherford saw the advantage of cultivating the suspicion that was clearly forming in Tilly's mind. "Oh, Mrs. Colling, please stay and let me introduce you to my friend and her companion."

The introduction was awkward. Mrs. Colling seemed bent on not meeting Tilly's eye, and Rutherford could see Tilly was squinting at Mrs. Colling suspiciously.

Rutherford began to feel nervous that his plan was going a little too well, that Tilly was interpreting Mrs. Colling's inability to meet her gaze as a sign of guilty actions, not just guilty interests. She flashed Rutherford an unimpressed look.

But then, as she caught another glance of Mrs. Colling, who was adjusting her veil to better cover her face and making to leave again, a look of realization crossed Tilly's features. Now Rutherford was in the dark. What did Tilly know that he did not?

CHAPTER 33

Tilly only permitted herself a single glare at Rutherford before regaining control of her face. So this is what he was doing out in the countryside while *visiting his uncle*. Having picnics on the lawn with the beautiful Widow Colling. What a load of bollocks. Why had she brought herself out here, only to watch this?

He introduced them. The woman could not even meet Tilly's gaze. Was she so ashamed at having been found out? Good Lord, she was involved in a tryst with him. So this was what his declarations of unwavering love and proposals of matrimony came to. As soon as he was out of sight he was off invading whichever pretty petticoat the wind turned up.

Well, that was perhaps not fair. Even with the limited view of her face, Tilly could see that Mrs. Colling was an uncommonly lovely temptation. This did not make Tilly like the situation any better.

Mrs. Colling finally made to break away from the lawn party. As she raised her arm to pull down her veil more securely, Tilly caught a flash of sapphire blue pupils through the lace. She stifled a gasp. Tilly recognized that beautiful face, those gorgeous eyes. The truth of the scenario arranged itself plainly before Tilly's mind's eye.

She could not suppress a brief look of amused superiority. Rutherford had no idea what sort of petticoats he had gotten tangled up with. She would lead him a merry chase. *Mrs. Colling*, as she called herself, saw Tilly's look of recognition, and met it with a fleeting expression of desperate pleading. Then she made her excuses in a barrage of mumbles and hastily departed.

Tilly considered the situation for a moment, then decided she would keep *Mrs. Colling*'s secret, for now. But she needed to have a quiet word with the *widow*. Rutherford, who had been smiling stupidly earlier, now looked dull—no, he looked confounded. He was feeling uncomfortably on the wrong foot. She suppressed a malicious laugh. Good. Served him right. Let him stay that way.

"Mr. Rutherford." She smiled sweetly at him. "I came to tell you some good news. I have come up with an idea to dispose of my—of those business assets that you so disapprove of. A very good idea, I think. And here." she pressed a flask and a paper with instructions into his hand. "This is a concoction that one of Lydia's servants makes. She is a clever herbalist, and she says it may help with—certain symptoms."

He raised a brow. "Well, that will be a welcome remedy, assuming it is not just *the devil that I don't know*."

Tilly shook her head. "She assures me it is not." But then, why should he trust anything that came from her hand? "She gave a version of it to Lydia for the delivery. As it has been successfully tested on a countess, it ought not kill a strapping buck like you."

"The delivery? So they are parents now?" Rutherford's features betrayed a twist of the jealousy that she herself had felt. "That is wonderful news."

She yearned to hold his hand, stroke his hair, soothe his longing heart, but she dared not touch him. "Perhaps we shall see each other, if we both happen to go pay a call when you return to town." What was wrong with her? Was she trying to arrange a meeting with the man that she was supposed to be giving up? Was she really that much of vain little ninny that she could be driven by jealousy to abandon all her plans to let him go be happy, free of her?

Rutherford looked for a moment like he thought she was referring to a rendezvous, but he seemed to dismiss the idea. "Perhaps we shall." He was still puzzling over something as he looked at her.

She chose to believe that he was intrigued by her lack of reaction to his flirting with the widow. Well, not flirting, perhaps, but up to no good, she was certain. She had seen a flash of admiration in his eye when he looked at *Mrs. Colling*. No matter how her stomach boiled, she would not give him the satisfaction of a response.

Actually, a little contest would be diverting. Her nose twitched. She could not deny that a part of her relished the challenge of winning back Rutherford's affections from the trollop of a widow who was trying to steal them. But no, she was only lying to herself. She was well beyond the point where any of it could be construed as a game. And it was nice to have someone else to blame, but the central problem was not the pretty widow.

However, she had the advantage over him now and she was going to enjoy it. Tilly forced her voice to assume a friendly, conversational tone. "So do you plan to stay long at Blackwood?"

He reached for a sandwich plate just as she did, and his fingers grazed hers, as if by accident. "Would you want me to return to London soon?"

"Well, to be honest, if I am considering your health, no. I must say you are looking much better after a little time away from town." It was true, and with a pang, she reflected that this was further evidence that all he really needed to get better was to get away from her toxic influence. "Perhaps country life agrees with you?"

"It does. But it would agree with me more if I could share it with the woman I love." His eyes were full of his heart.

She wondered if it was just wishful thinking that made her believe he meant her. Was she still the woman he loved?

She needed to change the subject, before she became maudlin. "I believe I have made it through the worst of the craving after sweets. I am down to one per day. I can see that you are also recovering."

"I have been following your daily dosing, but I have divided it up into smaller doses, taken more often. My body is less racked with tremors and pains, and I can feel my mind clearing, too. And I have been taking exercise. My uncle still has a fencing master on staff, and he has been only too happy to have someone to spar with."

"So we are both improving. And I want you to know that I took your strictures seriously. I have been trying to improve morally, as well."

"My strictures on moral improvement?" His amused smile was not arch, only warm and wolfish, like she remembered him when they had first met. "You make me sound like a governess. I hope you have not decided to give up all your wanton ways..."

The look he gave her was so inviting that her heart and resolve melted into a plasma of lust. She steadied herself and cleared her throat. "I was referring to your lecture on the evils of my *investments* in certain commodities. I have thought of a way of diverting them to good use."

He tilted his head sceptically. "Do tell."

"Do not be such a suspicious beast. I have decided that, rather than selling out to someone who might be even less well-motivated than I—"

Rutherford interrupted, "I hope I did not say you were ill-motivated when I was out of my senses with this drug fever. Tilly, you have an irreverent mind, which I love. It may lead you astray at times, but I can see, in your heart, you desire only to help your little parcel of urchins and foundlings, not to enslave incautious customers, like me."

Tilly petted one of the pups. She barely heard what he said after the point where he spoke the word *love*, which launched her into a dream of kissing the beautiful lips that pronounced it.

She shook her head. "You need not try to soothe me. I do not deserve it, and I did not mean that you gave me any offence with your observations. I flatter myself that I am liberal-minded enough not to resent the truth when I hear it. Anyway, do you want to hear my idea, or not?"

He chuckled and waved his hand for her to continue.

"I am going to make a series of healing spas for people to recover from their opium habits. They will be styled as private retreats. Patients will go on a regime of doses, reduced over time. The other aspects of the inmates' wellbeing will also be attended to through healthful food and opportunities for regular exercise and other amusements."

He surprised her by suddenly pulling her into an embrace. It was uncharacteristically chaste for Rutherford. He did not fondle any private part of her person. He kissed her cheek. She could only call it… affectionate. It pulled at her heart, but at the same time, she began to wonder why there was no passion in it. Was his heart already lost to her? Was friendship all that remained? And wasn't that what she had wanted for him?

He released her from his strong arms. "Tilly, you are a wonder! You have hit upon the very way to extract the most good out of the worst evil. I think the idea is a marvellous one."

She could not stop herself from blushing girlishly, which was such a rare occurrence for her, that she reached up and touched the hot spots on her cheeks with wonder. It was so nice to feel admired by Rutherford—not the object of his passion, nor the longing of his heart, but the idol of a higher consideration.

He thought her to be doing good, and that mattered to her so much. Though there was no risk that he would take her right there on the lawn, or propose to her again, her heart, her whole soul was now in peril of becoming his own. He knew of her dabbling in the demimonde and yet he still thought she was good.

No one but her brother and Mr. DeGroen knew this side of her. Would there ever be another man who could see past appearances, into her heart and see all the positive goals she strove for behind all the evil she did?

Her situation was horrid. She knew Rutherford was the man she wanted, *needed* in her life, and not only was she not good enough for him, but he probably was already well on his way to falling for another.

Desperate to escape the downward spiral of such thoughts, she brought herself back to the topic at hand. "And if this potion is efficacious, I thought we might use it as part of the treatment in the spas."

Rutherford busied himself with tucking the few pups who had collapsed on the lawn back in the basket with their mother and nursing siblings. "When you say *we*, do you mean you and Mr. DeGroen?" His voice had something perilously close to resignation in it.

Tilly blanched. Was there any hope? Was there any way that she could extricate herself from her obligation to marry DeGroen? Not without doing a great wrong. And yet, it was not DeGroen, but Rutherford that she saw as her partner in this effort. However it defied logic, in the back of her mind that had been her vision.

"I had hoped," she faltered, "as you have some experience, and as it was you who put me on this path, that you might be part of the venture."

"And yet, I cannot. Do you not see?" His smile was sad.

Tilly's heart clenched, because she knew what a sad smile meant. It was a white flag. A grimace of fury or an irritated brow meant a struggle of passion. A wistful curl of the lips meant surrender and disengagement. She was losing him, if she had not already lost him. She had persuaded herself that it was her duty to see him happy with another, but it was not her desire.

She lifted her chin in selfish opposition. "I do not see. Who better than you?"

"I have had time to do a lot of thinking while on this little retreat to Blackwood."

Yes, thought Tilly, bitterly, a lot of thinking about a pretty little dissembler who could not even give you her real name. She said nothing, but her shoulders drooped.

He continued with a grave sigh. "And this drug still has a hold on me. I am not yet free of its spell. Even speaking of your plans for the spas makes me aware of a great emptiness, like there is a hole inside of me. I do not wish to sound gloomy. My health improves, and my perspective becomes clearer every day. But I am not so far away from the ordeal that I cannot still see the brink that I stood upon. I am well aware of the chasm that yawns behind me. In short, I know that I cannot be trusted to handle any part of a project involving this poison." He shuddered. "I hope you understand."

She did understand. In fact, she understood, as perhaps he didn't, that his continued health probably also depended upon staying away from her. She sighed. "Yes. Of course I do. I should have thought of that. Forgive me for being selfish."

He laughed heartily. "Oh Tilly, I have learned a lot about you, since we first met. You are not what you seem. And you are neither greedy nor selfish, however things appear."

Her heart fluttered, and a tear came to her eye, but she was kept from replying by the reappearance of Mrs. Colling with a servant at her elbow.

Tilly cursed the sight of her. Just when their conversation was getting interesting, *she* had to arrive.

The beauty looked uncomfortable, but said, "His grace has awakened, and would like to meet your visitors, Mr. Rutherford. Stokes will clean up the picnic things."

Rutherford gathered up the dog basket. Neither Tilly nor Mrs. Colling were afforded his arm as they walked to the manor.

CHAPTER 34

Rutherford sipped his tea happily as the duke spoke to Tilly about her connections to see if they had any common acquaintance. The presence of Mrs. Colling was clearly helping his situation. He could see that, however composed she kept her features, Tilly hated the sight of her, and that was a very good sign, indeed.

Mrs. Colling also seemed highly apprehensive, however, and that concerned Rutherford. He did not flatter himself that it could be jealousy of Tilly. The pretty widow had only recently stopped showing a marked distaste for Rutherford's company—well not distaste, precisely. It was, rather, a sort of mocking dismissiveness, as though he were merely another young puppy and not to be taken seriously.

As loathe as he was to admit it, this acted on Rutherford much more effectively than flirtation would have done. It made him want to impress upon her that he was no puppy. But the only real way to do this was to behave indifferently toward her, which, to his irritation, appeared to suit her very well.

She was no Tilly, but she was fascinating. He could not suppress his curiosity about the real story behind the veil. Had she murdered her husband? Was she a misanthrope? Was she truly a fortune hunter with her sights on a rich duke?

His ear pricked up to an item of chit-chat between Tilly and Bartholmer. The duke had asked her about her upcoming wedding. Rutherford gritted his teeth.

"It is in two weeks, your grace." Tilly replied in such a demure, maidenly fashion that Rutherford could have laughed aloud at the fraudulence of it. But the substance of her words shot a pain through his heart, and the dull ache in his shoulder flared up.

"Well, then," said Bartholmer with a piercing look and a mischievous smile, not unlike that which Tilly's lips so frequently wore, "it is quite a wonder that you should be out here in the wilderness visiting Rutherford. He is very fortunate to have such a dedicated friend."

"It is I who am lucky," said Tilly, and all trace of dissembling left her features. "I do not know a finer person than Mr. Rutherford."

"Except, of course," corrected the Duke with a provoking smile, "your betrothed."

"Neither of us is deceived about our marriage, your grace. We do not wed for romantic reasons. Though I hold him in high esteem and great respect, and he is a very dear friend, I should not put even my betrothed above Mr. Rutherford."

Rutherford coughed. He wanted to cry out to her, *Then why don't you just ruddy well marry me?* But he could not. His shoulder throbbed, and a cold sweat ran down his back. He could feel a spell of tremors about to take him. "I hope you will all excuse me a moment." He dashed from the parlour.

When he had composed himself and taken his quarter dose of laudanum, he returned to the parlour, took a breath and opened the door. But in that very moment, Mrs. Colling ran from the room and directly into his arms.

Tilly shot him a look of disgust and turned away. Before he could disentangle himself, he saw the features of Mrs. Colling, bloodless with fear. "Whatever is the matter?" he whispered to her.

She only struggled to free herself, hissing, "For God's sake let me pass. I must go. I am indisposed." And she was gone.

He stood looking stupid for a moment, puzzling over what could possibly have transpired in his absence.

Then he started at a cold, creaking voice behind him. "Mr. Rutherford. Out to visit your uncle, are you? How good to run into you here." This pro forma address was devoid of any warmth, and had rather the effect of an icicle dripping down his back.

He suppressed a shudder and turned with furrowed brows to meet the gaze of Lord Screwe.

CHAPTER 35

Tilly cursed herself for not getting out of the parlour before Mrs. Colling, who had veritably bolted after Rutherford had left, when the butler presented Lord Screwe's card. Then she would have been the one caught up in Rutherford's arms, not the pretty little black widow. She wanted to claw her sapphire eyes out and have them made into a pair of earrings.

And she would have been away, not trapped, as she was now about to be, in a parlour with the person she least wished to see. There was no way of excusing herself without looking as though she were trying to avoid Screwe, which would make him certain of her guilt.

She swallowed, rapidly retrieved her sewing from Mrs. Carlton's workbag and threw herself into the tedious task just as Lord Screwe entered the room.

When the greetings were all made, Screwe slithered his scaly gaze over Tilly. "Miss Ravelsham. What a pleasant surprise to find you here. I did not know you were acquainted with the duke."

"We are recently acquainted," Bartholmer smoothly intervened. "But I am most surprised to see you here, Screwe. I recall your saying, many years back, when I spoke of my intention to retire to Blackwood, that I should do what I liked, but that for your part you should as soon be sealed into a vat of pickled cabbage as confined to the tedium of the countryside."

"Ah." Lord Screwe eyed the duke with a look that, though apparently expressionless, seemed to nonetheless emit rays of hateful ill-intention. "Well, we cannot all claim such constancy as you, Duke. That must have been about twenty years ago. I should not let a youthful fancy prevent me from visiting relatives. And then, as I was passing by, I could not deny myself the pleasure of calling upon an old acquaintance."

"Quite."

Screwe turned again to Tilly. "True, it is very odd to see you out here, Miss Ravelsham, and with your nuptials so close at hand."

Tilly looked up from the stitch she had just pulled through and smiled as blandly as she could. "Oh well, my lord, you know that it has been such a long engagement, everything has been planned to the last iota. There was nothing to be lost in a little trip to the countryside. I, too, have acquaintance in the area, you see."

Screwe pressed his lips together. "Indeed. Well, your betrothed is more forbearing than I should be under the circumstances, allowing his fiancée to chase after the company of an unmarried young buck like Rutherford."

Tilly saw the sinews in Rutherford's neck tense. She assumed a dull little frown. "I do not know what you mean, my lord."

As she had hoped he would not, Rutherford intervened. "I can do without your insinuations, Screwe, even if Miss Ravelsham is too much of a lady to understand them."

Screwe's laugh became a dusty, cracking cough as he said, "Oh, I can imagine you could do without them, Rutherford. But not to worry, I have no interest in interrupting your dalliance. It gives me such an advantage. But I am hardly your enemy. Just imagine how well things might go for you if I told Mr. DeGroen of your tryst. If he threw her off, she would be yours at last. Unless, of course," he cackled again, "you would prefer not to have her in any official way."

"I will thank you to keep your coarse insults to yourself," spat Rutherford. "This is not one of the low-rate clubs you crawl about in, now that White's will not admit your cheating hide." Screwe's face stiffened, but he forced a smile and ignored the insult. "Yes, I see. I can imagine you might prefer muslin of a higher quality, now that you are on the eve of becoming a duke."

Rutherford stood abruptly and looked ready to stride over and forcibly eject Screwe for his insolence to Bartholmer and his grave insult to Tilly.

But the duke raised a pacifying palm. "Rutherford, you should not dirty your hands with the task of seeing unwanted company out. I should wince even to put one of the stable hands to the work of scraping up and ejecting such as this. However, perhaps, Screwe, you would like to see yourself out. As you have remarked, I am not long for this mortal coil, and I have no desire to waste my remaining time entertaining filthy-mouthed bounders."

Screwe did not look at all disturbed by this rebuking dismissal. He fixed his evil gaze upon Tilly again. "Only know this, Miss Ravelsham. I will not remain silent for long. If the widow who robbed my home does not return what she stole from me, I will expose her, and she will be disgraced. And even if DeGroen does not cast you off, his grandfather will surely withdraw his approbation."

Bartholmer stood up from his wheelchair and raised his cane menacingly. "You have now added threat to insult under my roof. Do not expect this affront to go unpunished, Screwe. Out! And do not darken my door again!"

Screwe sneered at the Duke, but made to leave, only pausing at the door to drawl, "There, Rutherford, if the old man should throw a fit and die, that will be two good turns I have done you." Then he left them with a malicious laugh.

Tilly sighed in relief and consternation. She was glad to be out of such odious company, but he clearly suspected far too much about her involvement in rescuing Clara. His reference to *the widow* must mean he had found the torn piece of her black veil. Had he followed her out to Bartholmer's, thinking his former slave was hidden there? She shuddered at the thought and cursed herself for being so incautious.

On the other hand, it was clear that he had no idea where Clara and Sweep were. For that much intelligence she was grateful.

Just then the duke collapsed, shaking, back into his chair. Rutherford and Mrs. Colling rushed to see to him. She could see the affection they shared for the duke. Tilly hated the fact that it was in defence of her that Bartholmer had exerted himself to such a state of agitation. There was just no end to the ill-fortune she brought into Rutherford's life.

CHAPTER 36

*R*utherford turned things over in his mind as he paced the marble-flagged hallway outside of his uncle's chambers. The visit from Screwe was so completely unexpected. He had never liked the man, and now he detested him. If his uncle should die because of Screwe's malice, Rutherford would duel the ruddy bastard and kill him, even if it meant a life on the continent, evading a murder charge.

No. Death was too good for him. Rutherford had a better idea. He would run him into ruin—buy up all the man's debt and foreclose on him. And Rutherford was sure the man had financial problems, for otherwise why should he refuse to pay his debts of honour?

But he hoped his uncle's turn for the worse was just a temporary spell. He stopped pacing and listened at the door. The doctor was still examining Bartholmer, and Rutherford could hear the vague murmur of voices.

He began to pace again. And what was all that about a *widow* and *returning what had been stolen* from Screwe? Could he be referring to Mrs. Colling? Was that why she flew out of the room in such a state of fear? Was he seeking her out, or had he come all this way to menace Tilly? Tilly did dress as a widow when she came for a night-time rendezvous.

The thought of those occasions made him warm all over. God how he needed her. It had been too long. Only now he had to be careful. He could not just give in to his desire. If he wanted all of her, and he did, he had to play the long game. He suspected that she really did love him, and her reaction to Mrs. Colling only confirmed this.

So he had to be strategic. First, he had to best this dependency on laudanum and prove he was the man she needed in her life. What woman wanted a lame duck? And then she would have to be made to see that if she loved him and wanted him in her life, she would have to marry him. The threat of losing him to another woman had to appear real, even if it was not.

He did not like to play such games, but he was not going to lose her for want of trying everything at his disposal.

He looked at his watch. The dinner hour was approaching, and Tilly had gone to change half an hour prior. In his experience, she was adept at dressing rapidly, even without a maid. The memory made him smile, but he wondered what could be taking her so long.

CHAPTER 37

Tilly finally found *Mrs. Colling* in the library, where the widow was perusing the books. This displeased Tilly only for the peevish reason that a love of books was something the beauty would have in common with Rutherford. No doubt the two had spent several idle hours, haunting these stacks with their heads together over favourite passages… She shook her head to dispel black thoughts of sneaking up on the woman and clubbing her with a multi-volume binding of *Clarissa, or, the History of a Young Lady*.

"Well," said Tilly, "We are alone at last."

The woman started and nearly dropped the book she had been reaching for in the stacks. "Miss Ravelsham. I did not know you were looking for me."

"Oh, indeed? You could imagine a scenario where I would simply leave Blackwood without looking into the matter of a woman of my acquaintance passing herself off as a widow, under an assumed name?"

"You misunderstand the situation, entirely."

"Did you really believe I would just let you alone to continue imposing upon Mr. Rutherford and his uncle?"

"I am not imposing upon his grace."

"That remains to be seen. But you admit to imposing upon Rutherford, then?"

The woman's chin lifted. "You take quite an interest in Mr. Rutherford's affairs. Is he some relative of yours?"

"He is a friend."

"Oh, indeed. Have matters changed while I have been living in seclusion? Is it quite the thing these days for engaged women to be *friends* with single young men who are not their future husbands?"

"I will not grace that insinuation with a reply. We are speaking of you. You are the one who is passing herself off as someone she is not. And perhaps you have told the duke your proper name, but I doubt very much that his grace knows anything of your former profession."

The woman pressed her lips together. "You know even less of it. Like most meddling busybodies, you have not an inkling how great an injustice your officiousness might wreak."

"Ah!" Tilly's laugh had a razor edge. "You are the victim of injustice. Circumstance has forced your hand to defraud others, then take up residence hiding under the protection of a sick old man whose kind heart is easily exploited."

"I had thought you might be different, Miss Ravelsham. But it seems you are just like all the rest of them. Go. Tell what you know. I care not. I have to leave now anyway, as you or Mr. Rutherford have led that evil wraith of a man under this roof."

"Who, Lord Screwe?" This gave Tilly pause. She had thought the pretty widow's dramatic exit from the parlour had been an excuse to go off and throw herself in Rutherford's way. And in fact, when she *accidentally* dashed into his arms, they had exchanged some intimate whispers, which had confirmed Tilly's suspicions.

But what if her motivation had been much different? What if the imminent arrival of Screwe had driven her away? If she was, indeed, running from Lord Screwe, perhaps Tilly had judged too quickly.

"Shall you run to Screwe now and tell him what you know?" The widow's voice was bitter. "I cannot fathom how anyone could call both that fiend and Mr. Rutherford a friend."

This betrayal of the woman's admiration of Rutherford nearly drove Tilly to immediately march off to Rutherford and the duke and out the woman, just to spite her. But Tilly recalled herself and spoke through only slightly clenched teeth. "I believe you were present when I told the duke that I had recently made the man's acquaintance, but Lord Screwe is no friend of mine. Mentioning him in the same breath as Rutherford is an insult to Rutherford. Indeed, calling him a fiend is an insult to fiends."

Mrs. Colling laughed nervously. "Well, that is something, at least. You will not tell him I am here, then?"

Tilly considered the situation for a moment. The tart might be after Rutherford, but if Screwe was their common enemy, Tilly should proceed with caution. "No. I shall not do anything to help that slithering viper of a man."

"Do I have your word?"

"You do, as long as I have your word that you do not have designs upon Rutherford."

The woman's beautiful face was animated into the very embodiment of mirth as she gave into laughter. "I do not have designs on your Mr. Rutherford, Miss Ravelsham. You have my word. But I think you need to be honest with yourself about your own designs."

"That is none of your affair. Now suppose we have a chat about how you came to be a widow, *Miss Dervish*."

CHAPTER 38

Rutherford's heart clenched as Tilly's carriage drove away. He had begged her to stay, but she was determined to go immediately after dinner, to attend matters in London.

He smiled. It was nice that she was taking the task of getting out of the drug trade, or at least sanitizing her involvement, so seriously. It felt like she was doing it all for him. His heart filled, and he longed to pour out his love upon her, hold her close, give her everything she could desire, protect her, make her a duchess.

But he did not want to be a duke, not if it meant losing the uncle he had only just found. What an idiot he had been, waiting to get to know Bartholmer until it was almost too late. This brought him fresh pain and the now-familiar longing for oblivion.

But he would not take another dose of laudanum. He was almost out, and he wanted to cut back his dosing even more tomorrow. Some of the herbal decoction might help.

He went to his chamber and drank a few sips from the flask Tilly had given him.

Needing an outlet for his flood of feeling, he walked to the nursery. Molly and the puppies had been set up there in proper style, and Rutherford took to stroking ears and scratching bellies.

He would take them down to Bartholmer later, if his uncle was up to it. For the moment the old duke was resting. The doctor had chastised them all, saying that even the trip to the parlour to socialize had been a rash disregard for Bartholmer's health. He gave strict instructions against all future social calls by any but family or close friends.

Screwe. The man acted upon Rutherford like the appearance of a cockroach, at once invoking revulsion and a strong desire to crush the loathsome creature under his heel.

A sudden thought gripped Rutherford. What if he had followed Tilly to Blackwood? He had seemed to be watching her house on the day Rutherford left London. Yes, he certainly seemed to be watching her, for some reason, and Screwe's reasons could never be good ones.

He started suddenly, upsetting the puppy he was cuddling. Good Lord, she could be in danger right now. What if he had waited and followed her away from the estate? She had only Mrs. Carson and a couple of man servants along. Did they have guns?

He wiped his face. He was over-reacting. Screwe had no idea how long Tilly intended to stay. Surely a self-indulgent cur like him would not wait around indefinitely. But that was no guarantee that he would not continue to stalk her like a deer when they were back in London.

Rutherford was decided. As soon as his uncle had recovered from this most recent spell, he would return to London. He had to keep her safe.

CHAPTER 39

London had become dull without Rutherford. Tilly, having no resort to sugar, had occupied her time making lists of places to hunt for Clara and Sweep, and finding ways to discreetly investigate them. The degree of precaution she now had to engage in made the process maddeningly slow. She could not do any of the searching herself, and those she sent in her stead had to be made to take the most circuitous ways to get anywhere. It was ludicrous, really.

She was just returning home from a decoy hunt, having conspicuously left her house early that morning and gone to search out places and make enquiries which she knew would not get anywhere near to the two fugitives. In this way, she had hoped to mislead anyone who was watching the house. A good idea, but tedious and a dreadful waste of time.

She looked about her as she disembarked and walked to the front entrance. She spied, through the corner of her eye, a grubby lad in grubbier clothing skulking at the corner. He was one of Screwe's, not one of hers. She felt sorry for the child. Probably an orphan. If only she did not live in a world where poverty made you invisible, exploitable. Was England not a land of plenty? Only for a few.

She sighed and pretended not to see him. There was no point in drawing attention to the fact that she knew she was being watched.

There was an hour and a half until she was to depart for the Aldley estate, where she would stay to attend the christening the next day. She went to her chambers to let her lady's maid freshen her toilette.

CHAPTER 40

Rutherford did not love a ritual, but the christening of Beatrix Ruth Aldley, and the prospect of the gathering at the Aldley estate afterwards was rendered tolerable by the presence of Tilly. He had only just returned to town, and there had not yet been time to see her.

She looked beautiful, radiant even, in the stained glass light of the chapel sanctuary. He met her gaze as they each took their roles as godparents to the newest little Aldley. He could see the truth in her eyes, the same deep ache he felt. The yearning cries of her heart were the echo of his own, which pounded faster at the sight of her. He longed to run to her, sweep her up in his arms and carry her away.

But one did not do that in a church. More was the pity.

"You might want to be a little more discreet, Rutherford," Frobisher muttered at his side.

"I have not slung her over my shoulder and abducted her," he grumbled. "This is being discreet."

His friend's sad chuckle only slightly alleviated the gloomy cast of his features, which Rutherford knew was entirely affected for public consumption. Frobisher was quite jolly among the men, but anywhere he was likely to meet with an unwed lass, or a mother with marriageable daughters, he wore a sour, sickly look and feigned ill humour.

"I should thank you, Bish, for watching over her while I was out of town."

"How is the duke?"

"Better, thank God. He insisted on giving me a courtesy title, which I accepted, only to put him at ease."

"You had best get used to being titled, though I can understand your reluctance. Being an heir was bad enough. When I became a marquess, the marriage vultures were inflamed into a frenzy. Prepare yourself. But the next time you go to Blackwood, I shall tag along, if I may. Fenimore Hall is just down the road, you know. We could do some hunting."

Their whispering had to cease as the final benediction was under way. Rutherford stole another glance at Tilly. She smiled at him, and he felt light headed. He grasped his heart in a pantomime. She placed a trembling hand on her forehead in a theatrical gesture. God how he loved her.

When they were finally assembled at the reception in the Aldley estate manor, Rutherford procured two glasses of champagne and went to deliver one to Tilly. He was not interested in being discreet. They were both godparents, so performing the service of fetching her a drink should not be terribly scandalous. He knew not what Screwe had been saying around town, but surely the gossip-grinders had better grist for their mills.

She stood with Mrs. Carlton, chatting with some young woman, but the girl was soon drawn away. Rutherford seized his chance.

He leaned into Tilly's ear and whispered to her, as he passed close with the proffered champagne. "I wish I could lick it off of your naked body, but I hope you will nonetheless..." Then he said, audibly, "...accept the service of this little refreshment, Miss Ravelsham."

Her look was hungry, and her flashing eyes matched his. She took the glass. "I gladly accept, Mr. Rutherford, and thank you for this kind attention. Although, I am informed that I must now address you as *my lord*."

"Nonsense. Bartholmer has made me the Earl of Drake, but I have not been introduced at court. And you and I are both of a higher order of existence now, anyway, being godparents. We must rise above such worldly distinctions. You must continue to address me as ever you did before." He permitted himself a momentary waggle of the brow and murmured, "Preferably in the ecstatic, operatic tones that I have sometimes had the pleasure to hear."

She drew in her breath. "You are very bad, my lord. Do the Aldleys know what a libertine they have made godparent to their child?"

He gave her a piercing look and a mocking smile. "If your own character is to set the standard, I believe I am quite safe in my office. *You might look smart, however, for you may easily be ousted, if Red Martha should become available.*"

He enjoyed watching her pert little mouth form itself up, ready to deliver a scathing reply, but he was denied the privilege, for the soul-withering voice of Lord Screwe came from behind him.

"Well, how delightful to see you two again. In a tête à tête, I see. And Mr. DeGroen nowhere to be seen."

"Are you to be received here, Screwe?" Rutherford gave a look of distaste. "I shall have to have a word with Aldley about that."

"It is an open house to all members of *noble* families. I suppose that would include you, Rutherford."

Rutherford forbore to inform him of the courtesy title. It was unnecessary, as the rake-hell knew very well that Rutherford was the nephew of a duke.

"I believe it is customary to include the godparents on such occasions," Rutherford drawled without rancour. He did not like the man, but could be quite complacent, so long as Screwe constrained his lamentable manners to hurling slights at Rutherford. In fact he should prefer to distract the nasty little imp from having anything at all to say to Tilly.

Screwe, however, seemed bent on menacing Tilly and turned to her immediately. "But true, I am quite happy to find you chatting with this young cavalier in such an open way, Miss Ravelsham. If my property is not returned, it will lend credibility to all I shall have to say."

Tilly looked confused. "I do not know what you mean, my lord."

Rutherford remarked that her expression was of a sort that he had seen before, when she was dissembling. She seemed determined to assume a very uninteresting, dull persona when Screwe was around. Tilly was working quite hard to hide her true self from him. What was there between them?

"Oh, I think you do, Miss Ravelsham. Certainly your brother does—"

"No, I do not. And if you have some business with my brother, I hope you will consult him, and leave me out of such manly affairs. I have neither the nerves nor the inclination to contemplate matters outside of my sphere. I hope you will both excuse me."

As she left to go to Lydia's side, Screwe made to follow her, but Rutherford detained him, saying, "So, Screwe. What really brings you to this little party? You do not strike me as a man who cannot bear to miss a respectable gathering, and I did not see you at the church."

Screwe's chance to follow and further harass Tilly passed as she rapidly positioned herself with the countess Aldley. His face soured. "I do not attend anything so tedious as a christening, it is true. But I make an appearance at Christmas masses just like all the poor married souls of the ton. These womanish things seem always to be contrived to suck the last bit of joy out of a man's life."

Rutherford found them a tad boring himself, but that would not stop him from making some sport at Screwe's expense. "Yes, it must be rather difficult to sit through such obligatory sermons." He paused for effect, not betraying any inkling of a smile. "Particularly when one keeps bursting into flames at every mention of Christ."

Screwe mumbled something ill-humoured and walked away.

Rutherford looked at his watch. It was just as well that his sport had been ended thus, for he had to be in position on time. Aldley's plan was a cracking one, but it required properly concealed witnesses to be in place well in advance. It was good that the Aldleys had such a fine library, for he should need something to read.

CHAPTER 41

Tilly tucked herself behind the long velvet drape of the private parlour and slouched into the window bench. She retrieved a small novel she had borrowed from among Lydia's favourites, and began to while away the time reading the *Accursed Abbey*, with little moments of distraction when she contemplated where in the room Rutherford might be concealed.

It would be much more fun if they could be in hiding together, but knowing them, it would end scandalously. And anyway, the entire scheme relied upon the good character of the witnesses. If it were found out that they were tucked away in a closet together, all opinion would be against them, whether they had spent their time innocently or not. Tilly laughed quietly at this hypothetical improbability.

It was an hour later that Lydia entered the room and gave the little cough that was the signal that she was there, and that they should be at the ready. Tilly heard the sound of the countess seating herself comfortably on the chaise longue and arranging her skirts. There was only a brief interval before she heard another person, with a slight limp, enter the room.

"Mr. Delacroix." Lydia's voice held a very realistic strain of nervousness and strong distaste. "You are not welcome here. Leave this instant!"

"Not yet, countess. We have some unfinished business regarding that little sprig you just tended with the holy watering can. I am sure you would not like me to reveal her paternity."

"I should not like an unworthy such as you to speak of her at all. But her *father* is standing right behind you."

Apparently Aldley had entered the room quietly. Things were going well.

"Leave now, Delacroix, or I will remove you. I believe I made myself clear the last time you sneaked into my home to threaten my family that you were not to be received again."

"Your family!" scoffed Delacroix. "I am not sure who *your family* is. But that child you are lending your name to is mine. And I will tell anyone who will listen about the tryst I had with Lady Aldley."

"You have taken leave of your senses at last, Delacroix. There was never any tryst between us, despite your persecution of me."

"Do you think that will matter? Your child will be shunned. And it will not help matters, Aldley, that your own father was probably this Sir Gerard Beauchamps fellow that your mother has taken up with, *again*."

"Get out!" Aldley did not need to act his role.

Tilly could tell that the anger came very naturally. She could not even laugh disgust, as she might have once done, at the unequalled audacity of this nasty, ravening little cur of a man.

"Not so hasty!" replied Delacroix. "You may easily spare your child the grief of growing up under such a taint, not to mention sparing your wife's good name. All you need do is pay me the five hundred pounds, and I shall cause you no trouble."

"You will not get a farthing from me. I do not purchase the forbearance of lying bounders."

"Oh, get off your high horse, Aldley. No one cares for your moral pretences here. Is not your tender olive branch worth five hundred pounds? Such a sum is nothing to you. Do you hold her happiness so cheap as that?"

At this point the sounds in the room made it clear that Aldley was making for Delacroix, and that the little worm was shuffling away to evade him. Then the sound of a gun shot gave Tilly such a start that she fell off her window bench and became entangled in the drapes.

CHAPTER 42

Rutherford's hand had already been on the closet door when he heard the sounds that heralded a possible struggle between Aldley and Delacroix. The filthy little beast had already said enough to incriminate himself, anyway. There was no point in continuing until the confrontation turned violent. But he stepped into the room just in time to see Delacroix pull out a pistol and aim it, not at Aldley, but at Lydia.

Rutherford was behind Delacroix and lunged to grapple him. The shot that rang out sickened him. Had the festering little turd killed her? The question gave him pause to realize what his hands were doing. He looked down to discover that he was beating the face of Delacroix. The man's nose was gushing blood. Rutherford knew that he had to stop, but it felt incredibly good. He took a breath and held back his bloody raised fist.

Then he looked up to see if Lydia had been hurt. She was standing. Thank God. Aldley and Tilly had rushed to her side. Then Tilly looked up at him, and her face was lit up with admiration. Pure, whole-hearted, adoration of his valour shone from every corner of her visage. Her eyes said first, "You, sir, are my hero," and then, "If we were alone right now I would have you right there on the floor."

Warmth spread over his whole person. Tilly was his, and he knew it. She would not marry another, not now, not when she looked at him thus. He did not notice the entry of the men at arms and the magistrate. He almost did not feel the knife slicing into his left calf.

CHAPTER 43

The magistrate's chambers were comfortable enough, but Tilly was glad to quit them after she had given her statement. It seemed Delacroix would finally be brought to some sort of justice. She supposed stabbing Rutherford, *again*, would probably go unremedied, as it was a superfluous consideration in the face of an attempt on the life of a countess. At least Rutherford's injury was not life-threatening this time.

But Delacroix might hang, for blackmail and slander were one thing, but attempted murder was quite another.

Tilly would, under normal circumstances, not be eager to see capital punishment employed, from her general opposition to its use, and from numerous examples of its misapplication. But in this case, she was unwilling to devote pangs of remorse to an object who, if perhaps not entirely deserving of the noose, was certainly much more deserving than most of its victims.

In fact, she was still shocked to recall her own savage stirrings at the sight of Rutherford pounding the bastard's face bloody. She had thought, at that moment, that if he had asked her to marry him, she would have forgotten all she owed to others, all her obligations, and accepted his offer.

She shook her head. Of course it was pure selfishness. And yet, a tiny little spark of hope persisted inside of her. Perhaps she was not so irredeemable. Perhaps she could make herself someone not wholly undeserving of his love.

She sighed and dismissed such thoughts as she exited into the fresh air and was handed into her carriage. To believe she could become good enough for Rutherford was to conveniently forget the very real obstacle of her obligation to marry Mr. DeGroen.

As the carriage pulled away, she spied, through the window, a sight that made her gasp. She shuddered as she watched Lord Screwe and a man she knew to be a prominent barrister ascend the steps to call at the magistrate's.

CHAPTER 44

Rutherford was fidgety. Once again he had been wounded defending Lydia, and once again he was being cajoled into lying down and receiving treatment. What he wanted to do, should be doing, was chasing after Tilly, making her admit what he had seen shining in her eyes, and then running away with her before she could change her mind.

"That should do it." The doctor stood up. "It is all cleaned and dressed."

"Is there any serious danger?" asked Lydia, who stood with Aldley, watching nervously.

"I think not," replied the doctor. "The cut is not so deep. It will not slow him down much. I recommend no strenuous movement for the first day, and then after that, a little light exercise—but certainly no more foil play, fisticuffs or gallantry until it is healed."

"I hope I shall not be tempted, now that my enemy is behind bars." Rutherford shifted his bandaged leg to a more comfortable position and looked at Aldley. "Tell me, how is it that the man who is always menacing your wife has become my nemesis? And how comes it that I am always the one to be stabbed while saving her?"

Aldley only laughed and said, "Thank you, again, my friend."

"Yes, yes." Rutherford waved away this gratitude impatiently. "I am not clamouring after your thanks. But it seems to me that you are somewhat remiss in the valiant duties you owe to your lady. I rather wonder why she married such a stupid fellow."

But Aldley did not give Rutherford the satisfaction of rising to his comment. He only pulled his wife closer to him under his arm and said, "Yes, I wonder that myself."

"Cupid is a blind archer." Lydia's pertness was softened by a look of deep affection for her husband. "There is no accounting for the vagaries of love."

Rutherford coughed to hide his emotion. His heart cried out for wanting what they both had. Where was Tilly?

"I shall give you some laudanum for the—"

"No!" Rutherford spoke too abruptly, and was embarrassed to see Lydia and Aldley shoot him a glance. "I mean, the pain is not so bad. And I need to go attend to something, so I cannot have a head full of gauze and eiderdown."

"I recommend rest, my lord." The doctor looked hesitant to oppose his will.

Rutherford liked to have his way very well, but he was not sure he could get used to being *my-lorded* all the time. "I understand, however, I must speak with Miss Ravelsham."

Lydia and Aldley exchanged a look. Aldley spoke. "You should not speak with her until after you both have given your statement to the magistrate, upon his instructions. Miss Ravelsham is giving hers now. The magistrate witnessed your injury, and made a point of saying he would come to you, here, to take your deposition this evening. For Lydia and I both hope you will stay here, at least for the first day."

Rutherford sighed. "Very well, if it is necessary in order to keep that smoky little coward in gaol, I shall stay. But can you not invite Tilly to come for a late dinner instead of returning to London? I will follow her to town if she will not come, for I must see her."

"I suppose it might be arranged, if she does not have plans." Lydia smirked. "Perhaps she will stay by your bedside and read to you from her little book of poetry."

CHAPTER 45

Tilly stepped out of her lemon-sacheted carriage with the beleaguered Mrs. Carlton into the quiet Kensington neighbourhood, as the first red of sunset lit the neat bricks of her fiancé's home.

She hated having to refuse the invitation to Lydia's dinner, for she so longed to see Rutherford, her dear, brave Rutherford. But the message from DeGroen had been quite urgent, and he wasn't a man prone to flights of panic or nervous delusion.

Mr. DeGroen met them in the drawing room.

"How is Grandfather Fowler?" asked Tilly.

"He seems well enough, but he is not happy. It seems that Lord Screwe visited him yesterday in my absence."

"Screwe." Tilly was tired of even hearing the beast's name.

"His lordship had a few choice things to say about your relationship with Mr. Rutherford."

Tilly huffed. "Yes. I can only imagine. He has had, in fact, no scruple but to call at Rutherford's uncle's estate only to continue his persecution there—and in full hearing of his grace."

"His grace? Rutherford's uncle is a duke?"

"Bartholmer." Tilly could see the gears turning in DeGroen's mind.

"The crazy old childless hermit of a duke who sought retirement in the countryside? I am surprised you were admitted."

"It helped that I was presented as a friend to his heir."

"Rutherford is to be a duke then?" DeGroen pursed his lips. "Well, well. How can a mere rich man compete with a duke?"

"I think you, of all people, know that a title means nothing to me. Though I fear I have passed myself off as so mercenary and unromantic about marriage that Rutherford probably believes it gives him an advantage. But," Tilly heaved a sigh, "this is all by the bye. What did Grandfather Fowler have to say about Screwe's assertions?"

"We may, quite literally, thank God that my grandfather is somewhat sceptical of Lord Screwe's character. I assured him that your chastity was not to be impugned." DeGroen's lips only twitched very slightly in forming these words.

"Quite. I should expect nothing less. And so he has summoned me to hear the indictment denied from my own lips?"

"No indeed. He would pale at the suggestion of giving such an offence. He was apologetic to me for raising the point, but he felt he should put me on my guard against Screwe."

"Oh really?" Tilly was impressed to find that the old man was wily enough to sort out Screwe's character for himself. And she was surprised to hear that, far from believing every dark aspersion he heard about another, which is what Tilly had come to expect from overly pious people, Grandfather Fowler had opposed the rumour-monger.

"Apparently he has been making some inquiries about town and has satisfied himself that Lord Screwe is not only not to be trusted but is actively to be *mistrusted*. For this reason Grandfather, who assures me that he is not to be taken in by such an immoral rakehell, has come to the conclusion that Screwe means to interfere in his testamentary arrangements. He does not understand precisely why Screwe should do so, but Grandfather has a mad tendency to see conspiracies where his fortune is concerned."

"I should not call it *mad*, entirely." Certainly DeGroen's family had given the old man enough reason for suspicion. And even she and DeGroen had plans which were not all they appeared to be.

DeGroen waggled his head equivocally, then continued. "But the long and the short is that he wishes to make over the settlement to me now. In fact he has done so this afternoon, and he wishes us to be wed most expeditiously."

"Well," Tilly gasped and sank into a chair. Was their wedding within the week not expeditious enough? "So you are an independently wealthy man then." And together they would be titans of wealth, though not of passion.

"I am sad to say it," DeGroen conceded and his face looked troubled, "but I believe this latest shock has put the fear—or let us say *apprehension* of death into him. Indeed, he was consulting with his solicitor this morning. I imagine that means he has finalized his will."

Tilly grasped at this truth like a drowning man grasps at straws. If Grandfather Fowler should die before they were forced to wed she might be free to marry Rutherford. She shook her head to dispel such an evil thought. When had she become the kind of ravening ghoul that could actually wish the death of an old man? Grandfather Fowler, though irritatingly religious, had never done anything wrong to her or anyone that she knew of, and had been the member of Mr. DeGroen's family most inclined to value DeGroen and treat him decently.

A servant brought word that the old man was summoning them to his chamber. Tilly stood and straightened her skirts. Her feelings of shame would have to wait until she was finished her work of deceit and concealment.

CHAPTER 46

Rutherford had gone to the magistrate to give his statement, then immediate returned to London. There was no reason to stay when Tilly had gone. Why had she declined the Aldleys' dinner invitation? Was she trying to avoid him? Was she slipping away?

He wondered if he should risk sending Tilly a note, as he sat in his study and drank down a very weak draught of laudanum and brandy. The symptoms of his dependency had become quite mild now, and this dose was to be his last. No doubt tomorrow he would have a headache and feel out of sorts. And he would think about it. But the next day would be better, and the next.

He wished that he could celebrate this moment with Tilly. He had her to thank for rescuing him from his self-created peril. He burned inside when he recalled that he had once blamed her for his condition. What had he said? *The torment of seeing you slip away from me and knowing you will soon join with another man has driven me to this.* He cursed himself for a weak coward. How could he have laid that burden upon her? And yet, he had been unwell. He hoped that Tilly had considered that, and not taken the words too much to heart.

It had been his own decision to dose himself with poison rather than feel the pain of losing her. And she had never misled him about her plans and feelings. The fact that it now seemed she had misled herself did not change anything.

She had told him repeatedly that she would marry another, and he ignored her words, persisted in trying to charm her out of her engagement. He had been so certain that a little seductive persuasion and the certain knowledge of his love was all that it would take.

But she had held firm in her resolve. Why? What hold had this DeGroen fellow over Tilly? It could not be mere money. He had once believed her when she spoke of her mercenary motives, but now he did not.

All the good she tried to accomplish had endangered her reputation and cost her time, care and money. Rutherford could see this now, and he knew that Tilly, though perhaps a little licentious, was not motivated by money or social standing.

If only she were, then his title and his future prospects might induce her to accept him. In fact, he had once entertained that hope. But he had not been thinking clearly. The Tilly he knew and loved was, in addition to being delightfully irreverent, also strangely noble. He had to talk to her and make her tell him the truth, so he could find a way to persuade her to join her life with his.

Just at the moment that he was hobbling about and preparing to take the risk of calling on her, Frobisher turned up.

"Well, Lord Drake, you did not have your title long before you took up gallantry to lend it distinction." Frobisher was smirking.

"Bish! Good to see you, but I shall have to disobey the doctor's directions and duel you if you insult me by calling me Lord Drake. Do I call you the Marquess of Fenimore? I am always Rutherford to you."

"Very well. And how is the leg?"

"I have had worse. I dare say it will heal up in a trice."

"You know the whole situation is the talk of London. Every available heart is swooning with your heroics. And every available tongue is wagging about you and Lady Aldley."

"Good Lord. What nonsense. Does Aldley know about this?"

"If not, I imagine he shall, as soon as he next visits with his mother. But do not frown so, Rutherford. Their suspicions will blow over as soon as the next little thing happens. Gossipers have bird brains that peck at whatever seed falls in front of them."

"Yes." Rutherford was thoughtful. He supposed it might also prevent them from pecking at whatever stories Screwe might be spreading about him and Tilly. He still wondered what could possibly cause that dirty dish to so persecute Tilly. Had she taken something from him, as Screwe kept insisting? Rutherford needed to ask her, if they ever managed to find some time alone together.

Just then a servant delivered an urgent message. It was from Bartholmer. "You will have to excuse me, Bish, I must read this."

As he perused it, he realized it was not from his uncle's hand, but had been dictated. He had only just returned to town, and he was once again being summoned to Blackwood Manor. This was a very bad sign. Rutherford's face darkened.

"What is it?" Frobisher looked concerned. "Is something wrong?"

"I am afraid my uncle has taken a turn for the worse." Rutherford lost his breath just pronouncing the words. No, no, no. Bartholmer could not die and leave him alone again.

He tried to keep the pain and fear out of his voice. "Do you still fancy a trip to Blackwood?"

Frobisher tilted his head and shrugged. "Why not?"

"Good." Rutherford strode to the bell-pull. "I shall brood less if I have your company."

"Are we to leave right this instant, then?"

"As soon as I get Molly and the puppies gathered up. I hope you do not mind sharing your seat."

CHAPTER 47

As Tilly descended the steps of DeGroen's house, leaning on his arm, Mrs. Carlton in tow, she was thankful for the nightfall that concealed her struggle against a flood of tears. They were to marry in two days. Grandfather DeGroen felt his death coming and he wished to see them wed before he went. They could still have their planned reception in a week's time, but, after this absurdly long engagement, the old dictator would have them wed immediately.

Rutherford would be lost to her. She had to go tell him in person. She would not let him discover it from anyone else. She knew not why it should shock her so, the difference of several days was not such a big one, after all. But the ache in her heart and the feeling of panic in the pit of her stomach felt like they would kill her. For the first time in her life, she thought she might actually faint.

"Ah dearest Tilly." DeGroen held up her suddenly slumping weight on his arm. "You are not happy, I can see that. True," he stopped and tilted her head up to look in her face, whispering, "those are tears. I can scarce believe my eyes."

He pressed her into an embrace, and it was all she could do not to dissolve into sobbing. Mrs. Carlton stepped into the shadows and pretended to minutely examine the leaves of a tree.

When he released her again, the glib, mocking humour of his face was entirely gone. "My lovely little Tiddly-wink, you know I will never oppress you. Never make you give up... anything that makes you happy. Indeed, I shall always do my best to... accommodate your access to everything that can possibly amuse or charm you."

"Amuse me? Charm me?" She could not keep the disdain out of her voice. Did he think her heart so shallow as that?

"Ah, I see. Am I only now to realize..." He sighed sadly and shook his head in disbelief. "Can it be possible that you are," he hushed his voice yet lower, "in love with him?"

"I—" This was hard. She had never before said it out loud. "Yes." She croaked, and tears poured down her cheeks.

"My treasure, my dear one, I love you now more than I ever have. Save for your brother, I have no closer friend. But you are such a ruddy little fool." The mocking look was back on his face, but his eyes glistened.

She laughed and snorted as her nose began to run. "Do you think so?"

DeGroen looked askance at her. "Oh yes. Yes, indeed. I am afraid we may have to redraft the marriage settlements, now that I know you are feeble-minded and do not even know enough to blow your own nose. You should have told me this before." He handed her his pocket handkerchief in a quick, squeamish gesture. "Keep it."

CHAPTER 48

Rutherford drank a dose of Ole Maeb's concoction as he rolled along in the carriage beside Frobisher. He returned the sterling silver flask to his pocket with a sigh. He had picked a rather bad time to stop taking laudanum. To further console himself he stroked the soft ears of Molly and tucked one of her puppies into his jacket, positioning it over his scar.

"Rutherford, it does my heart good to see a man who loves his dogs so much." Frobisher's lip twitched. "However, have a care who sees you in such throes of tenderness. It could hurt your reputation at the sport club, you know."

Rutherford tried to rouse himself and play along with the jovial banter. "And you know I care such a great deal for my reputation *there*."

"If you do not, this must certainly be a recent change. For I can see no other justification for the degree to which you put on airs and swagger about the place, as though you were the very king of the Corinthians."

"I do not put on airs, and I certainly should never wish to be known as the sort of brute who could not appreciate an exquisite little pup. And anyway, kings do not need reputations. If any man should question my title in that kingdom, I should be happy to put him to rights with the foils or at boxing." Rutherford tried unsuccessfully to make his voice sound less peevish.

Frobisher decided to change the subject. "But this is not the most expeditious way out of London, surely? Where are we going?"

"It is only a little out of the way." Rutherford did not know how to confess his penchant for slinking by Tilly's home in the hopes of getting a glimpse of her. He tried to sound nonchalant. "I like the view in this neighbourhood, so I always make this little detour when I am leaving town." He did not add, *and at every other opportunity.*

"Quite. The view at night must be well worth a half hour's detour."

In making their way to Tilly's neighbourhood, they passed the house of Mr. DeGroen. The moon had come out, and Rutherford gazed upon the front step with some curiosity, seeing that there were people gathered there. The internal yearnings of his mind detected by instinct, before his eye could do so, the figure of Tilly.

His heart soared at the sight of her, before he could check himself. For of course she was there to see Mr. DeGroen. But then he gasped as he saw DeGroen crush her into a fond embrace, which she returned.

He was stricken. His heart throbbed, and he stifled a cry. He had never before contemplated that Tilly might love Mr. DeGroen, might be marrying Mr. DeGroen because she loved him, and not because of the fortune to which she made constant reference. Had Rutherford been such a fool is that? Had he dismissed DeGroen as a mere banker, when he was, in fact, a rival for Tilly's heart?

Frobisher seemed to perceive what Rutherford was staring at through the window, for his heart did not sound entirely in it when he gibed, "I suppose the view in *this* neighbourhood is not quite so enchanting."

They passed by the scene of the two lovers, and Rutherford roused himself. "Do not be a philistine, Frobisher. The prospect from this street may not enchant, but it certainly enlightens."

He used the speaking tube to tell the driver to make directly for Blackwood. Then he hugged the sleeping puppy closer to the scar that twitched above his heart. This would be a miserable drive if he did not distract himself.

"Fancy a drink and some cards, Bish?"

"Aye, aye. Thank God. Anything if it lifts you from this devilish mood."

Rutherford lit a candle and produced two tumblers and a bottle of brandy. He tried to make himself smile despite the relentless feeling that he was losing everyone he most wanted to hold on to.

CHAPTER 49

Tilly sipped a cup of creamy coffee in her carriage, savouring the charming interplay of its bracing, bitter flavours against its smooth, teasingly faint sweetness, which she had never properly appreciated before she stopped drinking it with enough sugar to choke a horse.

She glanced at the tired eyes of Mrs. Carlton. The woman was a saint, and Tilly was an utter savage to bring her out in the early gloom of the morning. But she heard that Rutherford had not stayed at the Aldley estate. He must be back in London, and she needed to see him as soon as possible.

She knew that it was foolish to so openly call on him, with Screwe circulating rumours about them around town. But she did not care. She would be wed the next day, and she could not let Rutherford find it out by reading the paper, or hearing it from the gossips.

At least, that is what she told herself was the reason for her call. She would not permit her heart the satisfaction of telling itself that she called because she secretly hoped that somehow, if she saw him, something might happen to rescue her from the mess she had gotten herself into.

No, that she would leave in the periphery of her mind. It was a mercurial little willow-the-wisp of a thought that, once acknowledged, would disappear in a puff of rationality. And Tilly did not want it to disappear.

As her servant handed her out of the carriage, Tilly wondered at the fact that Rutherford had not come out to greet her immediately. It was usual for her to visit in secret, dressed as a widow, and to enter through the servants' entrance. But on those rare occasions where she came without concealment, he generally met her enthusiastically on the front stoop, to the visible irritation of Smythe, who was always jealous for the credit of his master.

She supposed it was because she was calling so early, and Rutherford was probably still abed. In any case, he would not yet be dressed. With such appealing images to tease her imagination, she ascended the steps eagerly.

She was surprised to see that the man who opened the door was not Smythe.

"The master is not in, I am afraid. Shall I take your card, Miss?"

"No. Do you know when he will return? Is he still at the Aldley estate?"

With this, the servant apprehended that she knew something of his master's business, so he did not scruple to reply without concealment. "No, Miss. He has taken himself to Blackwood Manor again. I do not know when he will return."

Blackwood Manor? But he had only just returned from that place. And his leg could not have healed so quickly as that. Surely he must have received some news of the duke that took him back there, wounded leg and all.

She thanked the servant and turned back to the carriage. "Mrs. Carlton, I do not suppose that you would object to a little voyage to the countryside again, would you?"

As always, Mrs. Carlton agreed to whatever Tilly wished. Tilly supposed that was the lot of a companion, but appreciated Mrs. Carlton's long suffering compliance with all of Tilly's flying about and strange arrangements. She would have to increase the woman's stipend.

She did not relish the idea of going to the duke's manor again, only to give Rutherford news that would make him miserable, and at a moment when his anxieties must already be excited by the state of his uncle's health.

But do it she must. It was the right thing to do, after all, even putting willow-the-wisp considerations aside.

CHAPTER 50

Rutherford sat in the gloom of his uncle's chamber, listening to the shallow rattle of the old man's somnolent breathing.

He did not know how to deal with what was happening. His uncle was living his last days and slept all but a few hours of every day. It filled Rutherford with dread to lose him, and with deep sorrow and regret that he had waited too long to get to know such an excellent man.

This was a miserable form of distraction from the horrifying thought of losing not just Tilly's hand, but also her heart to another, as seemed now inevitable.

Beyond this he was surrounded by people whose behaviours and motivations seemed odd and entirely petty, given the context.

Smythe made himself a source of irritation by hovering around until he was ordered away. Rutherford knew that he was concerned for his master's wellbeing, but found the constant attention intolerable. And worse, it seemed that Smythe had taken a disliking to Sandes, the butler who was to continue as a fixture of Blackwood Manor.

Smythe had begun preying upon the butler's patience, by going about with white gloves and checking for dust, or shaking his head and sighing at some element or other of the household management. Smythe even carried a little notebook around with him for the purpose of scribbling a quick notation with a disapproving look, whenever Sandes might be in view.

No doubt Smythe was smarting under the idea that he should not be butler as well as valet in every household that Rutherford occupied. Or perhaps, less forgivably, Smythe had not yet apprehended that Sandes was not going anywhere, and the valet was merely whiling away the idle hours in tormenting the man he meant to depose.

Whatever the case, Rutherford could not take amusement in this bad behaviour. He had enough to stew over without worrying about a civil war breaking out between the servants.

And then there was Mrs. Colling. Right after Rutherford arrived, she had given him an accusing look of recrimination before dropping her veil and slipping away. She only sneaked into the manor again secretly to see Bartholmer early the next morning, but rushed off, almost rudely, when Rutherford and Frobisher disturbed her. He noticed that, as soon as Frobisher took his leave to go to his own nearby estate, Mrs. Colling was back, sitting almost ceaselessly at Bartholmer's bedside.

This behaviour was puzzling, but Rutherford could not attend, and only relegated it to the list of stupid irritations that he thought he should not have to support in this sad hour of his life. And so he hid in the sickroom, sharing the last hours of his uncle's life the only way he could.

Tears threatened him constantly. His eyes fell, propelled by some evil genie, to one of the medicine bottles at his uncle's bedside.

Rutherford rubbed his hands roughly over his face. What was wrong with him, thinking of filching his uncle's laudanum while he slept, like a common thief? He reached a faintly trembling hand into his pocket to retrieve the silver flask and took a drink. The mere gesture calmed him, but his heart still ached.

He rubbed his shoulder in the place of his old wound. It had healed under the tender ministrations of Tilly, reading him dirty poetry and beguiling him with her beautiful eyes and impish little ways.

But she was a fairy, it seemed. Unbeknownst to Rutherford, some of her mischief had embedded itself in the wound, sealed away under the scar tissue, from this position to whisper delights and torments to his heart ever after.

And now he must endure loss. So much loss.

He left his uncle's room and walked to the nursery, merely holding up a hand to dismiss the hovering Smythe. He petted Molly, selected two sleeping puppies, and tucked them into his jacket. They were growing fast. Very soon they would be too big and active for this, but for now, he needed their warmth and purity and unconditional love.

He recalled, as he returned to Bartholmer's dim chamber and seated himself once again at the bedside, that he had once heard of a French king who believed that illness could be cured by sleeping surrounded by puppies. Perhaps this was part of some now-lost magical practice, or perhaps it was madness. But situated here in the darkness, with his only sources of comfort cuddled into his chest, Rutherford came to believe that the king, however mad, was right.

Rutherford had observed that madmen often saw the truth with a clarity that the concealments and hypocritical pretences of the world would not permit. The fatal flaw of the mad was being unable to keep their visions to themselves.

The door opened and Mrs. Colling slipped quietly into the room. She seated herself without a word, her face the gloomy mirror of Rutherford's own torment.

He looked at her a moment. Saying nothing, he reached into his jacket and handed her one of the puppies.

He could not say how long they sat like that. The puppy awoke and peed on Rutherford, but he did not mind it. His sadness made him insensible to anything as frivolous as dignity. He moved the furry little beast to the other side of his chest and continued to sit in silence.

Bartholmer awoke just as the puppies were starting to stir. "Ah Rutherford, Mrs. Colling." The old man's voice was gravelly. "And the puppies." Even in his severely weakened state, delight glimmered in his rheumy eyes. "What a lovely assembly to wake up to." He coughed, and Mrs. Colling rushed to pour him a drink. She held it to his lips, and he took several sips before his head fell back into the pillows.

"Do not be selfish, lad. Bring me a puppy."

Rutherford set his own puppy beside Bartholmer, as it had already relieved itself.

The old man raised a feeble arm and, with effort, petted the pup. "Mrs. Colling, would you be so good as to read for me?"

She picked the very large book up and, finding the page, began to read.

"No, no! You have already read that. Do not keep me in suspense. You were coming right to the point, last time." He drew in a ragged breath and croaked, "I will have my due."

With desperate reluctance, Mrs. Colling advanced several chapters in the book, and began to read afresh. Rutherford was gripped by a superstitious dread.

He drew his chair closer to the duke, and entertained the puppy so it would not wander away from his uncle's side. Forcing back the tears forming in his eyes, Rutherford used his free hand to clasp Bartholmer's.

As the puppy chewed on his other finger, Rutherford listened to the story and watched a smile forming on Bartholmer's lips.

"Ah-hah!" said the man at a crucial point in the narrative. "I knew that was how it would be. I knew all that trouble could not be for nothing. You see, it all worked out as it should." His voice grew more quiet, and his eyes drooped sleepily. "As it should."

Just then the puppies, first one, then the other, began to whine.

The old man roused himself. "You must take the wee darlings back to their mother. They are hungry."

Mrs. Colling, though it obviously pained her to leave Bartholmer's side, picked up the two squirming masses of fur and carried them out.

As soon as she left the room, Bartholmer grasped Rutherford's hand with an alarming ferocity. "I love you like a son. If I had had a son of my own, I would have wanted him to be just like you."

Rutherford's heart caught in his throat as he spoke. "I can think of no higher honour than being loved as your son. Think of me thus. Command me as your own child. What can I do?"

He sighed. "For me, nothing, my beloved boy. But in my name, and upon your honour, I ask you to watch over Mrs. Colling. She is not what she seems, but she is something far better. Do not force her to tell you anything. Only help her however you can, and protect her."

"For you, father of my heart, I will. I swear it."

"I do not ask you to marry her." His tired face animated suddenly with a weak but wicked smile. "For I do not suppose she would have you."

Rutherford laughed sadly. "I appear to have that effect on young women."

"Though I admit," his uncle's voice grew quiet, "it would make me very happy if you did wed. If that Miss Ravelsham will not have you, try to keep an open mind."

Rutherford chuckled, but wondered how the duke had ascertained that Miss Ravelsham was the object of Rutherford's affections. By the time he had reflected enough to realize that it hardly took a sage to puzzle that out, Mrs. Colling had returned.

"My dear, come," said the old man, feebly stretching out his hand to gesture. "In that top drawer over there, you will find a leather purse. Go fetch it to me." When she hesitated Bartholmer said, gently, "Would you refuse a man's dying wish?"

This produced a flood of tears and a look of tormented contrition, but she hastened to obey.

"You will find inside a sum of money. There are several large bank notes, in case you should need to make an impression, and there are an assortment of smaller coins, in case you should need not to make one. In all the sum is five hundred pounds. I would give you more, but I do not wish to make you a target for unscrupulous opportunists. In the sight of my heir, and with him as witness, I wish to make a living gift of this. And in your hearing, Mrs. Colling, I wish to instruct my heir to otherwise supply you as is necessary."

She made to object, but the duke raised his hand, panting now with the effort it took after such a long speech. She was silenced. "I have directed William to assist, protect and watch over you. You can trust him, Mrs. Colling."

She looked miserable, and the look she flashed at Rutherford was, he thought, resentful. It seemed very hard that he should be compelled by a dying man to assist her, and have his last hours with his uncle thus interrupted by a woman unknown to him and whom he still did not trust, only to have her treat him to her bitter looks.

Rutherford tried, however, not to return her resentment. He spoke in earnest. "I shall do all I can to protect and assist you, Mrs. Colling. I will not compel you to tell me your story. You have my word. And better, you have my pledge to my uncle."

But when he turned to look at his uncle's face, hoping to have the pleasure of seeing him smile with gratification, the glassy-eyed mask of death was all that remained. Bartholmer's hand was limp in his own. And a panic-stricken *No!* echoed through every chamber of Rutherford's heart and ran screaming down the hallways of his veins.

Mrs. Colling pressed her face to Bartholmer's other hand and wept. Rutherford saw this with a numbness that made him feel he only hovered above this tableau of grief and finality. His gaze turned to the bottle of laudanum, and he almost spat in disgust at himself.

What made this worse was the sudden, mortifying realization that some creeping part of his mind had been thinking about that bottle all along. It had been just waiting, as though later the little flask would surely find its way into his hand. The evil worm had been lurking like a vulture until his uncle's death. *Then,* it had said, *it will no longer be theft, for everything here will belong to you. And anyway, then you will really need it.*

Without a thought beyond escaping this evil, Rutherford grabbed the book, the last story heard by his uncle, and dashed from the room.

He almost got as far as the staircase, when Mrs. Colling caught up and threw herself in front of him, yelling, "Is it not enough that you have forced yourself upon my last few hours with him? Must you take my only memento of our time together, too?"

Even as distraught as she was, her face was still lovely. There was an energy and genuine sensibility in her eyes that made him feel, for a moment, the wrong in his having taken the book. But then a selfish, angry voice inside of him asked, *what about my grief?* What about all the time that he could have had with his uncle? Why did a complete stranger like Mrs. Colling get this time with him, instead of Rutherford?

Rutherford let the worst version of himself come to the surface and speak for him. "You got your memento, Mrs. Colling. Why do you not go fetch your purse and leave me to mourn the loss of *my* uncle?"

He held the book away from her grasp when she reached for it, for he was much taller than her. He was surprised to find how much pleasure he took in withholding it.

A fierce anger crossed her features. "So this is how you keep your word to your uncle. You withhold comfort from me at the first opportunity, before that dear man's mortal shell is even cold."

Rutherford would not admit the justice of this comment. "If I were persuaded that this book could in any way advantage your safety or material wellbeing, I should consider myself honour-bound to relinquish it. But as it is, I see no reason why I should give over this last little piece of him, this object of our last hours together to the very interloper who, by inserting herself into my uncle's company, prevented him from summoning me to his side sooner. How much more time might I have had with that excellent man?"

The features of her still lovely face contorted themselves into a look of murder and accusation. "I? A woman who, as you pointed out, is a complete stranger to you, *I* prevented you from coming to see your uncle? You tell yourself pretty stories, but the truth is that you only came to see your uncle when you knew there was something to get out of it. The fact that you never valued him is your own shortcoming. And you only value this book because holding onto it will deprive me of its comfort, you dog in the manger!"

She leapt in the air suddenly, meaning to reach high enough to grasp the volume. This jostled him, and he took a few steps back, but still held the book out of her grasp. He could not see why she should have it.

They struggled on in silence, her grasping, him dashing out of the way with the book, until she stepped dangerously close to the staircase, and he grabbed her waist to pull her back. This only further evoked her ire. She slapped his face, but he did not let go of her.

Then she deftly placed a leg behind his knee and, so quickly that he could not puzzle out how she did it, toppled him backward. He dropped the book and pulled her down with him. She landed on top of him on the ground. When she made to sit up and take a proper swing at him, he grabbed her arms and pulled her back to him, rolling over to pin her on the floor beneath him.

At that moment the ridiculousness of the situation struck him. He began to laugh, though tears were still streaming from his eyes. What on earth was wrong with him?

CHAPTER 51

Tilly and Mrs. Carlton were received at Blackwood Manor by Sandes, who was looking harrowed. But Tilly was not of a mind to pay attention to the moods of the domestics. She needed to speak with Rutherford.

"I am afraid his lordship has had some bad news just now." Sande's voice was grieved. Tilly could now see far enough past her own self-absorption to apprehend that the man was deeply attached to the duke and was suffering.

"So..." Tilly hesitated, not wishing to speak abruptly lest she cause the butler further pain. "The duke has passed then?"

"Yes." It came out as a sigh of resignation. "The old master has left us for a better home. However the new master is here. It is a great comfort that the dukedom never dies so long as a descendent of the Bartholmer line takes his seat at Blackwood Manor."

This uncharacteristic amount of talk from the usually reserved Sandes surprised Tilly. But his loyalty and dedication touched her heart.

So Rutherford was a duke now. But she would not let that frighten her away.

"Sandes, I know I am coming just at a bad time, but I really do need to speak to Mr. Rutherford—I mean Lord Drake, even if briefly."

It seemed like Sandes' station was too heavy for him at the moment. He must be grieving as much as any member of the old duke's family might do. He gestured weakly to the stairs. "He is upstairs in the chamber. I will show you the way."

As Tilly stepped up to the top of the stairs, her jaw dropped. She was treated to a view of Rutherford and Mrs. Colling, as she called herself, rolling around on the floor. A gasp escaped her before she turned and hastily re-descended the stairs.

So that was how things were. She had trusted the pretty young widow to keep her word and not to pursue Rutherford as she had said she would not. And Tilly had believed that Rutherford's heart could not so quickly be turned from herself to another, no matter how pretty the face.

But she had been a fool. She was beginning to believe that credulous optimism was just an indelible defect in her character. What a simpleton she had been.

They probably had found that they had a lot in common. They were both attached to the old duke, both grieving at his loss, both had complicated lives in many ways. Tilly had been an arrogant idiot to believe that Rutherford would remain unattached, that he would preserve his heart to her forever, regardless of how she mistreated it.

And what woman would not melt at any attention from such a beautiful man, with such a noble heart and mind—even without his being a duke?

Tilly shook her head in disgust. Well, perhaps taking Mrs. Colling on the floor outside of the room where his uncle's still-warm body lay was not precisely *noble*. But he was mad with grief. And no doubt that little minx threw herself at him while he was vulnerable.

Her eyes burned with tears as she headed for the door.

Sandes rushed to open it for her. "My apologies, Miss Ravelsham. You find this house in something of a disarray. But it is a house of grief, so I hope you will make some allowances." The man seemed to be desperate to make a defence, some defence, any defence for what Tilly had just witnessed.

But then, no defence was really necessary. This was nature taking its course. This was the retribution that Tilly deserved, and the happiness that Rutherford deserved. And it was what she wanted for him, after all, was it not?

Then why did she feel like the bottom had fallen out of her soggy, tear-soaked heart? Oh, yes, that was right: because doing the right thing costs you something. She could hear the glibly philosophical voice of the pre-Rutherford Tilly saying, "That is why it is called *doing the right thing*, and not *doing the advantageous* thing."

She wanted very much to punch that Tilly in the face.

She could barely force her legs to carry her wretched being into the carriage. She was all but insensible to what went on around her.

When she had collapsed into the carriage seat, and they were rolling away down the drive, she noticed Mrs. Carlton looking nervously out the window.

Tilly wondered what trivial little problem might be added to her burden. She huffed. "What is it, Mrs. Carlton?"

The woman craned her neck, straining to maintain a view of whatever it was that had caught her attention. "It seems we were not the only visitors to Blackwood Manor."

Tilly shook her head. "What you mean, Mrs. Carlton? Speak plainly."

"Did you not see the carriage that was pulling up as we were leaving? I am certain it was Lord Screwe's."

Tilly was once again struck by the fact that Mrs. Carlton was clearly not deaf. But she didn't care.

She leaned her head back and held a hand to her eyes. Perhaps Screwe was only out there because he had heard from his spies that Tilly had gone to Blackwood to see Rutherford. But there was little she could do about it.

Mrs. Colling was Rutherford's problem, now. Anyway, Screwe could not touch the pretty widow if she were under the protection of a duke. And when the conniving little vixen became a duchess, she could amuse herself by punishing the filthy bounder. Tilly's heart cried out against this inevitability, no matter how unpleasant it would be for Screwe.

The fact that Screwe was their mutual enemy no longer mattered. The truth was that Tilly's true enemy was her own glib arrogance. She thought she could always fix things. Now it was too late. The only thing fixed was the day of her wedding to DeGroen. She was rushing toward her destiny and away from the longing of her heart.

She wept miserably as her lavender-scented carriage rolled her back to London.

CHAPTER 52

Rutherford heard the gasp, and began trying to disentangle himself from Mrs. Colling's blasted skirts, receiving several good cuffs, which he knew he deserved, in the process.

Why was he behaving like such an ill-bred child?

He stood and straightened himself, casting about for the person who had witnessed his ridiculous conduct. He looked down the staircase, only seeing a skirt disappearing into a hallway at the bottom.

A feeling of apprehension came over him. He rushed down the stairs, stopping to peek hopefully into the south parlour. It was empty except for Smythe, who was standing by a book shelf with his white gloves on.

Rutherford made for the front door, Smythe following behind. He hailed Sandes. "Who was here just now?"

Sandes looked uncomfortable. "It was Miss Ravelsham, my lord..." his voice trailed off. Then he corrected himself. "I mean, your grace."

"Did she—" He wanted to say *see me with Mrs. Colling*, but that would sound far too much like an admission of guilt. "Did she come upstairs?"

"Yes, your grace. I showed her to the sickroom."

Ruddy hell. He had really put his foot in things this time. Smythe's snicker was audible, and Rutherford resisted the urge to turn around and yell at him to stop being such an irritating little turd.

Instead, Rutherford ran to the door and flung it open to see if he might still catch Tilly and stop her from leaving. The leprous pale face and grinning yellow teeth of Lord Screwe greeted him, as Tilly's carriage rolled away down the drive.

"Well, well. Is the duke making economies by having his nephew do doorman's duties?"

Rutherford only just restrained himself from letting his fist fly into Screwe's face. "You have been told not to come here, Screwe. Do not make me take action against you in trespass."

"*You* take action? Ah, I see. Am I addressing the fifth Duke of Bartholmer, then?" His lips pursed in a mocking smile. "My condolences, and my congratulations, Duke."

"You disgust me, Screwe. I hate the sight of you. I will repeat and affirm the edict of my excellent predecessor, may he rest in peace, and tell you that you are not welcome here. You will not be received by me anywhere. Get off my property and do not ever return. You may expect a formal letter to this effect from my solicitor."

Rutherford made to reenter the manor.

"Very well. I am banished. I will just say what I came to say."

"Why should I hear anything from your filthy mouth?"

"Because it concerns Miss Ravelsham."

Rutherford clenched his fist and turned around, staring at Screwe in seething silence.

"I hope you will use your influence with Miss Ravelsham to persuade her to return my property." Screwe's gaze was menacing. "It would very much be in her best interests to do so."

"I have no idea what property you could be speaking of, but you are misinformed. I have no influence with Miss Ravelsham." He did not add *especially now*, but the words still tasted bitter in his mouth. "If you wish to engage someone's influence with her, why do you not petition Mr. DeGroen? No doubt if you catch him in a week he will be feeling in a benign mood, having secured his future marital happiness."

"In a week?" Screwe's laugh came out like the sound of a rusty nail scraped against a piece of slate. "Have not you heard? I assumed that was the felicitous news Miss Ravelsham came to tell you, for I saw her carriage departing as I arrived. She is to be wed *tomorrow*, happy girl. It is all the talk. Some say they are merely in a hurry to hush up rumours about you and her, but I know nothing of *that*."

"Tomorrow?! You lie!" Rutherford felt like a cannonball had ploughed into his stomach. Could it be true? It must not be.

"I know you do not like me, Duke, but you must admit, in your heart of hearts, your dislike revolves around my tendency to tell the truth, rather than to tell lies."

Rutherford's fist swung back involuntarily.

This was enough to make Screwe step away quickly and head for his carriage, only speaking over his shoulder as he retreated. "If you care at all about Miss Ravelsham, you will try to persuade her to return what is mine before I expose her. Oh, by the way, I have posted Mr. Delacroix's bond. He says he intends to press a suit against you for your assault against his person."

Rutherford knew this last shot was meant to incense him, but it bounced off of him without notice. He stepped inside the door, closed it, and leaned his back upon it, sliding down until he collapsed on the floor.

He knew not how long he sat there. Smythe had began to hover nearby, but with a single look Rutherford sent him scampering away.

What could he do? His instincts were divided. On the one hand he wished to curl up in a ball with a bottle of soothing poison and make the realities of his life go away. On the other hand, he wished to dash after Tilly, catch her and beg her to jilt DeGroen—or, if she would not listen, to make off with her. This scheme was equally mad. He knew it. After the eyeful of him and Mrs. Colling that she had received, she would think him an utter cad.

There was no hope. And yet, something else was gnawing at his brain. What was it that Screwe had said about Delacroix? The little shit was taking legal action against him. Rutherford laughed bitterly. Good luck with that. No, something else.

Screwe had posted bond.

Delacroix was no longer rotting in the gaol. He was rotting in public, free to stink up the streets of London. Rutherford stood abruptly. What if Delacroix was still up to his old tricks? Could Lydia still be in danger? But if Screwe had posted bond, it was no doubt for some nefarious purpose of his own.

He knew, in the pit of his stomach, that Screwe's plots would be directed at Tilly. And she probably was ignorant of her peril, thinking Delacroix was safely locked up.

"Smythe!" he bellowed, knowing that the man would be somewhere nearby. "Call for a carriage and the fastest horses! And round up Molly and the pups. Sandes, take care of—" He gasped. It was indecent for him to be running off now, so soon after his uncle's death. But he forced himself to continue. "My uncle. I know you will make the very best arrangements."

He dashed up the stairs. He should apologize to Mrs. Colling and reassure her of his protection before he left. But when he entered his uncle's chamber, she was nowhere to be seen. The leather purse of money lay on the bedside table. The magnetism of the laudanum bottle drew his gaze.

He swallowed his bitter self-loathing and went back to the hallway, looking for the book that he had left on the floor. It was gone. A stream of curses cascaded from his mouth. He had meant to give her the ruddy book when he apologized. If she had made off with it, she had probably left the manor and was God knows where.

He knew that he had done wrong, hoarding it to himself and then tormenting her with it. He knew it, and was ashamed for his own sake, and for the sake of what his uncle would think of such conduct. Wrestling with her on the floor was an especially pathetic flourish to his asinine behaviour.

Just then Sandes appeared. "The Marquess Fenimore is calling, your grace. Is your grace at home?"

Now he ruddy-well asks. Why not just show him into his uncle's chamber, as he had done with Tilly? Rutherford suppressed his bitterness. The situation was no one's fault but his own. "Thank you, Sandes. I am always home to Frobisher."

Rutherford made for the entrance room to greet his friend and led him to the south parlour, but in an afterthought, paused to call the butler back. "Sandes, see if you can locate Mrs. Colling. She probably has no desire to see me, but tell her I wish to apologize."

Sandes' face did not betray what he thought as he bowed and left again.

"Bish, it is good to see you."

Frobisher's face wore a mocking smile. "Apologize to the mysterious widow, eh? Whatever can you have done now, Rutherford?"

"Behaved like a bloody beast, is what."

Frobisher suddenly gestured at Rutherford's leg with a look of alarm.

"You are bleeding."

"Am I?" So he was. Blast it. "Well, the doctor did warn me about getting into fisticuffs." The good physician could not have imagined that he would need to forbid wrestling with young ladies under Rutherford's own protection. Rutherford winced at the memory. "I am sure it is nothing, for I hardly feel it."

"And is this in any way related to your need to apologize to Mrs. Colling?"

Rutherford did not wish to make a full confession to Frobisher. "I regret to tell you that my uncle has finally passed. I shall just say that, in the despair of the moment… Well, I did not take it very well. In fact, I hardly know what I am about, even now."

The smile fell from Frobisher's face. "I am sorry, my friend. I am sure Mrs. Colling understands what you must have been feeling."

"Perhaps, but I acted as though I was the only one grieving. She was very attached to my uncle, too. She loved him, I believe—no, do not give me such a look. It was not like that. Anyway, she was distraught, and I behaved like a perfectly savage brute. And even worse, I am sworn by my uncle to protect and support her." Rutherford's shoulders slumped. "I am such a failure, Bish. Such an arse."

Frobisher patted his arm. "You are not a failure, Rutherford." Then his old smile was back. "I say nothing about the *arse* bit."

It worked. Rutherford laughed, though sadly.

"What can I do to assist you?"

Rutherford brightened at this query. "You may, indeed, be able to help. I must leave right away and return to London. I know I look flighty, but believe me I am not mad—not yet anyway. Only I have business of the greatest import and I must get back to town tonight."

"I shall be ready to leave in a trice."

"Ah, but I hope you shall do me a very great service and stay behind. I need someone to make certain all the matters relating to final arrangements for my uncle are properly handled. Sandes is a very competent man, but there are some things that need a gentleman's touch."

Frobisher nodded. "Very well."

"And, more importantly, I have a somewhat delicate task for you. When Mrs. Colling is located, will you convey my apologies to her? Make her understand that I am sincerely sorry, Bish, and assure her in the strongest terms of my commitment to protecting and providing for her."

"Consider it done."

"You are an excellent fellow. I do not know how to thank you."

"I shall stay here for the time being and reward myself for doing you these heavy favours by killing every pheasant in your forest and helping myself to the wine cellar. The Blackwood collection is legendary."

"Good." Rutherford's smile was faint. "See what you can do to reduce it to mediocrity while I am away. Only now, I am sorry to say it, I must leave you. I have already delayed too long."

He found Smythe and gave him orders to follow him to London with Molly and the puppies.

"I will leave now in the faster equipage. You may take my carriage, it will be more comfortable for the little darlings. Take good care of them."

Smythe gazed in dismay at Rutherford's attire. "Shall I not dress you first, your grace?"

"I've no time for it."

Smythe looked crestfallen until Rutherford added, "And when you return, throw out all my colourful clothes, I shall not want them."

Smythe's face lit up with hope, as though he had just received a promise of a large raise and an extra ration of brandy. His voice quivered with joy. "Certainly, your grace."

"Have everything made over in black." Rutherford gave a comprehensive sweep of his arm. "Nothing but black. Neck cloths, too. See if you can have at least one set ready for tomorrow, and rush the other things."

Smythe's shoulders sank again. "Yes, your grace."

As he rolled out in a light carriage pulled by Bartholmer's four fastest horses, Rutherford sunk into sadness. His heart hurt to be leaving Blackwood. It felt like he was abandoning his uncle, which he knew was not rational. His uncle was gone. But still, some mad impulse taunted him to turn back, as though, if he returned and waited, his uncle might awaken.

The pain of the final truth was crippling. And rumination on Tilly, though slightly more amenable to some kind of hope, did not offer him any less painful distraction. He could only redirect his thoughts to how best he might protect her. At least that would keep him active and away from the laudanum.

CHAPTER 53

Tilly was exhausted when she awoke the next morning. She had returned to London in misery the day before. And now she faced the ravages of sleeplessness and tears as she looked in the mirror, preparing herself for her wedding day.

It should be joyous, shouldn't it? But there was no joy in Tilly's heart. She felt like an utter failure.

She had lost track of Clara and Sweep and could no longer protect them. She had failed Rutherford, even as she failed her own philanthropic vision, by getting involved in the trade of that insidious poison. She had broken his heart and, through her neglect, let him find consolation in the love of another.

Now all that was left to her was the one thing that she could do right for someone else. Mr. DeGroen would have his inheritance and his happiness. She had failed at all else, but DeGroen she would not fail.

Just as she was having this thought, a servant delivered her a note. There was no address, but she knew the writing.

It is not too late, my love.

That was all it said. If only it had been written by Rutherford.

But it was DeGroen. He was willing to give up everything only to see her happy. His good heart made her wish all the more to help him. And anyway, DeGroen was wrong. It was too late. Rutherford had moved on. There was nothing to be gained by cancelling the wedding, except to utterly scandalize Grandfather Fowler.

She threw the note into the fire, just as Miss Grey arrived to dress her hair. She was accompanied by a very modish looking lady, tall and willowy, with golden ringlets, and a young footman in tow—an archaically clad little boy, decked out in a powdered wig and cosmetics from the last century.

Tilly squinted at the woman, then dismissed the servants. "You too, Marie." Marie looked sullen, for fancy dress and weddings charmed her girlish heart like nothing else and gave her weak understanding a sparkly trinket to play with. Tilly actually felt sorry to deprive her, but out she must go.

Tilly locked the door behind them then rushed back to inspect the two newcomers. "Clara? Sweep?"

"Not at all, Miss," supplied Miss Grey, with a little wink and a tap of her nose. "This is my house guest, Mrs. Steele and her boy servant, Oakley."

"Ah." Tilly smiled broadly at the subterfuge.

They really were all but unrecognisable. Clara's petite form had been elevated by a very clever pair of shoes. Powder covered the darker undertones of her complexion, and her brows had been lightened to match the wig she wore. And no one would ever suspect that the perpetually grubby-faced Sweep resided somewhere under all that painted skin and frippery.

"Well, I am very pleased to meet you, Mrs. Steele." She winked in acknowledgement at *Oakley.*

"The pleasure is all mine, Miss Ravelsham. We have been living quite quietly with Miss Grey. But when we heard of your wedding, we could not be content until we came to wish you joy."

"Thank you." Tilly forced a smile. So Miss Grey had hidden and disguised them and kept it from Tilly. This showed some courage.

"You are not angry with me then, Miss?" Miss Grey sounded apprehensive.

Tilly could well imagine that Clara had frantically begged Miss Grey to keep her secret, even from Tilly. And, considering how closely Tilly had been watched, that secrecy was probably what saved them from Screwe's detection.

"Not at all, Miss Grey, I assure you. I am only very happy for everyone's good health."

They all had a nice long chat as Miss Grey dressed Tilly's hair. Then Tilly sent them all away, saying, "It might be best not to come here again, just to be safe. When I have sorted some things out, I will send for you, Miss Grey."

When they were gone, Tilly permitted Browning and Marie to reenter and bring the dress.

Tilly's breath caught as the dress was unwrapped. She had forgotten how beautiful it was. Her mother's design was rapturously lovely. And, when she was carefully cinched and draped into its silken folds, she beheld herself in the mirror with some satisfaction. It was not so much the swell of vanity, or of any romantic inclination that she had toward wedding dresses. It was the simple appreciation of the gown's undeniable beauty, and how perfectly it suited her.

A knock came on the door.

Tilly was shocked to see her mother enter. She looked with hopeful eyes at that aloof figure of Tilly's maternal dream, as though she were not a mere mortal, but a divine visitation.

Had she come to wish Tilly joy and to partake in it with her? Had she come to dispense some last minute counsel, as had passed from mothers to daughters on such occasions from time immemorial?

A little, painful "Oh" escaped her lips, as she realized that her mother only had eyes for the dress.

"Yes," pronounced Mrs. Ravelsham with satisfaction. "It fits you almost perfectly."

"Almost?" Tilly wished she could strip away the vulnerability, the desperate need for approval that clung to the word as it left her tongue.

The artist sighed and tilted her head thoughtfully. "The line is distorted just there." She gestured. "The mid-section should not intrude itself upon the graceful drop of the fabric."(Ooooooooo!!!)

Tilly was speechless. Was she trying to say that Tilly was fat? Had this woman roused herself from the ivory tower of dreamy maternal negligence only to admire her own work and insult her daughter? The merciful onslaught of anger drowned out the little spark of pain this comment had kindled in Tilly's heart.

"Is that really all you have to say?"

Mrs. Ravelsham stretched, then shook her head in recollection. "Oh no, I got distracted and nearly forgot. I shan't make it to the wedding today, I am afraid. I am working on—"

"A series of sketches?" Tilly supplied bitterly. "So I suppose father will not come either."

Her mother smiled as though Tilly had made a jest and waved her hand in a self-indulgent gesture. "Oh, you know us both so well. But, indeed, he shall be there to give you away. For, as I told him, he is a crucial part of the display. The work must be seen in its proper context."

The dress was nothing but a piece of art to her. The wedding was merely a theatrical pedestal upon which to install it, and the bride an imperfect model. Tilly supposed she should not be surprised.

Mrs. Ravelsham leaned in and kissed the air beside Tilly's cheek. "Only he will not stay to breakfast, for he must come back and assist me. Have a lovely time. I shall get back to my work."

And she was gone. Just like that, Tilly was an orphan again.

She returned her gaze to the mirror. At least she had inherited this beautiful dress. She remarked how the sadly downcast gaze of Browning contrasted with the oblivious grin of Marie.

"You look like a princess!" exclaimed the latter, clasping her hands together in rapture.

Tilly muttered, "A fat princess." She made ready to leave.

CHAPTER 54

Rutherford had spent a sleepless night. He had sped back to London faster than was safe. Then, only stopping to change his horses, he proceeded on to check Tilly's house.

He did not knock, for it was an indecent hour, and what could he possibly say? But he checked around the grounds. A likely looking urchin sighed sleepily in the shadows, but there was no sign of Delacroix. All seemed calm and undisturbed inside.

He then moved on, searching every second-rate club and third-rate hell where Delacroix might be found. But he was nowhere, and no one had seen him. If Delacroix was not out on the town, where might he be staying? There were thousands of places he could have taken a room. Rutherford could not check them all.

Then it occurred to him that Screwe may have given the little goblin shelter in his own home. They were a well-matched pair.

The streets were quiet as he came to Screwe's house. Screwe was not an early riser, but candles were visible through the windows. The house servants were beginning their day's work while it was still dark.

Rutherford rubbed his hand over the scratchy stubble forming on his chin. His stomach growled. There was no way of knowing if Delacroix was inside, but Screwe must certainly still be abed. What if Delacroix were not here? What if he were after Aldley's family again?

He found a woman on the way to market with baking, and bought a sack of food from her, then rolled on to check in at the Aldleys', just as the first rays of dawn were breaking.

He munched on a meat pie, wiping his hands on his burgundy pants negligently, as he surveyed the Aldley house. Again there were signs of servant activity, but all seemed otherwise quiet. The only person watching was him.

He rubbed his eyes. Was he mad? Had he just lost his mind with grief and heartbreak, and dashed off to tilt at the first windmill that presented itself? Just because Delacroix was no longer in the nick, that did not mean that he had any more plans for evil. After all, further charges against him now would surely result in his never getting another bond. Self interest should compel him to behave himself.

But then why had Screwe mentioned it to him? Was he just trying to be menacing out of habit? Lord, perhaps Screwe only meant to drive Rutherford mad. That was probably the truth of it. And here he was, eating food on the street in yesterday's clothing, spying upon everyone he could think of. This certainly had the appearance of madness.

He turned his thoughts reluctantly back to the torturous subject of Tilly. Surely that was who Screwe meant to punish, for whatever misappropriation his diseased mind lay at her feet. But Rutherford had already checked her home. There was only one other logical place where Delacroix might accost her. And it was the last place, the last event, that Rutherford had any wish to see.

But he had to put his own feelings aside. Tilly was in danger. He could feel it. He could do this one last thing for her, before he relinquished her to another man's care. He had to make sure she was safe, and then he had to let her go be happy with another.

He cursed as he watched the ash-man roll his cart down the alley to the servants' entrance. Rutherford squinted. Not Delacroix. No such luck. He had to go to the church, and he had best hurry, for these types of things were always abysmally early. With any luck he could intercept Delacroix lurking about ahead of time, and be conveniently out of the way before any of the wedding party made an appearance.

When he arrived at Saint Margaret, it was astoundingly quiet. His was the only equipage on the street outside. He searched the grounds and the surrounding alleys. No sign of Delacroix. He made to go inside, but the doors were not yet open. Surely Delacroix would have to enter at some point. He went back to wait in his carriage. He would watch the attendees arrive and make sure Delacroix was not among them.

He woke from a doze to the sound of keys jingling, and the great iron loop from which they hung banging against the oak door of the church. He wondered what time it might be. How long had he slept? What had he missed while he snoozed like a ruddy loafer?

He cursed himself, but took some comfort in the fact that, as the man was only now unlocking the building, Delacroix could not possibly be inside yet. He waited. It occurred to him, after half an hour of quietude, that it was odd that none of the wedding party had yet made an appearance. Surely the groom, at least, would be eager.

He decided to risk a foray into the church to make enquiries about the wedding.

The look of pity that the clergyman gave him told Rutherford how rough he must look.

"I am sorry to trouble you, but may I enquire at what hour the wedding is to occur?"

"The wedding?" The elderly man looked confused. "There is a christening, but no wedding here this morning."

"No wedding?" Rutherford's heart was buoyed up by a treacherous little wave of hope. "Are Miss Ravelsham and Mr. DeGroen not to be wed today?"

"Ah." The cloud of confusion lifted from the man's face. "The DeGroen wedding. Yes, quite right, it is today. You see, they suddenly changed the date. The grandfather is quite ill, may the Lord bless him. But we could not accommodate the change, for we have the christening, you see, the Viscount Brynwark's first s—"

"Do you know in which church the wedding is to be held?" Rutherford asked abruptly, before the priest could squander precious minutes congratulating himself on christening a future viscount. Why had he assumed it would be in the same church? Stupid, stupid error. And he had wasted all this time.

The cleric tapped his fingers on his lips and rolled his eyes upward.

Rutherford retrained himself from shaking the man. He already looked half mad. Assaulting a priest in his own church would put him well beyond the pale.

"I have the direction. I will copy it for you."

Rutherford impatiently followed the plodding holy man into a small office with neatly arranged stacks of paper on a desk, surrounded on three sides by shelving lined with the treatises and books of devotion attending his profession.

Rutherford wished the man's hand were faster and not half so neat, as the cleric copied out the direction. He snatched the paper from the priest, then recollected himself. "Thank you." He dashed away.

Rutherford ruminated as his horses fleetly navigated the streets, and the patter of rain began to sound upon his carriage. It would take him at least half an hour to get there, assuming the lazy world of the rich did not wake up and take it into their heads to congest the streets with their carriages.

An ominous feeling clasped his spine with icy fingers of dread. What if he was too late? Surely the ceremony had already started.

He caught himself in the thought. Did he mean too late to intercept the hypothetical Mr. Delacroix, or too late to stop Tilly's wedding by striding in looking like a homeless bounder who routinely washed in ditch water and had been forced by dire straits to eat his valet?

He pressed his hands to his face and tried to calm his mind. He would not interrupt the wedding if he could help it. But he would protect Tilly at all cost. He took a long swig from his silver flask. He was not sure the mixture did very much, but at least he was no longer plagued with headaches.

As he bolted from the still rolling vehicle and ran to the doors of the church, his stomach sank. There were no other people ascending those steps. He tried to pull the door softly open, but it seemed to his frayed nerves to be the loudest portal in London. Thankfully, there was an antechamber in the entry, whose wall blocked the sound, and Rutherford crept up to the intersection of the two hallways that led to the inner sanctuary.

He took the passage to the left and made his way to the very back of the church, where he might scan the attendees for any sign of Delacroix. Tilly was walking down the aisle with the man he supposed was her father, and it took every ounce of his determination not to gaze upon her beautiful back. *Don't look. Don't look, you damned fool. You are here to find Delacroix.*

There were not so many people. Rutherford felt certain that he would make out the somewhat hunched form of Delacroix, if he should be there. But he was not. Of course not. He would be concealed, not out in the open. However Rutherford started when he saw, not ten feet away from him, Lord Screwe.

The hairs stood up on his arms. There was no legitimate reason for this man to attend Tilly's wedding. The lord's wicked eye flicked in his direction. Had Screwe seen him? But the man's gaze fixed itself on the front of the church.

He would deal with Screwe later. Delacroix had to be somewhere. He scanned the upper gallery, but was not satisfied with his view. The balcony was narrow, designed for the passage of one or two people, but someone could easily conceal themselves up there.

He swiftly returned to the outer entry to locate the passage to the upper gallery. There was a small door inside the hall he had entered through, he opened it and found the staircase.

The church acoustics carried the sound of the priest's voice to him, as he rushed up the stairs as quietly as he could. The ceremony had started, and Rutherford suddenly felt he was running against the hourglass of the fates.

He scanned the enclave that housed the pipe-organ and saw only the organist, positioned sedately in his seat. Then suddenly Rutherford's eye spied a shadowy figure, concealing himself next to the bulky stone statue of some saint.

As Rutherford crept closer to the man, he saw that it was, indeed, Delacroix. Then he saw the little turd raise a hunting rifle to his shoulder.

Rutherford abandoned all stealth and charged upon the man, grappling him in a blind fury, oblivious to the gasps from the sanctuary below.

CHAPTER 55

Tilly remarked, as she walked down the aisle, on the arm of her distracted father, that a surprising number of the invitees had shown up for this new date and location. They had to have it in a smaller chapel than originally planned, for they could not get the larger church on such short notice. Still, there was plenty of room. Most of the guests were DeGroen's friends and members of his horrid family. She resisted the urge to stick out her tongue at the latter, as she passed them.

And there was her brother standing next to DeGroen, each of them staring at her with eyes full of love, admiration and gratitude. Her heart felt full. This was her family. She was doing the right thing.

She did not see, but sensed, the love of Lydia, who walked behind her. For Lydia to attend her meant a great deal to Tilly, especially given the recent scandal and the suggestion of some three way tryst with Rutherford that Screwe had insidiously been circulating.

She supposed that dispelling this rumour would be more practically accomplished by Lydia's standing as her matron of honour. However, many a lady would shrink from the humiliation of it, and the short notice of the wedding would have been all the excuse that Lydia would need to extricate herself.

But Lydia stood by Tilly, despite everything, despite even the conviction that Tilly was supplying Aldley's brother-in-law with his favourite poison. This was a true friend. She saw Aldley staring in admiration at his wife from the front pew. He diverted his gaze long enough to flash Tilly a grin.

Even Grandfather DeGroen, sitting in a wheelchair, away from the hard pews and covered in a warm blanket against the stony chill of the church, smiled and nodded at Tilly.

She was surrounded by love and good will. She really had nothing to complain about. True, she could not have Rutherford, and that hurt. True, her parents would spend all the rest of their days in the negligent fairy-realm of art. But she could still be content if she focussed on all the love that she did have—much of it undeserved. At that moment, she resolved to become a better person, so that she might be worthy of all the hearts that were so dedicated to her.

As she reached the front to stand before the priest, she stole a final glance at all her well-wishers. Her eye caught an unfriendly face at the back of the church.

Tilly was jarred from the moment of reflection upon her friends by the sudden appearance of her enemy. How had she not seen Screwe before?

DeGroen was smiling at her. The priest was clearing his throat. What could she possibly do—stop the ceremony and have him ejected from the church? Preposterous. She would have to endure his presence and hope that even he would not use the church as a venue for his malice.

"Dearly beloved, we are gathered together here in the sight of God, and in the face of this congregation, to join together this man and this woman in holy matrimony..."

Tilly recollected herself and remembered to look solemn. She supposed the nervousness would seem pretty authentic. They were really going to do this. She would not let Screwe ruin things for DeGroen.

"...And therefore is not by any to be enterprised, nor taken in hand, unadvisedly, lightly, or wantonly, to satisfy men's carnal lusts and appetites..."

Here Tilly felt a slight pang, not for guilt over her carnal lusts and appetites, which she lamentably was giving up in this undertaking, but for the fact that she was not only taking this marriage lightly, as was DeGroen, but worse, using it as a subterfuge. She shuddered. Would God punish them all for this? Surely God was bigger than the church portrayed Him. Surely He would understand her heart.

"Like brute beasts that have no understanding..."

Suddenly Tilly was aware of sounds of a struggle somewhere at the back of the church and the rustling of heads turning. The look of horror on the face of the priest made her turn to look, just as a shot rang out and screams echoed amid the hallowed walls.

CHAPTER 56

*A*ngry and shocked faces stared up at Rutherford from the sanctuary below. They could see the struggling form of Delacroix, but could they see that Delacroix held the gun that dangled over the edge of the balustrade? Rutherford was not certain. And he became suddenly aware that his presence there, especially imposed in such a conspicuous way, would ruin things for Tilly. It would certainly affirm the filthy rumours that Screwe had been circulating.

As quickly as the gazes had turned upon him, they turned back to the front, as cries of "We need a doctor! Someone fetch a doctor!" rang out in the otherworldly acoustics around the pulpit.

Rutherford looked about for Tilly. His eye caught side of her hurrying across the front of the sanctuary. She was not injured, thank God, nor was Lydia, who followed her as they rushed to attend to someone. He could not see who it was, for others had gathered closely around and blocked his view.

Feeling an apprehension that Aldley might have been hit, Rutherford leaned forward to see if it would afford him a better look.

Delacroix seized his chance, and swung the butt of the rifle at Rutherford. It was a weak blow, but it smacked his cheekbone painfully. Rutherford easily disarmed the cowardly little man and punched him hard enough to knock him out. It was tempting to tip him over the balcony, but there were people below.

And the man was unconscious. It would be dishonourable to kill him, or even to give him the beating he deserved. Rutherford removed his now grubby-looking, canary yellow neckcloth and bound Delacroix's feet together. He tore more fabric from his shirt and tied the miserable cur's hands behind his back. Then he made sure there were no more bullets on his person, and left him there to be discovered.

As Rutherford descended the staircase his body shook with the residual energy of his fury. He was oblivious to the pain in his leg and the welt rising beside his eye. Leaving quietly, he hoped, would at least prevent any more grist for scandal than he already had supplied.

Some of the attendees were streaming out of the church in confusion. Rutherford moved among them, making his way to the vehicle where his driver awaited, trying to keep the look of curiosity off of his face.

Just then, Rutherford heard a "There he is!" and two large men approached him through the crowd. His instinct was to run, just to avoid speaking to anyone. But he resisted it. That would appear cowardly.

They placed themselves in his path and one said, "We have orders to detain you, sir, until the men from Bow Street have arrived to question you."

"Question me?" Rutherford was incredulous. "Question *me*?"

"Aye."

"And by whom, pray, were these orders given?"

"I prefer not to say, and that's of no import."

Of no import. Those were definitely words supplied to the ruffian by someone of a higher station. A suspicion began to form in the awakening mind of Rutherford. "And did Lord Screwe, who has no authority over me, by the way, tell you who I am?"

The men looked uncomfortable at the mention of Lord Screwe, but one of them replied, "We were given a description, which matches you to the last tittle."

"And yet," contended Rutherford, "you must be mistaken. For *I* am the Duke of Bartholmer. You were not instructed to accost a duke, I am sure." Rutherford did not like to invoke his rank in this way, but thought it would be the most expeditious means to be rid of the two bully-ruffians.

"A duke? You?" The more talkative man laughed and swept his gaze over Rutherford's person. "Aye, and I am the Queen of Sheba. This here," he jabbed a thumb in the direction of his comrade, "is King Arthur."

Both men laughed heartily at this wit and made to grab Rutherford, who evaded them, stepping back. It did not, until that moment, occur to him how he appeared in his dirty, torn, puppy piddle soaked, meat pie splotched clothing—having one leg caked in blood, unshaven, devoid of a neckcloth, and nursing a bruised cheek, besides. He did not smell especially fetching, either.

His colourful attire would also do nothing to lend him distinction. When displayed in such a horrid estate, it could only make him appear more ridiculous. Good Lord. He must look the very picture of a madman, and his claiming to be a duke would not help matters.

"The Earl of Aldley will vouch for me. He is inside."

The looks on the men's faces betrayed that they considered this further mad utterance highly amusing. They probably had no idea who Aldley was either.

"Look," Rutherford made one more attempt to reason with them, "you see that carriage over there? You see that coat of arms on the door?

That is my vehicle, and those are the colours of the Bartholmer duchy. Let us go ask the driver."

The men seemed to be over their mirth now, and one said, more menacingly, "Aye, and let you try to escape by making off in some nobleman's rig? That would suit you as right as mud suits a pig, wouldn't it? No. We have our orders."

Rutherford had hoped to avoid drawing attention with any further altercation, but realised that they would not hear reason from a man they considered mad. However, they also did not consider him much of a match and were not properly on their guard.

One man lazily made to grasp Rutherford's arm. Rutherford slipped behind the two, and before they knew what he was about, deftly knocked their big, knobbly heads together. It was enough to stun them.

He made quickly away to his carriage. The people around him were now aware enough to get out of his way and looked somewhat alarmed. Fortunately his driver was looking sharp and had the door open for him when he arrived, closing it behind him with a withering stare at the two brutes that now made their way to the carriage.

Apparently, when they saw that the driver knew Rutherford as master, they thought the better of their former conduct. They doffed their hats and bowed, mumbling some apology that Rutherford did not hear through the door, then shuffling away.

He signalled the driver to take him home. His work was done. Tilly was safe, and was probably married by now, or would be soon enough. He heaved a sad sigh. He had at least earned a proper bath and a change of clothes.

CHAPTER 57

Tilly hardly had time to think as she rushed to push her way through the crowd. She heard a whispered gasp of "Thank God!" escape Lydia, who was hard on her heels, as they made their way to a clear view of the victim.

Aldley was beside Grandfather Fowler, who sat bleeding in his chair. The earl was trying to push the crowd back, while unsuccessfully calling for someone to fetch a doctor.

Lydia knew how to get rid of the recalcitrant onlookers. She raised her voice. "I am sorry for the shock you have all received, but as you can see a man has been shot. Whoever did this may still be in the church, reloading. For your own safety..."

The rest of what she had to say was drowned out by the sound of a herd stomping towards the door.

Tilly looked sadly at the face of the old man. She caught her father's arm. "The art exhibit is over. You may consider your duty here discharged, Papa. But on the way out, will you instruct my driver to fetch a doctor to us immediately?"

He nodded his ashen face, patted her arm and left her.

Frederick gave her a theatrical look of disbelief as he ushered his wife out of the church.

Mr. DeGroen took her arm, murmuring under his breath. "This is unbelievable. Do we actually live in England, or have we been transported to the wild lands of the Americas? We must get you out of here, my dear. It is not safe."

"Do not worry. It was Delacroix. I saw him. And I saw Rutherford make light work of him."

"Rutherford?" DeGroen gave her a penetrating look.

Tilly only nodded. What more could she say? Who else but Rutherford should be the hero? But she had seen him leave. Her heart was breaking all over again. But this was not the time for her mawkishness.

"I am glad Frederick has made Genevieve go home. She does not need to see or hear what will follow. If you send some men, they will no doubt find Delacroix's corpse up there." Tilly gestured. "We are quite safe now."

Having sent his wife home with the carriage, Frederick returned and fetched some men to retrieve Delacroix.

DeGroen went back to his grandfather's side to take his hand, but the old man only stared blankly.

Certainly they must fetch a doctor, but his eyes were so glazed, so still. Tilly knew that no physician could do any good.

The priest, whom Tilly had to admire for not lifting the skirts of his robe and scampering away at the first sound of gunfire, came to the other side of the old man. He looked at DeGroen consolingly and began to pray over Grandfather Fowler.

DeGroen now wore an expression of bitterness and disgust. "He only had such a little time left. Why would anyone want to take it from him?"

"If it is any consolation," the noisome voice of Screwe slithered into Tilly's ear, "I do not think the madman was aiming at your grandfather."

Everyone, including the priest, turned in shock to look at the nasty man.

"No, it is true." Screwe ignored their disgusted looks. "It was Rutherford—I beg your pardon, Lord Drake. No, no, no. I mean the new Duke of Bartholmer. You will all forgive me, but the man's titles are almost as difficult to keep track of as his mistresses." He cast a knowing look at Lydia and Tilly.

Aldley stood to full height. "I believe we have heard enough from you, Screwe. Remove yourself!"

Screwe ignored him. "I saw him, you know, waving his gun around. The duke, I mean. But I assumed he was aiming at his rival." He winked at DeGroen. "Not the grandfather. Though I suppose it is possible that he thought, in a moment of embittered passion, 'If I can't have her, nobody can!' and took an ill-aimed shot at the object of his affection."

The man broke out in a mocking laugh that so lacked the support of any true merriment that it collapsed into a dry cough. "But I suppose we shall never know unless he makes a full confession."

Tilly could feel the blood draining from her face. She had not thought of it, amid all the turmoil, but of course Screwe would try to make out that Rutherford had fired the shot. She wanted to cry out, to defend him, but she knew anything she said would just lend credence to Screwe's assertions about her and Rutherford, and make him look more guilty.

DeGroen walked over to Screwe. "You are either mistaken—which would be understandable, the doddering often get confused—or you are lying. In fact, that would be understandable too. Or rather, it would be all of a piece with your having posted bond for the villain the last time he took a shot at someone. For I can positively affirm that Rutherford was not the shooter. Delacroix was. I saw them both. Rutherford wrested the weapon from your murderous friend."

Tilly could kiss DeGroen. Who would not believe his word, under the circumstances? He had the better vantage point. He was the most injured party, save his grandfather. And if anyone had a right to cry foul against the affair that Screwe alleged, it was DeGroen.

Screwe waved his hand dismissively. "Of course you are trying to defend your bride from scandal, but really, Mr. DeGroen, you are telling tales."

"We shall see whose testimony is believed, should it come to that," DeGroen continued. "But it seems to me that your own testimony must be somewhat suspect, as, if Delacroix took another shot at Lady Aldley while he was out on your bond, you would lose all that money, would you not? Seems to me a man who cannot even pay his debts of honour might be willing to do a great deal not to let such a sum escape his clutching little fingers."

Tilly had to admire DeGroen's supple mind. Pure genius to deflect attention from Rutherford and Tilly by alluding to Delacroix's shooting at Lydia.

Frederick called from the upstairs. "Delacroix is here all right. And so is his gun. He is all tied up with bits of colourful cloth. Looks like a Christmas gift, or perhaps a Christmas goose. But he is alive, more is the pity."

"There!" said Screwe. "Where is Rutherford—I mean the duke? If he were not a guilty man, why would he run away? Looks to me like he left poor Delacroix to take the blame and stole off."

But by now no one was really attending Screwe, for the doctor was arriving, followed shortly by two men from Bow Street. The priest exerted his authority and ushered everyone but family out of the sanctuary, so that the doctor might have quiet for his examination.

Tilly stood by DeGroen, awaiting the determination which she knew was inevitable. She wished she could run out those doors and escape. She wanted more than anything to be certain that Rutherford was not injured. And she wanted to keep him safe from the machinations of Screwe.

CHAPTER 58

Rutherford wished he could sketch Smythe's countenance when he greeted his returning master. The valet permitted himself a sweeping look of despair over the attire of the new duke. This seemed to disturb the fastidious servant more than the contusion on Rutherford's face or the bleeding leg.

Smythe lost his stiff upper lip all together and grasped at his own neck in an unconscious gesture of strangled horror at the completely missing neckcloth.

It was a few moments before the stunned valet could recollect himself. "Shall I have a bath prepared for his grace? Or perhaps some luncheon?"

Rutherford had pity on his faithful servant's nerves. "A bath, a shave, and some fresh clothes would be just the thing. I shall nap while I wait."

When he saw Smythe rally, he added, "This is a house of mourning. I shall wish to wear all black henceforth. I hope you have procured a few mourning garments for me."

Smythe looked quite pleased with himself. "Indeed I have, your grace. They are ready made." His lip curled. "But that is only temporary. The tailors are hard at work on his grace's new wardrobe. And they deigned to make adjustments to the ready made things at first light this morning. So you have a full mourning suit at the ready."

This was not bad for a valet who had only arrived home the night prior. Smythe was clearly enjoying the prestige and power of his position in a duke's household. Rutherford thought that he enjoyed being a duke far less than Smythe enjoyed serving a duke.

When he was refreshed with a little sleep, a little cleaning, and the tender ministrations of Smythe to his bruised face, leg, and toilette, Rutherford did not look half bad.

The black attire made him look older, he thought, as he examined himself in the mirror. Or perhaps he simply was older, now. When he reflected on the Rutherford of one year ago, he could only think of him as a feckless young lad. He did not think the mantle of grief and dukedom was the lone cause of his new gravity.

Yes, properly dressed in the extreme of all black, but the elegance of perfect tailoring, he looked well. Even the wound on his cheekbone gave him distinction. He looked interesting and heroic, rather than shoddy and mad. This was just as well, because he had serious business to attend to.

His lawyer, Mr. Borland, whom Rutherford had summoned, arrived around the same time as his uncle's lawyer did.

When they were all gathered in his study, Rutherford poured them each a brandy. "I am glad you are both here. It will save some time. Mr. Hastings, I assume you have come to discuss the testamentary arrangements of my uncle?"

"Yes, your grace. As I believe your grace is aware, the entail passes to the fifth Duke of Bartholmer as of right. But your grace's late uncle bequeathed his entire estate to you, besides. Here is a list of all the assets."

"Give it to Mr. Borland, if you please."

Mr. Hastings handed over the papers. "There is also the matter of a more recent project undertaken by your uncle. I should like to know if it would please your grace to direct me to continue in its execution."

"What is this project?"

"Put succinctly, his grace wished to procure all the debt anyone held, that was claimable against a certain Lord Screwe."

"Oh yes." Rutherford caught a glance, in the glazing of a dark oak cabinet across from him, of his own merciless smile, framed in the black of mourning. "That is an undertaking I very much wish to continue. In fact, I want you both to expedite it as much as you can. I also want you to use every means at your disposal to make a list of all Lord Screwe's assets. Anything of any value."

When the meeting was over, Rutherford succumbed to the inevitable gravity of rumination. He wondered what Tilly was doing. He should not think about that, but he could not resist. Had they proceeded with the wedding, as planned, despite the shooting? They certainly seemed to be in enough of a hurry for anything.

Or had the disruption been sufficient to delay them? In short, was Tilly still free? A tiny ray of hope, that relentlessly tantalizing but treacherous fairy, pierced the brooding gloom of his heart.

He sprang to his feet, suddenly. Surely he could find out. True, even if all was lost, he did not want her to go on believing what she must believe about him and Mrs. Colling. He called for his carriage.

CHAPTER 59

Tilly was feeling faint as she sat on the hard front pew. It had been a stressful day, and she was half starved.

DeGroen sat next to her, his mother on the other side, staring in concern as the doctor completed his examination. This was entirely pro forma, for Tilly had it from DeGroen that his mother, Grandfather Fowler's eldest daughter, did not care one fig for the old man.

But she managed to muster a single tear to wipe away, as the doctor straightened and said, "I am very sorry to say it, but Mr. Fowler is dead. It is a small comfort, but I believe he died immediately and did not suffer. My condolences to you all upon your loss. Now if you will excuse me I must go speak to the Bow Street runners."

And he was gone. No one was shocked by the announcement, but DeGroen took Tilly's hand and squeezed it. "Poor old man. He did not deserve this violent end."

Tilly nodded and squeezed his hand back. It was not the proclamation of woeful grief that DeGroen's mother was now attempting to feign with the rest of his unfeeling, hypocritical relatives. But it was honest. In his own way, DeGroen was going to miss the old prude. With his grandfather's passing, he had lost the only blood relative that cared for him.

Tilly whispered, "He is receiving his reward for his devotion to God. And do not forget that you have friends who love you as family. You are not alone."

Frederick returned, and the three of them went together to see the men from Bow Street. They each gave a statement and left their cards. Then they made to quit the church.

But Mrs. DeGroen came calling after her son. "My dear!" she said in a voice so obviously without real warmth that it cast a frost over Tilly's back. "You must come with me to help select the casket. We want the best for him. He deserves the very best."

DeGroen did not look at all deceived by her words. He must know, as Tilly certainly did, that the woman was thinking only of working her way back into DeGroen's life so that she might somehow get her long fingers into the purse of the old man's heir.

"I should be very surprised if Grandfather has not already made those arrangements. I shall send a note to the solicitor to see what he knows. But I shall go home now, Mother. You may go look at coffins if it pleases you."

And with that, Frederick, DeGroen and Tilly squeezed into the wedding carriage and made for DeGroen's home—what would by now have been Tilly's home, had events of the morning gone differently.

When they arrived, DeGroen sent off a message summoning his grandfather's solicitor. Tilly exchanged her wedding dress for something from her trousseau. She was too stunned even to remark what. And Frederick set about ordering a meal and fetching them all champagne.

Tilly and DeGroen drooped as they sat down to luncheon. She felt as grey as the clouds that drizzled over London, casting a gloomy air through the dining room window.

"Drink your champagne, you two silly creatures! Do not be so dreary! True, it has been a hell of a day, but things are not so bad."

DeGroen tilted his head and looked at Frederick in disbelief.

"Do not look at me like that. Neither one of you especially liked the old man. I am sure he grew on you, but frankly, I can bear witness that his strictures have been a constant topic of mockery and complaint."

"Frederick," Tilly tried to rein in her brother's glib babble, "think how DeGroen must feel, and do not run on so."

"Oh!" Frederick was not to be repressed. "I do not mean to speak ill of the dead, but you know it is true. And a quick death must be better than the lingering suffering of illness and old age. Yes, yes, I know it is very indecent of me to speak the truth on such an occasion, but no one ought to feel sorry for the old gaffer. He died in church, a boon his heart probably never dared hope for, and he died in the happy estate of watching his heir marry."

"Well, you are right about that much. He is happy." DeGroen's spirits seemed to lift. He even raised a glass to meet Frederick's, and drank his champagne.

Tilly did not drink any more wine. Her stomach, though it had earlier been complaining of hunger, became unsteady now that it was being fed. It quailed at the thought of anything stronger than a cup of tea.

"I think the question that none of us is mentioning, but must hang upon all our minds, is *what now?*" DeGroen mused.

"I think you mean, *shall you and I now wed?*" Tilly put up her hand to ward off Frederick's offer of more champagne in her untouched glass.

DeGroen nodded. "Precisely. But I suppose we will know more when we speak to the solicitor."

"Still, it will look very, very odd if we do not wed, after all this. I mean, Frederick is married now, so I suppose that much is taken care of. But if you, to put it indelicately, make off with your inheritance and leave me in the lurch, what will people think?"

"I suppose they would think me a villain." DeGroen's lips curled. "But what of it? The rich never suffer for their villainy, real or imagined."

Frederick laughed and the two toasted again, drinking deeply to this bit of truth.

DeGroen continued. "I would only be too happy to jilt you, my darling. My dearest wish is to abandon you and make off with my ill-gotten wealth so that you might marry the Duke of Bartholmer. And all the ton would approve your stellar recovery from such a crushing blow as letting me evade your grasp." He chuckled darkly. "Well, at least publicly. Privately the ton would gnash their teeth in bitter mistrust of your good fortune and in anger that their nastiest darts of scandal had been blunted."

Tilly pursed her lips in distaste. "No doubt. But it seems Rutherford has other ideas. I believe his heart may be elsewhere engaged."

"Impossible!" Frederick and DeGroen said it together, then laughed merrily at themselves.

Tilly was glad someone was happy. Her stomach churned. "Oh God!" She ran from the room.

She made it to her chamber and was sick. Her nerves were getting the better of her, she supposed.

After some time, Frederick tapped and called though the door. "Tiddly? I am sorry if I distressed you with my glibness, darling. Is there anything I can do?"

Tilly opened the door. "Oh Frederick, do you not know that I am quite accustomed to your stupid way of going on?" She smiled at him, and he looked relieved. "I have just been sick."

"Sick?" He squinted at her. "My Tiddly? That is unheard of. Well come along, if you are all done with that nasty business, and wait with me in the parlour. DeGroen is talking to his solicitor, and I don't suppose we can get away with eavesdropping by the office door."

When the solicitor left, DeGroen had a dazed look.

Tilly and Frederick watched his face, waiting for some explanation.

Frederick finally huffed. "Out with it, man! What news?"

"The best news." DeGroen shook his head as if trying to wake himself from a dream. "My grandfather did not merely change the will. He transferred everything to me while he was still living, though he asked the solicitor to delay notice to me. All the residue in the estate is also to be mine, though nothing remains in it except a collection of old bibles."

Tilly gasped. "So…"

"So, with your usual deft cunning, you have narrowly escaped marrying one of the richest men in England, sister." Frederick was grinning as he made for the bell-pull beside Tilly. "This calls for more champagne!"

Tilly managed a smile before falling in a dead faint.

CHAPTER 60

A fit of nerves seized Rutherford, as his carriage pulled up at DeGroen's home.

What was he doing? What sort of idiot went to the home of his rival to congratulate him on stealing away the only woman he could ever love?

A noble idiot. Rutherford laughed bitterly at his own reply. The same sort of idiot that sat in his carriage having conversations with himself, instead of getting on with the task at hand.

He took up his bouquet and stepped out into the rain, eschewing the offered umbrella and instructing his men to carry the crate of champagne to the servants' entrance.

The door was answered by a very merry looking butler, who took his card and his bouquet, and ushered him into the entry room.

"My men are delivering my gift to the happy couple around back. I hope you will deliver these flowers, with my compliments. I know my coming at such a time is unpardonable, but I should like to request five minutes of Mr. DeGroen's time, if he would oblige me."

"My lord," the man straightened his spine to look sharp, "I am afraid the master is not to home."

Rutherford did not bother to correct the man about his title. His card still bore the style of the Earl of Drake. There was no point in scaring the servant further. "Do you expect him back soon? May I wait?"

"I cannot say when he will return. I know he will be very sorry to have missed such a distinguished caller. But we have sadly had a death in the family, my lord." The man looked very properly sombre. "He and Mrs. DeGroen have gone to make final arrangements for Mr. Fowler."

He and Mrs. DeGroen. There was the answer Rutherford had dreaded. He stepped backward as though he had been struck, rubbing his shoulder.

The servant looked concerned. "Forgive me, my lord, for my careless abruptness. I had no idea that Mr. Fowler was an acquaintance. May I order a restorative for your lordship?" The man quickly retrieved a chair from the far wall.

"No. Thank you. I shall be well," Rutherford croaked, as his last hope trickled out of him. "Only give the happy couple my sincerest felicitations."

Then, not waiting for the door to be opened for him, he bolted from the house.

CHAPTER 61

When Tilly awakened from her faint, she was laid out on a chaise longue. DeGroen was holding her hand, and Frederick was wafting smelling salts under her nose.

It all came back to her. She was free. Nothing but appearances kept her bound to this engagement. And appearances could be managed.

"All right. Enough. I am well." Tilly sat up. "Odd. I never faint."

"True." Frederick nodded, jiggling her arm as he was wont to do. "A bit prone to fits of arm waving, but definitely not the fainting type."

"Must have been the prospect of all that money slipping through your fingers." DeGroen smirked.

Tilly rolled her eyes and slapped Frederick's hand away from her arm, as she replied to DeGroen. "A wiser woman might pay double your fortune, just to be rid of you."

DeGroen grasped his heart as if mortally stabbed. "Do not let the fainting spell fool you, Freddy. She is still as much of a termagant as ever."

Frederick laughed. "You know you might want to take this fainting business up as an accomplishment, dear sister. You do it so elegantly."

"True." DeGroen joined in. "You grabbed the bell pull as you fell. That might never be fixed. And you kicked over the blue urn. It was not so much a faint as a falling paroxysm of destruction. Neatly done, darling."

Tilly shook her head. She knew nothing would keep DeGroen down for long. It was nice to see him merry again. "You are in a good mood. I suppose the fact that you shall be free of me agrees with you."

DeGroen gave her a wicked smile. "Not at all, darling. I could always set you up as a mistress."

Tilly laughed for a long time. "That, as Crump would say, would be about as much use to you as a teat on a bull ox."

"Not so, not so! Think of my credit as a distinguished man about town. A *carte blanche* or two would be just the thing."

Just then Mrs. DeGroen was announced.

DeGroen screwed his features into a pained look. "She wants to make everything up to her rich son by assisting with funeral arrangements for the father that she loathed. Lord, I have to get out of this town."

"And I have to get out of this parlour. Good luck, DeGroen." Tilly ran for the door. She did not wish to be forced into company with that horrid, tedious woman.

"But what about the Bow Street lads?" Frederick enquired.

"Hang them!" Tilly called behind her as she dashed away. Whatever questions they had would keep until tomorrow. She had to go see Rutherford.

It was probably pointless, and it would be humiliating to throw herself at him like some desperate, cast off strumpet, but she had to try. She owed their love that one attempt. And moreover, she owed herself the gift of extinguishing the poisonous little taper of *what if?* before its fumes choked her.

She did not wish to become some hand-wringing old maid, haunting windows that only afforded views of the past. Maybe he loved another, but if he did, she would pick up the pieces of her heart and try to get on with things. However, if it had been a mere dalliance… could she not forgive him that?

As she made to step into her carriage, the scent from the sachet wafted out. She stopped. "God no." The odour of roses brought a fresh wave of nausea over her.

"No roses." She swallowed and stepped back. "Bring around one of the unmarked carriages, but hang up some lemon sachets." She heaved a quavering sigh at the debasement of it all. "And put a bucket in it."

CHAPTER 62

Rutherford stood a stone's throw from Tilly's warehouse, eyeing the door where the smoky lads had hung about when he made his last desperate visit.

The area did not smell any better, but the last rays of the sun made it less shadowy. And there were fewer urchins now. Just several large men, who were clearly standing guard.

He doubted Tilly had halted her sales entirely, but perhaps she was already in the process of changing over her business to integrate with her projected clinics.

He smiled, then frowned when he recognized the stupid hypocrisy of that smile. Tilly had changed for the better, and for his sake. She was moving forward. But here he was back at the same place, and for the same reason.

Only now all was lost. He had lost.

That's true, said an insidious little voice inside of him, *but there is comfort to be had. You do not need to feel any of this. It can all go away.*

He hated the voice, but a small part of him loved the promise, longed for the blissful oblivion. And another, larger part wanted to punish himself. Wanted to lower himself into the gutter where he belonged.

He took a few steps back. No. This was not what he wanted. If he needed a distraction, he would find a purposeful one. He rubbed his scar. Losing Tilly was a torment, but it would be so much worse to sully the memory of their love by betraying her trust.

He had promised her to stop. He would keep his word.

He kicked a stone. No, it was not just that little manifestation of honour that subsisted on the promise kept. It was the very well-spring of honour that was at stake. If a man could not take his proper pride in both hands and say that he did right because it was right, not because of any other benefit or obligation, what sort of man was he?

A man without true honour. True honour was not transient. It was not a commodity to be bargained for with punishments or inducements.

Rutherford would walk away from this place, from this poison, and he would do it because he owed it to himself. Not to Tilly. Not to the memory of his uncle. To his own essential nature, to his pride of character, to his honour.

And all honour aside, his basic self-interest also demanded abstinence. He never wanted to be sick like that again. He would feel his broken heart, focus on the tasks before him, distract himself with exercise, and get well again. He had the will and he would do it, damn it all!

He shook his head at his own foolishness. What was he doing here? He was about to return to his carriage when a blow to the back of his skull made the world go grey.

CHAPTER 63

It was risky, calling at Rutherford's front door again. Tilly had hunted down Mrs. Carlton at her parents' house, so that much countenance she had. But showing up on his front stoop, on the day when her wedding had halted for a murder of which Rutherford was suspected? That could not be interpreted favourably —not if she had a half dozen chaperones. What of the Bow Street investigation? And worse, what of the gossip?

Tilly surprised herself by not really caring anymore. She was too tired, too disordered, too sick, too broken-hearted, and if the gossips had something to say, they would say it. Evidence was hardly necessary, anyway.

"I am sorry. His grace is not to home." Smythe looked even more above his company than usual.

And this was only his first day as head servant to a duke. Tilly feared that in a year's time he would be intolerable. She decided to loosen his lips with a little white lie. "I had understood that I was to meet his grace here. Perhaps I was mistaken."

Faced with the prospect of displeasing his master by turning away a person whom the duke had particularly summoned, Smythe capitulated. "I do not know when his grace will return, but you may wait in the parlour, if you will, Mrs. DeGroen. I shall have the fire made up."

Tilly froze. He had called her Mrs. DeGroen. Was he just surmising, or did Rutherford think she had married today, too? Could Rutherford imagine that she had just lifted her silken hem to kick the old man's corpse aside, and then, pounding on the pulpit for order, demanded that the priest continue, as if nothing had happened?

She could almost laugh at the image, but she was not in the mood.

Indeed, Rutherford might think her that heartless. She had certainly done her best to persuade him she was marrying for money, and that nothing would stop her.

"I am afraid I am not *Mrs. DeGroen*. I am still just Miss Ravelsham."

He bowed his head. "I beg your pardon for the mistake, Miss."

"Not at all. It is quite understandable. May I enquire whether his grace was also labouring under this false impression?"

"He may have mentioned it, Miss." It was not until then that the look of concern upon Smythe's face caught Tilly's attention.

She threw caution to the wind. "Did his grace say where he was going?"

"He did not." Smythe's face was now a beacon of worry.

"Thank you. I cannot stay." She returned to the door.

"He took the Bartholmer carriage." Smythe tried to look like he had not murmured the words, as he saw her out.

Well, that would narrow it down. But she was already forming a surmise. She would look first in the place where she most hoped he would not be.

CHAPTER 64

When Rutherford came to his senses, he was lying on a comfortable bed with a quilted-topped down duvet, behind the bars of a dimly lit cell. He lifted his hurting head to look around.

A large man was making up a fire in the adjoining chamber, his back turned. Rutherford looked around to see if he might slip free. The iron-barred door had monstrous large lock. There was nothing he might use as a weapon. He slumped back in despair.

The man heard him stirring, and turned to face him. It was Crump.

"You ruddy bastard!" Rutherford sprang to his feet. "I should have dispatched your worthless soul when I had the chance."

Crump sighed. "I reckon there hain't much point in talk. I have my orders, and talk won't change 'em."

Rutherford did not accept this dismissal. "I am glad for this much, that you are showing your true colours. Miss Ravelsh—Mrs. DeGroen will at least be taken in by you no longer."

A strange look passed over the man's broad face. He seemed to be contemplating something, but then thought the better of it. He planted himself in a chair by a small table, apparently resolved to keep his own counsel.

Rutherford found this calm snub extremely provoking. "You must work cheaper than I had guessed, for Delacroix cannot have two farthings to jingle. Indeed, I am surprised to see such an elaborate dungeon—especially when it is patrolled by such a low-rate yahoo."

The man still said nothing, but calmly opened a book on the table, picked up a pencil and began to work at something.

"Well, now I am astonished! Does the great lummox pretend to write? Indeed, his no-count little worm of a master has furnished him with paper for this pantomime of literacy? This is a wonder."

Crump persisted in his labour. Rutherford thought he should try a different tack. "I do not suppose anyone told you that I am now the Duke of Bartholmer."

The man turned a page in the book and continued his work.

"You are slow-witted, so let me explain to you what that means. You see, when the authorities know what you have done, I will finally see you locked up. You might even hang for this, Crump. And there will be no hiding behind a good lady's need to protect her own reputation by concealing your crime. This time, you will pay. And believe me, I will have my pound of flesh."

Crump suddenly stood up.

Rutherford saw that a figure had entered the room while he was delivering this last tirade. He blinked.

Mr. DeGroen, dressed in black mourning, held up his hands in surrender as he approached the bars. "I hope you will not include me in your wrath, your grace. I am only here to rescue you. But before I let you out, I need you to promise me that you will not attack, Mr. Crump. He was only following orders."

"I will not attack him." Rutherford did not like the confused sound in his own voice. What was going on? Was DeGroen somehow tangled up with Delacroix? "But pray, who has given these orders? Surely not you."

DeGroen chuckled. "Oh no, not me. Can you not guess, your grace? Who is the master of this man?"

"Not Til—not your wife." The correction was bitter.

"No, not my wife. But yes, Tilly."

"You are speaking in riddles." What could he possibly mean? Was Rutherford still unconscious and just having some sort of bizarre nightmare?

Mr. DeGroen walked to retrieve the key from a hook on the wall. "Mr. Crump, will you leave us? I know you were following orders, but I assure you, Miss Ravelsham does not wish Rutherford to remain locked up. I have dispatched a message to her, and I am certain you will be hearing from her soon. You may guard the door until you have word from her, if you wish. The duke and I have much to discuss."

CHAPTER 65

Tilly felt quite awful as she rolled up to the warehouse, but at least she had not been sick again. Then she stepped out of her carriage and into the disgusting stink of the local air. She had forgotten how bad it smelled in this area. Tilly lunged back into the carriage and tore down the lemon sachet, clutching it to her nose and mouth. She did not have time to be sick.

She scampered through the gloom to the back entrance, not knowing even what to hope for.

On the one hand, she wished to be proven wrong in her suspicion. She hoped that Rutherford, after all that had happened, had not lost his resolve to be free and succumbed to the deadly siren-call of the drug.

On the other hand, her warehouses were not the only place one could procure it. He could as easily go to an apothecary, though there was an even greater shortage now that she was tightening down on her distribution. Or he could find his way to one of the nasty opium dens that had sprung up around London. And, if he went out seeking the poison, it would be much better that he came here.

At least she would know exactly where he was. Crump would have him in the hidden cell. She rubbed her temple. The situation would require some explaining, but that was nothing. She did not even mind if he was angry with her, so long as he was safe.

She laughed mockingly at herself. "So much for your great commitment to free will, Tilly. You are just like everyone else. You do what is expedient and you find a justification for it later."

And yet, she did not feel repentant. He was safe, and to the devil with everything else. That is, unless he had gone somewhere else. Her stomach knotted at the thought.

She unlocked the door to the office and released her breath in a gasp of relief when she saw Crump standing watch by the large painting that hid the secret door.

CHAPTER 66

Rutherford paced the little prison room with a manic energy. "You can stop calling me *your grace*, DeGroen. We shall speak man to man, if you please."

"Very well." DeGroen was seated in the chair previously occupied by Crump, looking at the papers over which Crump had laboured. "He is coming along rather well. I have to say, Tilly was right about him."

"What?" It took Rutherford a moment to realize what DeGroen had said. "So, Tilly has been teaching the oaf how to write?"

He nodded. "She started off with reading. I have to admire Tilly's vision for humanity. She even makes a better person out of me."

"And she really gave him orders to lock me up here, if I should show up at the warehouse again?"

"I am afraid so."

"How did you know about all this?" What he really wanted to know was whether she had told DeGroen of his dependency on laudanum.

"I was there when she gave Crump the order. She did not discuss her reasons with me. I assumed they were good ones."

Rutherford winced at the truth of this, but there was no judgement in DeGroen's voice. "So you knew about her business here?"

DeGroen shrugged. "I know about all of Tilly's businesses. Frederick is my closest friend, and they are in all these ventures together, though she has the better head for business. But she is also too honourable to keep it secret from me. You see, she knew that my grandfather was a stickler for what he called 'good moral character.' Tilly wanted me to have full knowledge of the risk involved in marrying her, should Grandfather Fowler ever find out about her enterprises."

"And you might as well know…" DeGroen swallowed as he met Rutherford's gaze. "You might as well know that I have always known about you."

"About me?" Rutherford paused in his pacing.

"About your affair. It is amazing to me that you did not sort it out for yourself, but our projected marriage was not a love match. Tilly was trying to help me and she was willing to look like a fortune-hunter to do it."

Rutherford smiled. That was Tilly to a tittle. "I suppose it was hard for me to believe that anyone could be so lucky as to be engaged to Tilly and not be madly in love with her."

DeGroen chuckled. "I quite agree. And I do love Tilly. But there were other reasons why she was helping me… In short we love each other almost as a brother and sister, because," he gave emphasis to the words, "her brother and I are so close."

Rutherford squinted at DeGroen. His smile grew broader as understanding descended upon him like an angel of deliverance. He was speechless for a few moments. "I see. Well, I have been a blind idiot then, have I not?"

"Well..." DeGroen lifted his shoulders and tilted his head equivocally. "On the other hand, Rutherford, we were quite discreet enough. And Frederick is a married man, you know."

Rutherford chuckled. "Also arranged by Tilly, or so Aldley informs me. She is quite the little schemer, our Tilly." He met DeGroen's eye as he said these words.

They shared a look of fondness, and DeGroen said, "Yes, *our Tilly* is ever a schemer for a good cause. And it speaks very well of you that you can admire it in her."

"I love it in her, DeGroen. I love everything about her. She is the most fascinating woman I have ever met. She is an utter adventuress, but she has a heart of gold—no, more precious than gold. Tilly's heart is made out of the same stuff as angels' halos."

DeGroen laughed at this poetical effusion. "A devil's ingenuity anchored to an angel's heart. One wonders what God was thinking when He crafted that charming little hypocrite."

Rutherford's voice was dreamy and awe-filled. "He was thinking of me."

DeGroen inclined his head.

Rutherford's heart soared. She was perfect for him. And she was free. He leapt to DeGroen's side to shake his hand. "You are a good sort, DeGroen. A jolly decent fellow. And I am sorry for any ill-tempered thing I ever said about you."

DeGroen's lips twitched as he returned the handshake. "Likewise, Rutherford."

"Now I must go find her!" Rutherford made for the door.

"Wait!" DeGroen called him back. "I know you are anxious. But Crump is still on the other side of that door. Do you really want yet another altercation at this happy moment? He is only following Tilly's orders. Besides, I have not yet told you how I knew I would find you here."

Rutherford halted abruptly. That was quite true.

"I only bring it up because I mean to caution you before you go bolting off to find Tilly."

"Caution me?"

DeGroen held up a hand. "Let me explain. When I arrived home from making some last arrangements for my grandfather—"

"Oh yes." Rutherford was contrite. "My condolences. Forgive me for not offering them earlier."

DeGroen nodded impatiently. "Thank you. As I was saying, when I returned home, my servant advised me that you had been there, and that he had told you I had left with *Mrs. DeGroen*. He meant my mother, of course. But I was quite certain that you would have drawn a different inference."

Rutherford nodded.

"Tilly had gone back to her parents' house. She seemed to be labouring under the belief that you loved another." DeGroen's face betrayed no condemnation.

But Rutherford certainly condemned himself for this. He sighed. "It is not so—"

"Yes, I am quite sure of it. But I took it upon myself to lay the misunderstanding, at least as regards Tilly and I, to rest once and for all. So I went to your house. You had just left, and your servant did not know where you had gone. However, I noticed a dirty little smudge of an urchin lingering about in the shadows, so I decided to question him."

"Really?" A suspicion formed in Rutherford's mind. "And what was his business there?"

"He was so frightened that it took five quid to bring me into his confidence, but it seemed he was hired by Screwe to watch you."

"The filthy spying bastard!"

"Indeed. But to sum things up, the child had overheard your directions to the driver, and had already dispatched a message to notify Screwe. So thither went I to seek you out. But I suspect Screwe will be somewhere nearby by now."

Rutherford sprang back into action. "But do you not see, DeGroen? If you sent a message to Tilly, she will come here, and Screwe will be watching. I must go protect her!"

Rutherford flew to the door just as it opened to reveal Tilly, all dressed in black and peering out at him from under her veil with anxious eyes.

CHAPTER 67

Tilly looked from DeGroen to Rutherford as confusion, then relief, spread over her.

Her smile was tentative. "I see you have not been fighting. That is one good thing, I guess."

"Tilly." Rutherford's hand reached out to clasp hers, and her heart thudded madly in her chest.

There was so much remorse in his eyes mingled with the affection there. Was he about to tell her that everything had changed, that he was now in love with the sumptuous Widow Colling? And yet, if that were true, would he not be happy? Why would he have been driven to visit Tilly's warehouse?

"Ahem." DeGroen's assumed look of aloof amusement was a poor disguise for the happiness in his eyes as he looked at her. "I shall leave you two to talk. But before I go," he bent in and kissed Tilly's cheek, "consider yourself jilted, darling. I've got my money and have no intention of interrupting my amusements by anchoring myself down to a wife, especially one so drearily virtuous."

"Who knew you were such a scoundrel?" Tilly laughed. She actually felt tears forming in her eyes at DeGroen's goodness. When had she become such a weepy little ninny? But still, she was deeply impressed by his chivalry. He was going to make himself out to be a black-hearted infidel, in order to preserve her reputation.

"I believe Rutherford had some inkling of my scoundrelly ways. Which is why I have little doubt that he will console you in your hour of bitterest heartbreak, and some day, who knows what lovely blossom might spring forth from the root of such chaste compassion?"

Tilly could not quite formulate her feelings at this suggestion before Mr. DeGroen, with a wink, slipped through the door and left them alone.

Rutherford's eyes were burning when she turned to look at him again. "My love, Mr. DeGroen has told me all, and..."

"So you understand why I insisted upon the engagement? Oh, William —" She wrinkled her nose. "Would it be acceptable if I just call you Rutherford? I cannot quite get used to William."

He laughed and nodded.

She continued. "It pained me not to tell you, but how could I share a secret that was not mine to tell?"

"I understand, my darling. And I admire you for your heart, for your resolve to help your loved ones, no matter how bad it made you appear, no matter what it cost you."

"And yet, when I began... that is when you and I became entangled, I thought it would be a safe enough affair. DeGroen had bid me to enjoy myself, and I believed your knowledge of my engagement would shield you from giving me your heart. True, I even believed that your professions of love were only part of a seductive art of dalliance at which you had great practice. If only I had known..."

"Then I am glad you did not. For all this—even the mistakes—it has all led us here." He pressed her hand to his lips. "Tell me that you love me, dearest Tilly. My heart is yours. It will never love any other."

Tilly's heart was overflowing in the tears streaming down her cheeks. She hated crying, but in the moment, she simply could not help herself. And yet, she had to know. "And what of Mrs. Colling?" Tilly knew she sounded bitter.

Rutherford's face was so full of pain and shame that Tilly dreaded what he would say. But his beautiful lips formed the words, "What you saw was not an act of passion. We were squabbling like two children over a token of my uncle's life, of our last moments with him. I would laugh at how ridiculous I made myself, if I were not so ashamed of how I behaved toward Mrs. Colling. I was out of my head with grief, but she was suffering too. She certainly did not deserve such treatment. But I have no other feeling for her than this regret and contrition."

Tilly's smile could not stop her tears, but a warmth spread over her when Rutherford pulled her close to him.

"There is no room in my heart for anyone else. I love you. Now admit that you love me." He slipped down to her waist suddenly and hiked up her skirts, then stood to press himself against her mound. "Do not make me resort to special measures to extract your confession."

"Well." She gasped as he began to play with her with his finger. "You are dressed blackly enough to be a high inquisitor." She moaned with pleasure as he found her pearl and massaged it. "Oh, how I love you. But I still want you to extract that confession."

"Well," he gave her a wicked look, "how else will I know that you are telling the truth?"

Then he hefted her up in his arms and carried her to the bed in the prison cell, laying her down gently and stripping off her clothing, and his own.

She assisted him in this process, impatient to feel his skin, to see his rippling muscles and his beautiful manhood.

When all their mourning clothes had been cast aside, he kissed her deeply and ran his fingers lightly over her breasts, making them yearn after more until the nipples began to harden.

Then he took a nipple in his mouth, sucking and stroking it with his tongue, which threw her into such a feeling of happy submission that all she could do was moan, "Oh yes!"

She felt his erect cock slide closer to her quim. It was hot and hard like freshly forged iron. "Is that a red hot poker?" She smiled mischievously at him.

"Oh yes. And you will feel its brand." His gaze was searing through her. She could feel herself getting wet. "But first, I have another line of inquiry."

He dropped down and began to lick her pearl mercilessly, massaging her inside with his finger as he did it, stroking and stroking until she thought she could not hold back any longer.

Then he raised himself back up and kissed her deeply again, so she could taste her own body on his tongue. She groaned with longing. "Oh, give me the rod, Inquisitor!"

He leaned back and looked at her, his face deadly serious, his massive organ throbbing and almost glowing with his heat. He was silent as he lifted her hips and thrust his cock into her.

She gasped, and he held it there for a moment, watching her eyes dilate. Then he withdrew and pushed into her more deeply, leaning over her body and kissing her as he thrust into her over and over.

The pleasure mounted in her. More, she wanted more, and his passionate strokes came harder and faster until she screamed with pleasure. He clasped her hips and pulled himself so deep inside her.

She could feel him spasming with an ecstasy that matched her own, as his hot seed spread within her in trembling waves.

Then they both lay back, panting.

After she had caught her breath she said, "How I love you, my stallion."

"Well, I believe you." He was still breathing heavily. "But I like to be thorough in my inquisitorial examinations, you know."

She smiled her invitation as she saw his member growing hard again. Then she spread her legs and said. "Oh, I am ready for the rod, Inquisitor. For my soul's sake, you must not spare me."

"I shall show you no mercy," he growled.

CHAPTER 68

When they had put their clothes back on, Rutherford hugged Tilly close to his heart. "In situations such as these, it has become something of a tradition to ask you to marry me. And now you are free." He grinned. "Would you object to a proposal within the walls of your own prison chamber?"

Tilly thought for a moment. "Not at all. I think if one is to be shackled for life, a prison chamber is quite apropos."

"Well then." He dropped to one knee and placed her hand over his heart. "Will you be my wife, Tilly?"

"You will not try to take away my freedom, and make me do dull little screen covering projects to fill my time instead of trying to help humanity?"

Rutherford laughed. "I should have known this would be a negotiation. But let me assure you, dearest, most adorable of women, that I will not try to put a stop to any of your strange ventures. In fact, I think the two of us might work together for good. You make me want to be a better man, Tilly."

Her smirking mouth turned more serious. His heart caught in his throat as she looked at him with adoring eyes. "You have already made me a better woman, Rutherford. And you make me want to improve myself, too. You have challenged me, made me think about and question what I do more than you can realize."

"So does that mean *yes*, my love?"

"Are you sure you do not wish to change me?"

"I only wish to change your last name." His gaze was intense and expectant.

"Very well, then. Yes, I will be your wife." Her smile was radiant with love.

He gave a hoorah of joy and sprang up, lifting her in the air and kissing her. "You have made me so very happy, my darling duchess."

"Ooh." Tilly put a hand to her waist. "Be careful. My stomach has been a bit queasy. It only just settled down—do you know, I think the inquisition had a calming effect." Even in illness, her face still shone with a wicked smile.

Rutherford looked concerned and gently placed her back on her feet. "I am sorry, darling. But are you very ill?"

"It is nothing to worry about. If you think of all that has transpired today, I suppose I should be entitled to a nervous stomach."

"Quite true. Well, shall I escort you home? We are engaged now, after all." He wiggled his eyebrows. "And my carriage is quite spacious."

"I prefer my own carriage. It is less conspicuous. And we must consider how best to manage the news of our engagement, for you know Screwe will be trying to cast as evil a light on us as ever he can."

"Screwe." Rutherford had completely forgotten DeGroen's warning. "It slipped my mind, but he has been watching my house, and DeGroen tells me that Screwe knows I came here."

"Then we should definitely take my carriage. It is by the back entrance, which Screwe is unlikely to know about."

"True, and my carriage is some distance down the street. Near a tackle warehouse, I believe. I suppose I did not want anyone to know I was here."

Tilly gave him a concerned look.

"Tilly, you have not asked me about it, but I want to tell you. I did come here in a black moment, but I had already decided to leave again. Then Crump clouted my head."

Her eyes narrowed. "He struck you? I never told him to—"

"But how else was he to get me in here with the least injury to me and to him? For you know I should have fought him."

A funny look came over Tilly's face. "Are you defending Crump?"

"Will you stop changing the subject and let me finish? What I was saying is, I made a decision before I was knocked senseless. It was not just to keep my promise to you. I turned away from the drug for my own sake."

She hugged him tightly. "I am so glad to hear that, my beloved stallion. That is the very best reason. It means you have turned a new page in your life."

He traced a finger around the beautiful little devilish curve to her lips. His heart was so full. They would make a new life together. They would bring joy under the roof of Blackwood Manor, and he liked to believe that his uncle would be watching over them, pleased. Together they would work for the good of humankind.

"And what a happy, happy page it is." He took her hand. "But I suppose we must leave before we can make a fresh start."

When they emerged from the secret chamber. Crump and DeGroen were playing cards.

Crump looked from Tilly to Rutherford, then nodded to himself in approval. An hour prior, this presumption would have irritated Rutherford, but now he was surprised to find that it did not.

"There you finally are!" said DeGroen. "I am glad you two sorted things out before Crump here reduced me to poverty. So, am I to congratulate you, Rutherford?"

Rutherford beamed. "Indeed. The woman you have jilted has agreed to make me the happiest of men. Now we just need to get out of here, preferably without Screwe's detection."

"Yes, about that. It seems he has been spotted skulking about the place. One of the lads came to report it to Crump. But he has gone back to station himself outside the warehouse down the road, where your carriage is."

"Hah! That was a bit of luck!"

"Then it is settled. We shall take my carriage and go the back way." Tilly looked charmingly animated by the intrigue. "Mr. Crump, will you wait until we are gone, then get a message to Rutherford's driver that he may return home? It would be unkind to leave him waiting there all night."

"True." Rutherford rubbed the bruise on his cheek. "Though I do owe Screwe repayment on several grudges. I admit that the thought of leaving that bounder to wait all night for my return is tempting."

But Rutherford had much better plans for Lord Screwe. That piece of filth would rue the day he had ever tried to harm the woman that Rutherford loved. "What is it that he wants from you, Tilly?"

"I will explain it all in the carriage. Only now, let us go."

When they were alone in the vehicle, Rutherford drew Tilly into his lap and kissed her. What a strange day it had been. What started with despair had ended with the pinnacle of bliss. He enfolded her in his arms and dreamed of their future together.

CHAPTER 69

Tilly sat in her brother's breakfast room, trying not to let the horrifically clashing décor make her ill again. Genevieve's taste had not improved.

Frederick winced when he strode in to greet her. "God. I never get used to this hellish jumble." He kissed the top of Tilly's head. "It makes my eyes hurt."

"It makes me want to cast up my accounts." She placed a hand on her stomach.

He laughed. "Not that anyone would notice if you did. The servants would probably just take it for the most recent instalment of Genevieve's aesthetic genius. But are you really still sick, Tiddly?"

"I can't seem to shake it. And the smell of roses, or anything at all unpleasant just makes it worse. I do not think I shall ever be able to return to the warehouse."

"Well, that can easily be managed, particularly with the new direction you are taking with the business. I am glad about that, frankly."

"As am I. But speaking of business, how did your discussion at the club with *The Queen of Cups* go?"

"It was very enlightening. But I feel like a great idiot that you had to suggest it to me. Honestly, what is the point of running the sort of club we run, if it is not to have access to… well let us say, those sorts of ideas and accommodations?"

"Well, there is also the money, and the satisfaction of giving people a degree of liberty in their anonymous sport. But to be honest, Frederick, I have lost interest in it. Even the masquerade balls now seem dreary to me. I want to focus my efforts on a more worthy cause."

"More worthy than liberty?"

"I want to work for real liberty. The sort of liberty that permits rich people to amuse themselves as they like without detection is such a pale representation of true liberty, that I laugh at myself for ever thinking I was doing something noble." Tilly stood and walked about the room to relieve her stomach from the discomfort of sitting.

"So what is your vision for *real liberty*, then?" Frederick's voice was gently mocking.

Tilly knew this was out of a habit of teasing and not any real derision. She gave him an arch look in return. "I want to work to end slavery."

Frederick whistled. "You do not think small, Tilly. I will grant you that."

"But I *have* been thinking small, and a bit meanly, I must confess. And I have ignored my own sins. But anyway, what I meant to ask of you is whether you would take over the club and the enhanced membership? It cannot be managed by just anyone, you know."

"No. Quite true. But Tiddly, I simply cannot. I meant to tell you right away. I have conspired with DeGroen to come up with a scheme. Genevieve and I will make a lengthy trip to the continent. Then DeGroen will leave a day later, which will put the truth to his rumoured intention to jilt you now that he has his money. He has been spreading that all over town, you know."

Tilly nodded. "I thought as much. It explains some of the pitying looks I have received. And some ladies of the ton, whom I barely know, have made a point of calling on me just to see what they can find out. That I could do without."

"Well, you will not have to endure it long. When DeGroen bolts for the continent, no one will be in any further doubt about who the wronged party was. Then we three will all meet up in France and wander about having a jolly good time. And when we return in several months, you will be a duchess, and with any luck, on the way to becoming an aunt."

Tilly's brows sprang up. "So you have persuaded Genevieve to try the, um, accommodation?"

He gave a bewildered laugh and nodded. "I do not know where you found that girl, Tilly. I mean she is self-absorbed and somewhat indifferent to the feelings of others, and she has atrocious taste, though she loves to put on airs, but she is no prude. And her single-mindedness, once she has seized upon an objective, makes her extremely flexible about what means she uses to accomplish it. She is truly ruthless. I am almost afraid of her. She would be a bit like you, if she were kinder."

"I am not sure, dear brother, whether to be affronted by the comparison, or grateful for its qualification. But really, you cannot be entirely surprised, can you? Look at Delacroix. Though Genevieve is more clever."

"Oh and her brother is definitely on her mind. She thinks a trip to the continent is just the thing. She is quite anxious to escape the shadow of infamy that her brother has cast over her family." He laughed. "Is that not marvellous? I mean we all know she has aided and abetted him in his past crimes. I almost find her hypocrisy endearing."

Tilly smiled. "I know what you mean. Has the mother finally given Delacroix over?"

"Genevieve says she has not. She even visits him in gaol."

Tilly sighed. More of that undying maternal devotion. When did a virtue become a vice? "Well, I suppose that makes it easier for Genevieve to quit London."

"Oh, she is more than enthusiastic. We cannot leave quickly enough for her. And do you know, she has even taken quite a liking to DeGroen? For now that we cannot be seen to be on such friendly terms, she is always asking why he never comes to call, and should we not have him for dinner and cards, and so forth. It is quite odd."

"Not really." Tilly chuckled. "The Delacroix family also have a nose for money. DeGroen is even richer than you."

When Tilly quit her brother's, she went straight home and summoned a doctor. The sick stomach had persisted too long. She needed to know if there were some more serious illness behind it.

When he had completed his examination, the doctor sat down and remained thoughtful for a few moments. Then he said, with the air of a man choosing his words carefully, "Miss Ravelsham, if you were not an unmarried maiden of impeccable character, as you are, I should say that you were in the early stages of being with child."

Tilly's eyebrows shot up, and her mouth hung open. Oh no. A dreadful conviction gripped her, but she could not let the growing realization show upon her features.

"However," he continued, apparently flustered to have so shocked her, "that being impossible, I conclude that you are merely suffering from a stomach complaint. I shall leave a script for some medicine, but I recommend that you avoid rich foods and strong drink, eat small amounts several times per day, and never within two hours of retiring to sleep."

"Thank you. I shall be sure to follow your directions." Tilly grasped at the charade that protected her precarious reputation. This would be just what Screwe needed to exact his revenge.

When the doctor was gone, she collapsed in her chamber. Whatever would she do? She had to tell Rutherford, but how would he react? No. She had to wait. He would be overjoyed, of course, but he would want to marry immediately, and they had to be especially careful of appearances, now that a child was involved.

She sighed. In her heart of hearts she had wanted to have Rutherford's baby for a long time. But now she could not properly enjoy it, because of all the other intrigues in her life.

But in spite of the complication it presented, her heart flooded with joy. They were going to have a child.

She put a tentative hand on the little bulge and smiled happily. Then she whispered, "See here, little baby, you will have a very happy life, if I have anything to say about it. Only for the moment, you must not make your presence known. It is too risky. Help me to keep you safe, and please stop making me so sick."

CHAPTER 70

Rutherford was feeling a strange combination of sadness and nervous energy as he paced in his office. The funeral for his uncle was over, and that good man was interred in the Bartholmer crypt. It was sad, but also affirming in some way. Things had been done properly and Rutherford felt authorized to take up the mantle his uncle had passed and go on with his life.

And yet his life remained in suspension, waiting for the time that he could marry Tilly, or even let the world know of his intention to do so.

He tried to soothe his nervous spirit by fetching Molly and the puppies. The little whelps were getting big and adventurous. He watched them caper and gambol about his office, and smiled at poor little Mick whose long ears always proved an irresistible temptation for the tiny milk teeth of the others. Molly was beginning to be less indulgent of them when they tried to chew on her or chase after her tail.

He sighed bitter-sweetly and patted her head. "Ah Molly, you are wise. You know they must grow up and learn to behave properly. But I cannot help loving their little puppy ways." Then again, it was all very well for him to wax sentimental; it was not *his* tail being nipped.

A servant came to announce Aldley, and moments later Rutherford was greeting him.

"Well," Aldley said, when they were settled with their brandy. "I see Molly's pups are growing fast."

"Are they not, though?" Rutherford felt a surge of pride. "And how is your little darling?"

"She is marvellous. I think she will have her mother's green eyes." Aldley was grinning dreamily. "I have only ever been so smitten once in my life."

Rutherford reached down to rescue his shoe from the teeth of one of the pups. "I can well believe it. I know it is not the same, but I can only imagine how happy a child would make me, when I see how much I love these little hellions of Molly's. Honestly, Aldley, my life, until recently, has been such a series of blows. These puppies have been the little ray of joy that kept me going."

"I believe I know what you mean, at least about the series of blows." Aldley's face was black. "It would be very nice if my wife and I could hold a christening or attend a wedding without someone shooting at her."

"Or at Tilly." Rutherford smiled sardonically. "I do not mean to correct you, old friend, but your wife cannot hoard to herself all the distinction of being the target of a gun-wielding maniac. I have every reason to believe that Screwe arranged Delacroix's bond in exchange for the service of shooting Tilly."

"Well, Screwe certainly seemed bent on making you out to be the shooter. It made him look quite pathetic, really. As if anyone would believe a duke would do such a thing. But what does Screwe have against Miss Ravelsham?"

"It is a bit of a story, and I am bound in secrecy. Let us just say that he believes her responsible for foiling him in a deed so terrible you would not believe it, even of Screwe. But as recent events can attest, his bad character goes a lot farther than failing to pay his gambling debts."

"Hmm. Well, I am glad Delacroix is now permanently fixed in gaol—at least until the magistrate gets around to hanging him. I finally feel I can let Lydia out of the house without an armed entourage."

"I am relieved to have him locked away, too, though I am still concerned about Screwe. It is my hope that Delacroix will give evidence that Screwe hired him to shoot Tilly. That would land Screwe in the nick as well. I intend to make his life a misery."

"I will drink to that." Aldley toasted again. "But let us try to find happier things to speak of. You said earlier that your life, *until recently*, had been going badly. Have you some good news?"

"Indeed I have. But you must keep it a secret, Aldley." Rutherford was bursting to tell someone, to tell the whole world. It was maddening to keep such happiness hidden.

"Of course. You shall have my utmost discretion."

"DeGroen has broken off the engagement with Tilly." Rutherford's face hurt with grinning. "And she has agreed to be my wife."

"That is wonderful news!" Aldley leapt up and slapped Rutherford's shoulder. "Finally. Well, this will relieve Lydia's mind. She has been terribly concerned about Tilly *marrying the wrong man*, as she put it. She was steeped in guilt over attending as the matron of honour at their wedding, though she could scarcely do otherwise. You will never repeat this, but she said that the shooting was *a blessing in disguise*."

"Well, I should not say it, but I cannot disagree with your wife." Rutherford refilled their glasses. "I am sure Tilly will share the news with her. But you know, our engagement must otherwise remain secret for a time, for appearances' sake."

"I suppose." Aldley did not sound convinced.

"You will keep my confidence, will you not?"

Aldley waved his hand dismissively at Rutherford's absurd concern. "Of course I shall. After all the secrets we have shared, your doubt pains me, Rutherford. But you are thinking like a mere gentleman of the ton. You are a duke, now. You could have rode your horse into the church and abducted her from under the priest's nose, and everyone would be forced to admire it as a bold romantic gesture."

"I suppose. But there would still be those who would speak ill of it behind their hands. I do not mind it for myself, but I do not want Tilly to be hurt."

Aldley laughed for an irritatingly long time, then wiped his eyes, saying, "Oh do not look at me so, Rutherford. I like Miss Ravelsham very well—not just because she has been a true friend to Lydia, but for her own sake. No matter how much she has shocked me in recent times, she really is a remarkable woman. And her heart is in the right place."

Rutherford nodded. "So you can see that too, can you? I am glad. And you must see why I wish to protect her."

"You love her. Of course I understand. But Rutherford, honestly, she runs a brothel, and I shall not to speculate what other enterprises. She cannot be overly *hurt* by what the ton might have to say, can she?"

"Quite the contrary. She has been extremely cautious in preventing anyone finding out about her businesses. Let the *beau monde* get an inkling that she was less than faultless in the loss of Mr. DeGroen's affections, and she would be very vulnerable. Screwe has already been throwing accusations around town and spying on us both. We need not help him."

"But if you marry her, it will not matter. Not a jot. The whole town could be convinced that she is a veritable Jezebel. If she is a duchess, their opinions can all go to the devil, and they know it."

"Pardon me, but am I speaking with the same man who had an apoplexy when he discovered his wife's plan to own a shop?"

"Oh that was different." Aldley took a nonchalant sip of his drink. "*I am an Aldley.*"

It was Rutherford's turn to laugh. That was the gist of it. His good family name meant more to Aldley than his title. But it did not mean more to him than his wife. And though Rutherford laughed at the absurdity of his friend's fastidiousness, he had to concede that Aldley had the right of things, in one way. A man's honour should prevail over his title, no matter what the ton thought. But love trumped all.

When Aldley left, Rutherford's solicitor paid a call.

He laid out a list of assets and debts on the desk for Rutherford's perusal.

"And these are all the debts held against him?"

"Of course, I cannot be absolutely certain, but I believe the list is comprehensive. I found most of his creditors quite eager to sell the debt, some of them were willing to be rid of it for as little as two thirds of its face value."

"Well, to be honest, it is probably worth less than that."

"That is my conclusion as well, given the list of the assets. However, as his grace's instructions were to acquire the debt, I did not hesitate."

Rutherford nodded. "And you did just as you should have done."

"Thank you, your grace. The list of assets is certainly comprehensive. And his grace may foreclose against all of them, save for two. The property within the entail of the Screwe estate cannot be touched by creditors. However, the beneficial interest that Lord Screwe currently enjoys may be diverted to you at the order of the court. You could evict him and use the property until such time as he dies. Then the interest will revert to the heir, which is a nephew, it seems.

Rutherford nodded. All this was to be expected. "But what of the other untouchable asset?"

"That is more particularly what I wished to discuss, your grace. It is some sort of trust, over which Screwe holds a legal interest as trustee, but the money is not to Screwe's benefit, so his grace cannot foreclose upon it. I have made some enquiries, and it seems that this trust is substantial. I am still trying to get access to the will that created the trust, so I can learn more."

"Do you know who the beneficiary is?"

"No, your grace. That is part of the mystery. But, if I might have permission to speculate..."

"Oh, by all means." Rutherford was listening intently. He could see the expression on the lawyer's face and could smell blood.

"Screwe's finances have been so behind, and for such a long time, that the only explanation I have for his sustained spending, even just considering the upkeep of his London home, is that he has been diverting trust monies to his own use."

"Oh really? Does the law permit this?" Rutherford leaned in.

"No. Such spending would be justified, if the beneficiary were residing with him. But Screwe lives only with his wife, and I have been able to confirm that the trust is not for her benefit."

"So there is a good chance that Screwe is defrauding this trust?"

"Unless there is some rich friend who is handing over sums of money to him whenever he asks, he is almost certainly misappropriating funds from the trust, your grace. Though I will be more sure if I can get my hands on a copy of the trust terms set out in the will."

"Mr. Borland, this has been very enlightening. I look forward to hearing what you discover about the will. In the meantime, I want you to call in all the debts at the same time, and start foreclosing on the assets as soon as is permissible." Rutherford's expression looked as dark as his clothing. "Brook no delay, and show no mercy."

CHAPTER 71

Tilly collapsed into a well-stuffed chair in the Aldley library and accepted a cup of tea from Lydia.

"How is the little mistress?" Tilly had to stop her hand from going to her waist. It had become a compulsive gesture, since she had discovered her pregnancy.

"Wonderful and horrible." Lydia looked tired and smoothed a tendril of hair off of her cheek. "She awakes at all hours of the night."

"But you have a wet nurse to take care of that." Tilly wondered if she would be able to bear allowing another woman to nurse her child. It was not something that had ever before entered her mind.

"Oh yes. But that does not stop me from hearing the crying, and it always awakens me. My ears must be preternaturally sensitive, for it never disturbs Thomas. I must admit, it feels unnatural not to go to her. But I know if I do, it will only make it that much more difficult for the nurse to soothe her. So I am always tired." The countess smiled. "But I do not mean to complain. She is such a joy to me. Watching her grow fills me with wonder, and at the same time a little sadness mingles in, because a part of me wants to keep her so sweet and carefree and tender as she is now."

"I believe that is quite natural. I have heard it is so for all mothers. And it may just be the human condition. Who among us has not enjoyed a joy or pleasure and thought, *if only I could stay fixed in this moment?*"

"You are philosophical today." Lydia lifted a suspicious brow. "I half expected you to make fun of my weak-brained maudlin ways."

Tilly tried to laugh without concern. "Oh, my own brain is too weak today to think of anything clever." Then she sighed, and she knew that the weight of it would give her heart away.

"What is it, Tilly?" A crease of worry formed on Lydia's forehead. "I mean, you are marrying the man you love, you will very soon be a duchess, and you are tidying up your business affairs so that Lord Screwe will not have a thread to pull at. What can possibly afflict you so?"

What afflicted her? Only that the need to conceal her affair with Rutherford made it necessary to delay marrying, at least for a little while. But they had a child on the way, and the need to prevent anyone questioning the paternity of their baby made marrying expeditiously equally necessary. It was such an awful dilemma.

Tilly took a deep breath and fixed Lydia's gaze with a look so serious it seemed to frighten the countess. "I will tell you what troubles me, but first you must swear to me that you will not tell another soul, not even your husband."

CHAPTER 72

Rutherford stared at the special licence, his heart pounding with excitement. Today DeGroen had left town, and all the ton was buzzing with sympathetic words, sincere or malicious, for *that poor Miss Ravelsham*. Good old DeGroen.

He was that much closer to marrying Tilly. Tilly thought they should wait, but Rutherford did not want to. He would call on Tilly's father tomorrow and make a formal proposal. It did not matter that Rutherford was still in mourning for his uncle. The old duke would have thought him a bacon-wit if he delayed such an important event for mere appearances' sake.

And Rutherford felt an added urgency now. It was worrisome that his drive to ruin Screwe might make the man more dangerous. He should have thought of that before, but now he simply could not wait to get Tilly under his roof so he could better protect her.

Several men were discreetly watching her home and following her when she went out. But it was not enough for him.

He had thought she would resist this officiousness, for she had such an independent spirit, but the message she wrote to agree to his precautions conveyed a sense of resignation. He had only seen her once since the night of his confinement at the warehouse, for they had to be discreet, but she had not seemed herself.

At the Aldley dinner party, Tilly had looked unhappy and worried. Something was troubling her, and he wished she would tell him what it was. He did not see how it could be Screwe's gossip, for it was fast losing any power. Rutherford's foreclosure action had given Screwe more pressing concerns to deal with, and who listens to a bankrupt?

So what could be bothering Tilly? Whatever it was, he would address it as soon as they were wed. He was convinced that once she became his duchess, she would be carefree and merry again, free to throw herself into her philanthropic madness. And Rutherford would join her. He would be happy to be mad right alongside her.

Rutherford stood and began pacing the room. Then he stopped abruptly to hail a servant. It was daft to wait until tomorrow, he would call on Mr. Ravelsham immediately.

CHAPTER 73

Tilly walked down the steps from her parents' home. Fresh from the task of acting surprised at her father's news that the Duke of Bartholmer had asked for her hand. Of course she accepted the proposal. What else could a woman scorned do? They would not wait for the ink to dry on the announcement.

Tilly had given up on any foolish notions that they should delay further. Certainly the ton would talk, but she did not care. In a couple of weeks they would have moved on to other gossip. Tilly did not care for her own reputation. It was her baby she was concerned about.

Her discussion with Lydia had convinced her that her best chance of evading commentary on her child's paternity was to become the Duchess Bartholmer as soon as possible.

The gossips might then speculate about her involvement with Rutherford while she was still engaged to DeGroen, which would be preferable to their later thinking that the child was not Rutherford's at all.

She was still worried that something might happen to stop the happy resolution to her woes, but found enough joy to smile as she was handed into her carriage. Her impossible dream had come true. She would marry her beloved stallion.

But the smile dropped off her lips as she viewed through her carriage window a haggard and hungry looking Lord Screwe standing in the park, staring after her as she pulled away. She closed the curtain on his evil gaze, thankful for the armed men that followed in one of Rutherford's rigs.

CHAPTER 74

Lydia hugged Tilly tightly as they walked toward the carriages, and the bells rung merrily around the little chapel at the Blackwood estate.

"Felicitations, your grace!" Lydia looked as beaming and happy as she had been at her own wedding. Tilly could not believe her luck at having the love of such a dear friend, and having married such a wonderful man. Who deserved so much happiness? She feared it would displease the gods.

"Oh do not start *your-gracing* me, or I shall kick you!" Tilly wiped her eyes and sighed happily. "And you are also forbidden to call me *Duchess*. I am always Tilly to you, as well you know."

"Not something more formal, like *Mathilde?*" Lydia's tear-filled eyes were full of mischief.

"You know very well that I hate that name. And if you call me by it, I may have to have you beheaded. We are within the bounds of the duchy, you know. I am sure there is some old, obscure relic of law that permits me to order executions."

Lydia gave her a look of alarm and pressed a gloved hand apprehensively to her neck. Then she pulled Tilly to the side, out of the hearing of Aldley and Rutherford.

"So, have you told him yet?" Lydia's face was full of the joy that Tilly felt.

"No, Lady Nosiness, I have not. I am saving it for a wedding present."

"I must say, I have always admired your nerve, Tilly. I should be frightened to keep such a secret from a duke."

Tilly's smile was arch. "The moment of realization will be more joyous for the great surprise."

It was true that Tilly was being over-cautious, but her motives were not so glib as they seemed. She had not built a small empire in the *demimonde,* while preserving her good character in the *beau monde,* by having loose lips.

In her experience, the fewer who knew of private matters, the better. There was too much at stake for her to risk her overjoyed husband giving the matter away to Aldley in the hearing of a servant.

She gave Lydia a final squeeze of the hand. "I shall see you at the breakfast." She went to be seated beside Rutherford in the carriage.

The doors were barely closed before Rutherford pulled her into his lap and kissed her. "Do you think we have time for a little consummation before we arrive at the manor?"

Tilly assumed a prim air. "Your properties are extensive, Duke. But not so extensive as that."

"Hmm." He reached under the skirts of her dress. "I should like to acquaint you with the fact that my property grows more extensive by the moment."

"Well." She pretended to consider the matter. "Perhaps we might ask the driver to take the scenic route."

"Never mind the scenery." He set her back onto the seat, and had his pantaloons unfastened and her skirts up before she could respond to his quick movements.

Then he lifted her back to sit in his lap, reaching down to position his cock and tease her with it.

"Oh, Duchess, you are already wet."

In reply she only moaned with pleasure.

He thrust into her. "My God." He thrust again. "I have been waiting for this all morning." He pushed in deeper. "Mmm. I have been so hard for you, darling."

"Give me more." She was breathless. "I have been hungering for this, too."

He thrust all the way inside of her and reached around to massage her into ecstasy with his fingers.

"Oh God, yes!" she purred, then moaned with increasing intensity as he stroked her faster.

He began to drive into her frantically, faster and faster until they both cried out together, and he pinned her hips to him, his cock spasming inside of her.

"God I love you." he growled as his member shuddered finally.

"Mmm. My stallion, you are even more delicious now that we are married."

He kissed her collarbone, still panting with his exertion so that his breath tickled the little hairs on her neck. "So my property is extensive enough for you, then?"

She laughed. "Oh yes. And I love you, darling. You have my whole heart. But I regret to inform you that you shall have to share it with another soon."

He lifted her off of him and set her down in the seat so he could look into her eyes. "What do you mean? Now that you are finally mine, I shall never share you. I mean to be a very greedy husband."

"I thought as much, and yet you shall be forced to share me." She pressed his hand to the tiny bulge of her abdomen. "Only look what your greed has already done."

His eyes grew round as he drew her close to him. "Are you telling me that you are…"

She nodded, unable to repress the tears in her eyes or the smile on her lips.

He kissed her deeply for a long time. When he came up for air, he wiped the tears from the corners of his eyes and gave her a wolfish look of hunger. His member was once again standing at attention.

He grabbed the speaking tube, looking seductively at Tilly as he spoke. "Woods, take us around the park, and be slow about it."

CHAPTER 75

The wedding breakfast was an intimate affair. Only the Aldleys, Frobisher and a few relatives of Rutherford's, including his younger sister, were in attendance.

Smythe lurked about with his white gloves, clandestinely checking objects for dust, until Rutherford got tired of him and told him to go sit in his own chamber until he was summoned. He supposed he would have to have a word with the valet.

When the wedding breakfast was over, and the guests were going through for drinks and biscuits, Rutherford tore himself away from Tilly to speak to Frobisher.

"I must thank you for taking care of things for me, Bish. I have been so busy, I have not had a chance to express my very deep gratitude."

"Think nothing of it. I have helped myself to several bottles from the wine cellar, and I may stuff a few more in my pockets before I depart tomorrow. But that reminds me. I meant to tell you that I have had no success in one of the tasks you assigned. I could not convey your apology to Mrs. Colling, because she has left for parts unknown."

"She has left her cottage?" Rutherford was surprised. He knew he had behaved shockingly, but he had assumed the woman had nowhere else to go. "Did she leave some forwarding address?"

"No." Frobisher pursed his lips in thought. "And she did not even return to get that purse you told me to give her."

"Really?" Rutherford frowned. "That is odd."

"Very."

"And it is worrisome. Surely she must have little else to live on. Where can she have gone?"

Frobisher looked troubled too. "I do not know, but she most assuredly could not have gone far without assistance. She did not so much as borrow a carriage. Does she have any friends that might have collected her?"

"I have no idea of any. My uncle certainly made it sound as though her protection was entirely up to me." Had he failed in his promise to his uncle, already?

Rutherford sighed. With Screwe still skulking about, he did not want to leave Tilly even for a moment, especially now that she was with child. "I must find out where she has gone. I swore to my uncle that I would look out for her."

"I am not sure what you did, my friend, but if you want to apologize, you are going to have to work for it."

"Or perhaps," Rutherford's face looked hopeful, "I might rely upon you to do the work. You could look for her. After all, you like a mystery."

"You know what else I like?" Frobisher crossed his arms and gave Rutherford a calculating look. "That seventeen hand black mare in the stables."

"Lucifer? You could never manage her!"

Just then an awful racket came from the servant's area at the back of the manor.

"What could that be?" Frobisher asked.

But Rutherford did not stay to hear him. He rushed to Tilly's side to stop her from going to look into it.

"Let me look, darling." He dropped a kiss on the top of her head.

"Well, it has not taken you long to become a controlling husband." She was giving him a look that showed she had no intention of staying in the parlour like a good little wife.

"I cannot help being protective under the circumstances. Do not look at me so. Is it not reasonable for a man to wish to protect his wife, when she has so recently been shot at?" And with a look to her midsection he silently communicated, *and when she is in a delicate state.*

Tilly rolled her eyes. Then gunfire sounded through the walls.

Rutherford quickly scanned the room. Everyone had frozen, but no one was hit. A movement caught his eye. His little sister, Susan, was just reentering the room through the main door. She looked puzzled as he took her arm and hurried her over to Tilly's side. "You two stay here."

The other guests were beginning to look about curiously and speculate amongst themselves, as Rutherford headed back for the door. Tilly grabbed his arm. "Do not think you are going to investigate alone."

"It is not safe."

Tilly scoffed and settled the question by tucking her arm under his. He supposed it might be better to keep her close to him, after all. And there were armed men just outside who would go with them. He relaxed. It was probably nothing.

He addressed the guests with his practised *sang froid*. "Shall we go see what all the racket is about?"

A quick exploration led them to the hall just outside the butler's office. Sandes stood looking down in bewilderment at a gentleman lying on the floor with a chamber pot on his head.

The area was strewn with dried peas, and a single cord of embroidery thread wound its way down the hall and disappeared into the scullery. One of the servants retrieved a pistol from near the man's hand.

Rutherford ordered another servant to go clean up the pots that had fallen in the scullery, which had caused most of the racket. He was about to bellow for Smythe, whom he knew to be the author of this interruption, but spotted him skulking about behind the guests, looking as guilty as sin.

Rutherford was opening his mouth to order the scheming prankster to go help tidy the scullery, but just at that moment, the servant who was assisting the man on the floor removed the chamber pot from his head to reveal the face Lord Screwe. He was just regaining consciousness and was covered in the typical contents of that ignoble vessel.

There was a gasp of surprise, followed by snickering from all the guests, as the lord tried to wipe the filth off of his face.

Rutherford, though equally amused to see the bounder so perfectly rewarded for trying to sneak in through the servants' entrance, curtailed his laughter and fixed Screwe with a look of calm superiority. "My lawyer informs me that you have been served with my formal refusal of your company at any of my residences. So I can only interpret your attempt at unlawfully entering Blackwood Manor as an act of criminal trespass."

Screwe managed a sneer of contempt, despite the fact that he reeked of faeces. "You call me the trespasser! You have trespassed in my home. First your trollop steals from me, and now you are taking the whole house!" His words were slurred, and he wobbled as he gesticulated.

So the foreclosure had gone through. Good. But it was not a scene with which he wished to mar his wedding day. He looked at Tilly. She was holding a scented handkerchief to her nose and shaking with laughter.

They exchanged a look of merriment. She was not even a little shocked at being called a trollop, only amused. That was his Tilly. She was not one for letting a ruined formal occasion get in the way of a good laugh. How he loved her.

Rutherford turned back to Screwe. "You are not welcome here, Screwe, as you well know. But I must thank you, for you could not have made the duchess and me a better wedding gift than by presenting yourself on the floor before us, penniless, debased, and covered in shit. However, we shall not remain, as I cannot stand the smell of you, literally or metaphorically."

"You will regret making an enemy of me, Duke." The man spat.

Rutherford ignored him and ordered the men at arms to take Screwe outside, throw a few buckets of soapy water over him and store him in a shed until the authorities from London arrived.

When Screwe had been removed, Rutherford summoned Smythe back from the stairway that the guilty servant had sneaked off to. He hated to threaten the man, but no matter how well this prank had turned out, Rutherford could not permit such conduct to persist.

He fixed Smythe in his sternest gaze. "You will go clean up that filth outside Sandes' office. And when you are finished, *if* Sandes is satisfied with your work, you may still have a place as my valet."

Smythe grew pale and blinked with disbelief. This lasted only a moment, then he bowed and went to work.

Rutherford placed his arm around Tilly and kissed the top of her head, then turned to the guests. "Now that the light entertainment is concluded, let us return to our champagne and biscuits."

As they made their way to a cheering fire, Rutherford whispered in Tilly's ear. "I am sorry for that spectacle. But now you know why I am so protective. I will never let anyone harm a hair on your precious head."

She gave him a little smirk, the one he had first fallen in love with, that looked like the devil had just set his hook at the corner of her mouth and given it a tug. "As if you need an excuse for being protective, my love. It goes along with being a hero, I suppose. You simply cannot help yourself. However, I am very glad our baby will have such a wonderful father."

Her eyes were full of love and a flash of heat. He was only prevented from carrying her upstairs by the inducement of the good company and laughter of the friends that gathered around them to share their joy. He would attend to his duchess later.

AFTERWORD

Dear reader, if you enjoyed *Mistress of Two Fortunes and a Duke*, here are few things you can do…

Give it a review! With just a few moments and a couple of clicks, you can help to share Tilly and Rutherford's romantic adventure with others. It makes such a difference to new authors like me, and it helps readers find new books to love!

Sign up for my newsletter (at www.tessacandle.com) and get fun bonus content, alerts of new releases and special offers.

Follow or like me on one of my favorite haunts: Goodreads, Bookbub, Facebook, or Twitter.

Then turn the page and read a little snippet from my next release, *Accursed Abbey: A Regency Gothic Romance...*

ACCURSED ABBEY CHAPTER 1

*E*lizabeth Whitely stood shivering with her little dog, Silverloo. The alpine wind chilled her back as she waited, tired and anxious, for coachmen to change the horses and resume the journey to Friuli.

Mrs. Holden approached her, handing her a clay mug of some herbal infusion, sweetened with honey. "Here, this will warm you and settle your stomach. Many people feel unwell at these altitudes."

Elizabeth smiled as she accepted the cup from the kindly middle-aged woman. She was the most recent in a series of married ladies and widows that had met Elizabeth upon her long journey from England, and had compassionately offered her their protection.

But this was Mrs. Holden's last stop. As Elizabeth stared down the mountainside at the orange-bricked villages that sprouted up here and there like little mushrooms along the spindly road, Elizabeth wished her journey, too, ended here. She longed for a proper bed and a life without wheels beneath her.

But Elizabeth would travel on alone, further and further from the only home she had known, toward the place that was to be her new home, at what seemed like the edge of the world.

"That is my husband, now." Mrs. Holden waved at a gentleman in a beaver hat, then turned back to Elizabeth. "I wish you were not travelling on alone." The woman's face looked genuinely worried, which only agitated Elizabeth's own fears.

She embraced Mrs. Holden. "Thank you for your kindness."

When the lady tore herself away, Elizabeth felt utterly alone, and the light-headedness that afflicted her made her wish to curl up in a ball and sleep.

But instead, she finished her herbal tea, wrapped her shawl more tightly about her, and took Silverloo for a walk around the posting house. There was a little time until the coach departed.

As the little dog relieved himself on some scrubby bushes behind the stables, she listened idly to the many different languages spoken by the people passing around her. There were languages she recognized, and then there were others that were a mystery. They sounded like German, Italian or French, but were not.

It was disorienting, at once exotic and unnerving, to be in such a mixed cauldron of words. Back home in England, she had never heard so much as a smattering of French. But here, for all she knew, revolutions might be being plotted, or incantations recited, and she would be none the wiser.

The coach was brought around, and as she walked toward it, she was struck still by a sight of beauty. A young maiden stood ready to enter the same carriage. She was perhaps sixteen—or at any reckoning, she was certainly no older than Elizabeth's nineteen years, and neatly, but modestly dressed in a dove grey travelling habit.

Her straw bonnet was tied with a length of dull ribbon, and no jewellery or lace ornamented her. But the face that peeked out from underneath that bonnet was ornament enough.

The girl had features and skin that angels might envy, as though her face were delicately carved from unblemished ivory and framed in perfect golden curls. The pale, icy blue of her eyes gave her an otherworldly look, which was startling next to the air of innocence that pervaded her entire person.

Silverloo gambolled over to the girl, looked up at her with his best rakish smile, then rolled over to present his belly. This had the desired effect, and the girl grinned and scratched him.

Elizabeth laughed as she approached. "You must forgive my little dog. He has rather fast manners."

The girl smiled and said, slowly and with a strong accent, "He is a treasure. What is his name?"

Elizabeth spoke a little German, and the girl spoke a little more English, and so they got on and introduced themselves. Her name was Lenore Berger, and she, too, was destined, for Friuli.

By the time they rolled away, Silverloo had laid himself out to span both their laps, exposing his belly, and the two young ladies had settled into a proper chat.

Suddenly Elizabeth drew in a rapid breath, as she felt the carriage lurch into a very steep descent.

"What is wrong?" asked Lenore, resting a hand gently on Elizabeth's arm.

"I," she gasped as though the wind had been knocked out of her, "only just got accustomed to going upward, altitude sickness and all. And now it feels like we are headed down a cliff." This was so much worse.

Lenore stroked her arm sympathetically. Elizabeth gripped the wall of the coach with her other hand and prayed, closing her eyes to the sight of the looming emptiness that gaped between the carriage and the rugged peaks in the distance.

"You will get used to it." Lenore's voice was calm.

"Does it not bother you at all?"

"I was raised in the mountains, so I had not given it a thought until now, but I can see how it might be a little frightening."

A little frightening. Elizabeth's right hand ached from grasping whatever purchase her fingers could find. She made the mistake of opening her eyes again. The road was so terrifyingly narrow that it disappeared from view. Straining to see further out the window only persuaded her that they were already suspended in the air, ready to plummet at any moment and dash against the rocky depths below.

Lenore smiled reassuringly and tucked Silverloo under Elizabeth's left arm. "Close your eyes. I will tell you when we are at a better place."

Elizabeth peeked once, and to her horror, was given a full view down the slope of how tiny and narrow the road became, before it apparently ended in a cliff, requiring of her the very great leap of faith that there was a corner affording a continuation.

Just then a sudden gust of wind made the coach waver sideways. She squeezed her eyes shut again, waiting to feel the sudden drop that would precede her death.

It did not come. A plaintive whine brought her around, and she realized that she was clasping her little dog a bit too tightly to her chest. She relaxed her grip and petted him. "Sorry, Silverloo," she whispered.

"Just keep your eyes closed." Lenore spoke soothingly. "Perhaps we should continue talking."

"Yes." Elizabeth kept her eyes shut, but forced herself to make conversation. "Are you going to see family in Friuli?"

"No." Lenore's voice was sad. "I have no family. I am an orphan."

Sympathetic pain shot through Elizabeth's heart. "I am also an orphan. I lost my parents this month past." She could not cry about it any more, but there was still such an ache.

A day did not go by that she did not have a sudden realization that they were gone. The shock of the loss seemed to be ever recurring, and left her feeling as breathless and without anchor as when the carriage had threatened to plunge over the alpine cliff.

Elizabeth's emotions must have registered on her face, for Lenore patted her hand where it rested on Silver. "You have Silverloo." She smiled.

The sweet, kind simplicity of the gesture charmed Elizabeth and she was comforted.

"I go to my ward..." The girl faltered. "No. My *guardian*. It was planned long ago in my parents' will. I should stay in a convent school until I reached my sixteenth year, and then I should go to live with my guardian. That is why I have been taught English, for he is an Englishman."

"And I am to go and live with my aunt and uncle, whom I have never met, though they were apparently present at my christening." Elizabeth had recovered from the grave fear that she had felt when she first embarked upon the journey, but as she drew closer to its completion, she could feel a dread of the arrangement's finality settling into her bones.

"They own a vineyard somewhere outside of a town called Melonia," Elizabeth added. "I know not when I shall see England again."

Lenore nodded. "My guardian is also somewhere near there, in the countryside. I do not know him at all. I am a little frightened to meet him."

So Lenore, too, had been oddly consigned to the care of a distant stranger. But, unlike Elizabeth, she had no other family. It still puzzled Elizabeth that her own father should have made this estranged aunt and uncle the trustees of her person and her modest inheritance.

Why had he not made her over to her godparents, or to one of her other relatives who lived in the neighbourhood, instead of these two people, strangers to her, who lived in such a faraway place as a tiny outpost of Venetia?

She supposed her father's illness must have already been affecting his judgement when he drafted his will.

Elizabeth sensed her own troubled mood might be alarming Lenore, so she smiled. "We shall not be afraid. We shall look out for each other."

It was a fast friendship, but seemed natural, for their similar situations gave them a common bond. Elizabeth relaxed more as they talked.

Then Lenore finally said, "You can look now."

Elizabeth hesitated, but opened her eyes. She drew in a breath at the beauty of the mountain peaks floating about in pools of blue sky, clad in the holy raiment of white gossamer mists here, or in the ominous black robes of thunder clouds, there.

"It is so beautiful and so terrifying." Elizabeth laughed and shook her head. "I have never seen anything like it." Such convulsive geography could never exist anywhere in quiet, civilized England.

"I adore the mountains. Since I was a child, I have always roamed in the forests, collecting flowers for bouquets, or to press as specimens in my scrapbook."

"I love walks in nature, too, but I prefer hunting for mushrooms or fishing." It was not something Elizabeth would disclose in polite society back home, for it made her look a bit more sport-loving than society generally approved of among young ladies.

Lenore pulled a little lace cap she was working on from her reticule. "The sisters taught me all kinds of needle work. I like that too."

Elizabeth marvelled at the intricate craftsmanship. "I could never do anything so fine. It is beautiful."

"Our needles are guided by God," said the girl with a sweet plainness that Elizabeth had never encountered.

Where Elizabeth came from, pious proclamations were always for the sake of display, as was needlework. Making lace was not a suitable passtime for English young ladies, but Elizabeth's mother had tried to cultivate her daughter's ability with fancy embroidery.

And now that excellent woman was gone. Elizabeth thought, with a twist of her heart, that she should have applied herself more earnestly to her needlework, if only to please her mother. She fought to push down the surge of anguish and remembered loss that such thoughts brought back.

Seeing the troubled look on Elizabeth's face, Lenore led the conversation in another direction. They spoke of their favourite places in the meadows and forests they had known as children. And soon they shared the playful dreams of those happier days.

"Some day we shall live together as old maids in a cottage in the woods, planted 'round with wild herbs and berries." Elizabeth treasured the childish fantasy. "And pretty flowers for you."

"And I shall make our blankets and our lace caps," added Lenore, her heavenly blue eyes sparkling. "You will catch fish for our dinner."

Elizabeth smiled as she yawned. "Silverloo will patrol our home and chase away uninvited mice. And we will all be perfectly merry."

With such pleasant thoughts to seed their dreams, they fell asleep in the carriage, rolling toward their strange, unknown destinies in Melonia, with only the snoring Silverloo to guard them.

ACCURSED ABBEY CHAPTER 2

It was late when the last carriage of the journey finally stopped at an inn in Melonia. Elizabeth was grateful to get out of the carriage into the cooler night air, for once out of the mountains the coach had become insufferably hot.

The inn yard was gloomy, lit by a single torch. This was apparently sufficient light for the workmen to remove the trunks, bags and boxes, and attend to the horses.

But Elizabeth fumbled about, barely able to see, and when the workmen were done, even the one torch was extinguished, leaving her reliant on the dim glow from the inn window. She felt like she had arrived at the penumbral edge of the world, as though some final, blind abyss yawned before her in the deeper darkness outside the inn's yard.

Elizabeth had two trunks, and Lenore only a single small case and the little bag that she carried on her person. The two stood beside these possessions as though they were the only anchors tethering them to an earthly existence.

Both cast about for their guardians, but neither knew what face to seek. People milled about, entered the inn, or met their parties and departed, but Elizabeth and Lenore remained unclaimed.

"I suppose they shall have to find us." Elizabeth sat down on one of her trunks, and patted the other one to invite Lenore to sit with her.

Lenore fingered a little rosary while they waited, and Elizabeth did not speak while the girl silently went through her recitation.

She hoped this ritual would calm Lenore, for the girl sat so tensely that Elizabeth could almost hear her muscles creak, and the pretty little face that was faintly illuminated whenever the inn door opened and the lamplight poured out, looked drawn and pale.

When the girl was done her rosary, she sighed, and Elizabeth patted her arm. "All shall be well. He will come. And if he is not yet here when my aunt and uncle arrive, I shall ask them to wait with us until he does."

Lenore's smile was a little thin, but she nodded gratefully. "Oh thank you. That is very kind."

Sensing the girl's anxiety, Silverloo crawled into her lap and licked her arm.

"I am famished." Elizabeth rose. "If you will watch our things and Silverloo, I shall go fetch us some bread and cheese from inside."

She did not have so very much money, but she sensed that Lenore had none, and she must also be hungry. The girl did not argue but looked a little sad.

"I mean to treat you. True, you look so worn. I think a little sustenance will restore you."

When they sat, sharing a loaf of crusty bread and fresh goat cheese, the world did not seem quite so dark. Elizabeth amused Lenore by getting Silverloo to do little dances and tricks in exchange for his share of supper.

In this way he made off with a good quarter of the food, though he was the tiniest member of the party. But he earned his bread, for Lenore finally smiled.

"I do not have a direction for my new home. I wish I could give you one." Lenore looked earnest.

"I shall give you mine." Elizabeth wrote it down in pencil on a page from her travel diary, as best she could in the sparse light. "There you are. Now you may find me, or at least write me a letter, when you are settled."

"I hope so. I shall not be half so afraid now that I know you are nearby."

Elizabeth left her things in Lenore's care as she went to take Silverloo for another quick walk. She did not like ambling about in the dark, but she did not want him to do anything untoward on the inn wall, so she took him to the rough grounds behind the inn.

When he had peed, and she sensed that he was about to start chasing unspecified denizens of the shadows, she called him and turned back.

They rounded the inn just in time to see Lenore walking with a man toward an inky black vehicle, so dark it seemed to be made of shadow. He must be Lenore's guardian. Elizabeth could not make out much detail in the gloom, but he took Lenore's arm and appeared to propel her almost against her inclination toward the carriage.

Elizabeth quickened her pace, for she wished at least to say goodbye to her new friend. But the man seemed in a hurry.

When he loaded Lenore into the carriage, Elizabeth called out, "Wait!" Silverloo ran ahead of her.

Surely he could not make them out in the shadows, but he turned to stare directly at her, as though he saw her.

A chill penetrated Elizabeth's bones. She could feel the man's gaze upon her. Silverloo froze and emitted a low growl.

The man turned away again and got into his carriage, which sped off into the night.

Elizabeth's heart sank as she sat down once more upon her trunk. She wondered when her aunt and uncle might come for her. Silverloo crawled into her lap as the noise from the inn grew louder.

She pulled her shawl about her. If only she had some light, she might read her novel while she waited. She had but one book with her, and she had been saving it, only reading in the most dull moments, in order to make it last. There was light inside the inn, but it did not seem an entirely respectable place.

Just then another carriage pulled up. Elizabeth looked up hopefully, but it was not her aunt and uncle, only a young man, who stepped out and stretched wearily. He must be some nobleman, for there was a coat of arms upon his rig.

Why did they never come for her? The inn door opened, and a pool of light and a cloud of drunken fumes streamed out into the courtyard. Three young men frisked and swaggered, looking utterly foxed and unjustifiably pleased with themselves.

Then the door closed, and darkness reigned again. Elizabeth was not much accustomed to being around drunk men, but even those few encounters had always made her uncomfortable. And here, sitting alone in this dark, strange place, with only Silverloo for protection, she felt greatly uneasy.

She sat still in the shadows, hoping that they would depart without taking notice of her.

In fact, they did almost that. But in his drunken state, one of the men struck her trunk with his foot, and nearly tripped over her. He stank of days old sweat and liquor. Silverloo barked as the man swore in some foreign tongue—probably Italian or Friulian, so she supposed it was not really *foreign* in this place.

He said something incomprehensible to her.

"I am sorry, I do not speak Italian." She looked straight ahead and tried to keep her voice from quavering.

The other three men were now intrigued and swaggered over. They also spoke some incomprehensible words, and seemed to be joking amongst themselves. The first man, emboldened by this camaraderie, leaned in and said something leeringly to Elizabeth.

His breath reeked and she turned her face away. Silverloo was now growling.

"Please go away and leave me be. I should warn you, my dog bites."

The man reached to touch the curls sticking out of her straw bonnet, and missed, roughly stroking her cheek instead.

Elizabeth yanked her head away. "Do not touch me!"

Silverloo snarled menacingly.

The man laughed and looked at the dog, then foolishly reached out again—only just retrieving his hand before Silverloo's little teeth snapped in the air where it had been.

"For pity's sake, leave me!" Elizabeth cried out.

The other men seemed to be interested in the sport, and they began to move in on her.

Elizabeth grasped Silverloo and stood, making ready to run away.

But suddenly the young man who had just arrived in the carriage pushed through the group of men, then turned to them, his broad, muscular back to Elizabeth.

"You lot can clear off now." His voice was commanding and strong.

The other men looked at him, then at Elizabeth. All but the one who had pawed at her face made to shuffle away.

The remaining man said something, again in his native tongue, but in a sufficiently angry tone that the Englishman could infer a challenge from it. Her rescuer replied by drawing a sword.

"It is usually a coward who conjures up the courage to accost a defenceless lady only when she is alone, and he has two men at his back. Prove me right and walk away now, or taste my sword."

Elizabeth's heart fluttered. He spoke so well, like a gentleman, and in English. Could he possibly have been sent by her aunt and uncle to fetch her?

The drunken miscreant laughed and held up his hands in surrender, backing away. The three men made their way down the road, grumbling amongst themselves as they went. Not a minute later their merriment rang out again in raucous laughs and yells in the distant shadows.

Elizabeth trembled and petted Silverloo, as much to calm herself has to coddle the dog.

The young man turned to her. "Are you well? They did not hurt you?"

She could not see much detail of his face, but she thought it pleasing, and his voice was kind.

"No. They only frightened me. I am quite well. I must thank you, sir, for intervening."

"It was the least I could do for any defenceless woman being accosted by such worthless louts. But when I heard you spoke English, I knew I had to come to the aid of my fellow country-woman. To shirk such a duty would be a crime against the crown."

The smile in his voice warmed her. She stopped trembling.

"And what of this little knight?" he continued, gesturing at Silverloo. "He was very brave."

Silverloo's grin was wolfish as he cocked his head sideways to look inquiringly at the man.

"This is Silverloo. He is my keeper in all things."

"Good to make your acquaintance, Mr. Silverloo. I am Mr.—" Her rescuer shook his head. "I mean to say, I am the Viscount Canterbourne. Do I ask too much, or will you be so kind as to introduce me to your mistress?"

Elizabeth could not help beaming foolishly as she curtsied. "I am pleased to make your acquaintance, my lord. I am Miss Elizabeth Whitely."

"And may I ask how an English young lady and her four-footed champion should come to be standing out in this desolate inn courtyard in a remote part of Venetia—in remotest Friuli, of all places?"

"Your lordship may ask it, and I should very much like to answer, but I can scarcely account for it, myself. Only it was," she looked down in some confusion, "the testamentary wish of my father that I should be entrusted to the care of my aunt and uncle until my twenty-first year, or until I marry. And they live near this place."

He looked around. "And where are they, then?"

"I do not know. I must have arrived well over an hour ago. I had hoped they might be waiting for me."

"That seems a reasonable hope, if they are to be your guardians."

"But I do not even know what they look like."

"They are strangers to you?" He sounded surprised. "Have you no relatives in England?"

"Yes, my lord, many. My mother's brother and his wife are my godparents, and live in the village where I lived all my life, until now." She trailed off sadly.

"Why send you away then? I cannot believe it."

"If I may say so, your lordship's consternation about these strange arrangements can be nothing to my own. I have had a long journey to contemplate what my father's reasoning might have been, and I cannot find any logic to it."

"And you made this trip alone? Did your aunt and uncle not even arrange a servant to attend you?" His voice held restrained indignation.

She felt a pang of shame at his tone. "No, my lord. There was only Silverloo to attend me." She scratched the little cluster of silver curls above the dog's eyes. "Although there were a series of kindly older matrons travelling along the way. They took pity on me, and watched over me for the duration of their journeys. And I made a new friend, a young maiden who calmed me during the more frightening parts of the descent down the mountain."

"I am glad you inspired such kindness, at least in the hearts of strangers. I cannot believe anyone would leave you to make such a trip alone."

Elizabeth was surprised to hear so much concern in his voice. In her limited experience, most young noblemen were at least a little disinterested in the difficulties of strangers, and in many instances, so selfish and vain that they paid more heed to their attire than to even their nearest relatives.

She had never before been overly religious, but she now felt convinced that someone must truly be watching out for her, to send such an angel as this to intervene on her behalf.

"I hope I will not seem forward, Miss Whitely, but I propose to wait with you until such a time as your aunt and uncle arrive. My servants will be with us."

"Thank you, my lord. That is most kind. I shall feel much safer now."

"Only I am ravenous." He looked doubtfully at the inn. The sounds emanating through the walls had grown even louder and more raucous. "Let me send a servant to fetch some food. For I think you will be safer out here."

When he walked away to address his man, his face was illuminated in the beams from the little inn window. The yellow glow crossed the angles of his face showing his strong features and lighting his tawny hair. He was very handsome.

Elizabeth sat down on her trunk to wait, the feeling of abandonment that had gripped her when Lenore left now dissipating. At least she was not alone in this strange, dark world.

ACCURSED ABBEY CHAPTER 3

*L*ord Canterbourne returned from his carriage with a blanket, carriage candle, some wine and two mugs. For the first time on this accursed journey, he was enjoying himself. He hummed a little tune as he set up the rustic courtyard picnic, draping the blanket over one trunk to be their table.

"Will it be acceptable if we share your trunk as our seat, if I promise to sit on the far side? Else I can happily fetch chairs from the inn."

"I think there will be plenty of space, my lord." She added with a playful smile, "I shall try not to elbow your lordship very much."

He laughed. She was sweet and charming, but he so wished to see her face out of this frightful gloom.

The servants arrived with the food, serving each of them a mug of the wine he had retrieved from the carriage.

"You brought wine with you to Venetia, my lord?" She inquired. "Is there not some local wine god who would be angered by the affront?"

"No doubt, but this wine is some I procured in Treviso. How local can these gods be?" He grinned. "Besides, I am a Christian. My salvation goes out ahead of me and rousts out evil, evicting every bad spirit from my path."

He bit his tongue. He was accustomed to making such over-blown speeches. He thought they were amusing. But she was a stranger, unfamiliar with his humour, and he did not want to frighten her off or make her think him entirely irreligious.

He relaxed a little when he heard her laughter in the darkness, like the tinkling of a fine silver bell that dispelled bad faeries.

Then the servant lit the candle, at last, and he caught his breath at the vision of her incandescent smile, manifesting suddenly before him. The impression so made was permanently emblazoned on his mind's eye. His heart quickened.

The other sweet features of the lady's face were equally entrancing. Her dark curls were wearied from travelling, but framed her pale skin and fine oval face beautifully. The candle light added a special glimmer to her sparkling eyes and showed her long, inky lashes to best advantage.

However, he could not make out whether her eyes were blue or green in the limited light. Before he thought the better of it, he asked dreamily, "What colour are your eyes?"

"My eyes?" She looked a bit confused.

He cursed himself as a beef-wit, and apologized. "Forgive me, that was a crudely forward question."

"They are blue." She said plainly, with a little shy smile that made him wish to kiss her curving lips. "But not heavenly ice blue. They are a pedestrian, dark blue."

It was an odd thing for her to say. "And why should they be other than they are?"

She shook her head. "No reason at all. Only I met a girl while travelling. Lenore. She has lovely blond curls and comely ice-blue eyes. A true beauty, though I think it is her sweet disposition that is fairest of all."

"Yes," he agreed, meeting her eye, "a sweet disposition is more attractive than any point of physical beauty."

He thought she blushed then and looked down. He feared he would make her afraid with his forwardness. Only she was so lovely.

He decided to change the subject. "Shall we not eat?"

"Thank you, my lord. I find I am quite hungry again."

Silverloo made a little half-bark of agreement.

ACCURSED ABBEY CHAPTER 4

It was, perhaps, the strangest repast of Elizabeth's life thus far, but also the most enchanting. Dining with a lord, alone by candlelight was such a novel and exciting experience. Even the shadowy perils of the unknown land around them oddly lent themselves to the romance of the tête-à-tête.

So juxtaposed against danger, his strength, goodness and valour warmed her heart. And the vague sense that he was a little bit dangerous—being able to call forth a sudden streak of violence, all in the flash of a sword blade—warmed her everywhere else.

She had only met with noblemen but infrequently back home in England, just once or twice on the few occasions when she had visited London, and those lords were not nearly as amiable as this one. Nor were they half as exciting.

She had never had a proper London season as a débutante, for her father was highly apprehensive about her falling into dissipated company. He was highly apprehensive about almost everything, toward the end.

She remembered him saying, in one of the extremely agitated spells that plagued him, "You know not of it, my child, for you have grown up as a simple country flower. But the London roses have thorns soaked in poison, concealed behind their fluttering foliage. Oh, and the London bees speak through mouths full of honey, but are well-tailored wasps! And that is just the polite company. There are devils, there, real devils, I say!"

"Have I said something wrong, Miss Whitely?" Lord Canterbourne's face was suddenly serious.

In the candlelight he was a dream of masculine beauty, and his concern made her heart quiver with a pleasant scintillation. Or perhaps it was the wine, which was sweet and strong and insolent on the palette, so unlike the reserved French claret they drank back home.

"No indeed, my lord. I was just enjoying the savour of the wine. It is so different from claret. You will think me an utterly provincial weed from the countryside, but I have never had other red wine than claret."

His smile was all understanding. "You must not tell anyone, but until I made this trip, neither had I. I am not well-travelled at all, for all that I am a viscount. Outside of my education, I lived a comparatively retired life in the countryside, with occasional sojourns in Bath, until I succeeded my late father." His face turned grim. "Then I went to live in his house in London."

Elizabeth looked puzzled, but forbore to inquire further, for it seemed an impertinent intrusion. But was he saying that he had not lived with his father? Why ever should that be? Surely she must have misunderstood.

"You look puzzled. I quite understand. Like you, I have had a father with unusual reasoning, and perhaps undisclosed motives. And, like you, I am at a loss to account for his decisions. But it was his wish—nay, I must say his *order*, that after I was born, he would live apart from my mother and I."

"My lord, I should never intrude upon your privacy, but I must say, though it is presumptuous of me, that I cannot imagine why your father should not wish to know, to spend every available minute with his son." She did not add, *and such a marvellous son as you.*

"I have had some time to puzzle over it. And I believe he thought he was protecting us. I only ever saw my father but one time, at an assembly in London where we chanced to both be. He saw me and recognized me at once, for I could see it in his eye. But he looked alarmed. True, he paled and seemed almost desperate, before he pretended to stare past me as though he had not seen me. Then he quit the place forthwith."

"What a shock that must have given you, my lord." Her heart was moved at the thought of so cutting a rejection from one's own father. Her father's mind had been afflicted, but he had always been affectionate, even to the point of doting upon Elizabeth.

"I confess, I first thought that he could not stand the sight of me. But when I told my mother of it, she reassured me that his every thought was for me. She said that my father had been the one who ordered the portraits of me made every year, and had copies delivered to him. His only concern was for my well-being, she claimed. She was anxious that I should not try to contact him, however, for she said he would be angry enough that I had come to London at all."

Elizabeth shook her head. His mother's explanation was hardly satisfying. "My own father was full of dread that I should spend any more time in London than was strictly necessary. I suppose fathers may be consumed with strange fears that we cannot understand until we become parents, ourselves."

"You are very wise. Forgive me for the intimacy of it, but I must say I have never spoken to another of this matter. And you seem to understand me so well. I am grateful for your indulging my long tales of woe."

"Not at all, my lord." Elizabeth was anxious for him to know that she accepted his openness, without judgement. "I am deeply honoured by your lordship's trust. In fact, it makes me blush that I have been so stingy with my own confidences, only my father's decline is such a painful topic."

"I should never force a confidence from you, Miss Whitely, nor broach a topic that could cause you pain. Only know, that whatever you chose to tell me shall remain with me, and not be repeated."

"Well then," she took a breath, "it is only that, as terrible as it is for me to say it, I must admit that my own father's behaviour, though not unaffectionate, has brought me more shame than I think even that to which your father subjected you." She paused to drink more wine. "It is hard to confess, but his mind became so troubled with unreasonable fears and superstitions, that, toward the end, I could only call him mad."

"I entertained a similar suspicion about my own father, at one time."

"I believe your lordship may be forgiven for it, if he had been so alienated from his senses as to give you the *cut direct*, my lord. But in my case, my father's madness made him do things at such odd moments, and with so little apparent cause but caprice, that it became truly terrifying. Indeed, I would still have both of my parents, were it not for his taking it into his head that they had to go for a paddle about the lake one dark evening, when a bitter storm was brewing."

As the words left her lips, she shrank from her own bold loquacity and solaced herself with more wine. What might he think of her for saying such a thing, for, even indirectly, accusing her father of his own and her mother's death?

And yet, she always came back to that question. Was her father's madness so far advanced that he intended to—it seemed wrong to even ask. But it was such a relief to share the burden of that dark thought with someone.

"My God!" he said. "And I thought my misery was grave. What a feeling to carry around in such a young heart. I am sorry, Miss Whitely, truly sorry to hear of your doubly painful loss."

"My lord, you cannot know how much it soothes my feelings, merely to be understood. Your lordship is the only one to whom I have ever disclosed these thoughts. There are not many who could even hear of my father's strange mental state, without thinking it cast some taint upon me. I sense that your lordship knows this sort of unjust judgement only too well."

He nodded. "Indeed I do."

"I am afraid it has set me somewhat apart in the world these last few years, and especially now." She sighed.

His voice became warm and playful. "And saved you for me, set you in my path so that I might enjoy your company in this strange place. I cannot repine, selfish as it is of me to savour this blessing."

She blushed and changed the subject. "If I may be so bold, my lord, what brings you this far away from your home?"

He shook his head and gave her an oddly penetrating look. "Ah, that is a stranger tale still. Are you sure you wish to hear it?"

"I must confess to a certain love for strange tales. Perhaps a life so sheltered as mine leads to longing for variation."

The viscount chuckled. "Perhaps." Then he drew in a long, sad breath.

ACCURSED ABBEY CHAPTER 5

*S*ome sleepless bird cried out in the fragrant air of night, almost unheard against the chorus of yet another bawdy Friulian song, poorly contained within the walls of the inn. Lord Canterbourne's servants cleared away the remaining food from his makeshift table and refilled their cups.

He drank deeply and sat himself on the other trunk to face Miss Whitely.

It was so odd a tale. Should he even tell her such a story? Would it not disturb her? He could scarcely think of it himself without feeling goose flesh on his spine.

Still, he wanted to share it with her. It tied into the darkest parts of his past, his estranged relationship with his father, his father's peculiar mind and apparent obsession. He could not say why it was so important, but he wanted her to understand him.

He took another deep breath. "In addition to the documents strictly entailed within my father's will, there was also a testamentary letter, explaining one particular element of the estate, which was a specific bequest to me." He paused.

"What was the bequest?"

His brows knit together. "I cannot precisely say. Not because I do not wish to, but because I do not know, exactly. It was a certain box, and its unspecified contents, which were on deposit with the solicitor. I received it sealed within a silk bag, and I have not opened it."

"But was your lordship not curious what was inside?"

"Exceedingly, but the solicitor was careful to follow my father's directions. He made me read the testamentary letter before he released the bequest to me."

"And did the letter tell you what was inside?"

He smiled. She was a curious creature, and her face lit up with glee at the intrigue of it. He need not have feared she would be overly disturbed by the tale.

"No. The letter adjured me several times that I should never, under any circumstances, break the seal and open the bag, and that, should the bag be opened for any reason, I should never look inside. But should the box inside the bag be revealed somehow, I should most certainly *never* open it."

"It sounds almost like a fairytale." She clasped her hands together and leaned in.

He shook his head to dispel a strange feeling that she saw inside his own heart. "Indeed, *fairytale* is exactly the right word. I called it by a less kind name to the solicitor. But he assured me that my father was, though eccentric, in sound mind when he made the will, and that these directions were very much in earnest."

"But, my lord, why should he give you something that you must only hold, and are never permitted to see or make any use of?"

"A just question. There was more to the letter, you see." He took another long draught of wine. "The box was not to stay in England. I was personally to deliver it to the home of a particular man, who lives about Melonia."

"Could it not just be sent to him by special messenger?"

"One would think. But the directions were very clear, that it was a duty that I should discharge myself. I could not do so by any proxy. And so I have arrived here on this errand. I must present myself, as soon as may be, to this fellow, and deliver the sealed bequest to his hand."

"How very odd, if you do not mind my saying so, my lord."

"You cannot be as perplexed by it as I was when this missive was given to me. And my father was so adamant that I must follow the directions precisely and deliver the sealed box to this man, or that all would be lost. His sacrifice, he said, would have been in vain."

"What a thing to write to your lordship, after such a history. What sacrifice could he possibly be speaking of?"

She met his gaze, her brooding blue eyes full of compassion and understanding that made his heart flutter. He so wished to enfold her in his arms and kiss her. It was a preposterous thought to have about a young lady he had only just met.

And her vulnerable situation demanded circumspection from him. He could not make her feel ill at ease when she was so unprotected in the world. As much as he would like to take a few liberties, he must instead be her protector.

But where on earth were her blasted aunt and uncle? Some guardians they were turning out to be. This last thought was amusingly odd. It might be too much to call himself a rake, but not so long ago, inattentive guardians of fetching girls were his favourite kind.

He roused himself and replied, "I am deeply grateful for your kind sympathy, Miss Whitely. I must say that all my life I missed the presence of my father. I wondered what I had done to so lose him, and what I could do to get him back."

"You should not have tortured yourself, my lord. Fathers have their own strange minds. The children must not take the burden of these fixations upon themselves—it is unjust and it is never what a good father wants for his child."

He wondered if she had heard those words from her own father, or from some other concerned friend, for he could scarcely believe he was hearing them from the lips of a young maiden. She could not be yet nineteen, he thought. How could she be so deeply contemplative?

And yet this was a character trait he, himself, possessed. Perhaps it came naturally to all children who had been made to look out for themselves because of the strange obsessions of their fathers.

"But do you know who this man is, to whom you are to deliver the bequest, my lord?"

"In fact I do, but only just. He was pointed out to me at that same assembly where I saw my father for the first and last time. His name is Lord Orefados, which does not sound like a real name, if you ask me. Reputedly he is a man of great learning, and unfathomably rich. Eccentric too, which is attributed to his having spent so much time in the east, seeking out arcane knowledge."

Miss Whitely chafed the fabric of her dress, and her eyes grew big with wonderment. "What sort of arcane knowledge?"

He tried not to chuckle at her insatiable curiosity. "I know not. But he was tall and broad-shouldered, and tanned as an Arab. So I think it must have been a more practical sort of learning than that which one receives by poring over whole libraries of manuscripts."

Her voice was thoughtful. "It makes one wonder what might be in the box."

A sudden gust of cold wind chilled his back and the candle sputtered out, so that they were plunged into darkness just as a cart pulled up.

A servant stepped over to re-light the candle, and when it was done, Canterbourne could dimly make out a middle-aged couple, with broad straw hats and deeply stained hands. The couple climbed down from the ass-drawn cart and approached them.

"Might these be your guardians, at last?"

She was squinting toward them. "I should say that I hope so, only it would mean a termination to our wonderful al fresco meal." She turned to smile at him, though her face looked apprehensive. "I must thank you again, my lord, for rescuing me, and for staying with me, though it delayed you."

"It was no delay and has been my great pleasure." Did he see a glimmer of affection in her countenance? He needed to be introduced to her aunt and uncle, to be made acquainted so that he might call on her. For he had to see her again.

The couple made their way over to Miss Whitely. They both looked at her for a few moments.

Then the man spoke. "Are you Elizabeth Whitely?"

"Yes," said Miss Whitely, smiling and looking from face to face. "You must be my aunt and uncle. I am so glad you are come."

The couple did not smile, but shuffled self-consciously, and looked unhappily at Silverloo.

"This is Silverloo, our family pet," said Miss Whitely. She seemed to detect disapproval in her guardians and added, firmly, "Before he died, my father instructed me to take care of Silverloo."

"Ah, then so it must be," said her aunt, in unhidden dismay. "I hope he does not object to catching mice for his supper."

Her uncle seemed to collect himself suddenly, and added what Lord Canterbourne thought should have been among their first words to their niece, "I am sorry we are a bit late. We were delayed by grape work. And we had to leave two of the donkeys, so we only had two to pull the cart. Slow going."

"It is quite understandable, uncle," said Miss Whitely with a kind graciousness that Lord Canterbourne could not help admiring.

His own feelings were not so temperate, for he was irked by the insufficiency of the explanation. If they had lost a cart wheel, this would be some excuse. Still, he ought not start out on an evil foot with these people. However shoddily they were treating her, Miss Whitely was in their care.

Lord Canterbourne spoke up. "Miss Whitely, would you do me the honour of introducing me to your aunt and uncle?"

"With pleasure, my lord. Lord Canterbourne, may I present my uncle, Mr. Wallace Whitely, and my aunt, Mrs. Myrtle Whitely. Aunt and uncle, this is the Viscount Canterbourne, who is travelling here on business."

They all made their bows and acknowledgements. Lord Canterbourne could not help but note a sort of constant apprehensive reserve about the aunt and uncle. He did not know what to make of them.

"His lordship has been guarding me from the local rabble who pour out of that inn." Miss Whitely filled in the silence, anxious, perhaps, about how things might look to her aunt and uncle, coming across them alone together, but for the servants.

"Aye," said Mrs. Whitely. "It can be a rowdy place in the evenings, when the vine-workers are about."

Lord Canterbourne wondered at their so cavalierly leaving their niece to sit upon her luggage outside of such a place, if they knew it to be so.

But he only said, "I was surprised to find Miss Whitely travelling without so much as a servant. When I saw her accosted by some young brutes, I could not but intervene."

When Mr. Whitely looked horrified, Lord Canterbourne thought the man might finally be realizing the position he had put his niece in. But neither he, nor his wife, uttered a word of shock or concern that their ward had been accosted.

Instead the odd man said, "Oh, the journey itself cost a pretty penny—but to bring a servant all that way." He shook his head gravely. "Think of the expense, my lord!"

"Aye the expense. The expense!" echoed the aunt, almost as though the very thought threw her into a ghastly fugue.

Lord Canterbourne did not feel equal to a vulgar discussion about money, especially when he was already vexed by their indifferent attitude toward Miss Whitely. However, it seemed to him that if Miss Whitely's inheritance were in their management, they might have used some of those funds to make sure that she was protected on her voyage. They displayed rather odd priorities.

But he decided to change the subject. "I am staying this night here, at the inn, Mr. Whitely. But hope I might have the privilege of calling upon you and Mrs. Whitely, while I am in Melonia. I should very much like to see Miss Whitely settled in, and I will not have much other company among my own countrymen in this place."

Their faces betrayed consternation, but apparently they had not so completely taken leave of their sense of propriety that they could bring themselves to refuse a lord.

Finally resolving some internal conflict, Mr. Whitely said, "That would be most condescending of you, my lord. Our home is humble… oh, but I shall write the direction down for your lordship."

Lord Canterbourne could not even take amiss this begrudging reply, for he was too engrossed in the lovely, sweetly blushing smile of Miss Whitely. Surely, if no one else would be happy for his visit, at least she would be. And this was all he could want.

ALSO BY TESSA CANDLE

Three Abductions and an Earl, Book 1 in the *Parvenues & Paramours* series. Get links to buy my books on all your favourite retailers on my website: www.tessacandle.com.

Accursed Abbey, a Regency Gothic Romance—coming soon! Sign up for updates on my website.

Three Abductions and an Earl, audio book, as read by the author—coming soon! Sign up for updates on my website.

ACKNOWLEDGMENTS

Mistress of Two Fortunes and a Duke relied heavily on the encouragement, work and support of several people.

Thank you for your edits, your feedback, and your talking-me-off-the-ledge sessions.

I don't know what I would do without you.

ABOUT THE AUTHOR

Tessa Candle is a lawyer, world traveler, and author of rollicking historical regency romance. She also lays claim to the questionable distinction of being happily married to the descendant of a royal bastard.

When not slaving over the production and release of another novel, or conducting *research* by reading salacious historical romances with heroines who refuse to be victims, she divides her time between gardening, video editing, traveling, and meeting the outrageous demands of her two highly entitled Samoyed dogs. As they are cute and inclined to think too well of themselves, Tessa surmises that they were probably dukes in a prior incarnation.

Those wishing to remain apprised of the status on her patent for the *Rogue-o-matic Self-ripping Bodice* should subscribe to Tessa Candle Updates at www.tessacandle.com.

You can follow her on:

Facebook

Goodreads

Bookbub

Book Hub

Twitter

Amazon

Or visit Tessa Candle's website:
www.tessacandle.com

Printed in Great Britain
by Amazon